ReCREATIONS

RELIGION AND SPIRITUALITY IN THE LIVES OF QUEER PEOPLE
Edited and with an introduction by Catherine Lake

QUEER PRESS, TORONTO

This collection and biographical notes copyright © 1999 by Queer Press.

First paperback edition 1999.

All rights reserved. No part of this publication may be reproduced in any form or by any means whatsoever without written permission from the publisher, except in the case of a reviewer who may quote brief passages in a review.

Canadian Cataloguing in Publication Data

Main entry under title:
(Re)Creations: Religion and Spiritually in the Lives of Queer People.
Includes bibliographical References.

  ISBN 1-895564-06-9

  1. Homosexuality—Religious aspects.
  2. Gays—Religious life.
  3. Lesbians—Religious life.
  I. Lake Catherine 1964—
  II. Title ReCreations

  BL65.H64R43 1999   291.1'7835766   C99-900749-1

Le Conseil des Arts du Canada | The Canada Council for the Arts

We gratefully acknowledge the support of the Canada Council for the Arts for our publishing program.

Cover art: Harreson Cebiliak and Michelle M. Threndyle
Design: David Christian
Printed and bound in Canada
Queer Press P.O. Box 485, Station P, Toronto Ontario M5S 2T1

Acknowledgements

This anthology has been a long time coming, to which any of the contributors can attest. I wish to gratefully thank the writers included in this anthology for their patience and encouragement throughout this process and for their insight and experiences which are expressed in their work.

I would like to thank the Women's Centre at the University of Toronto which offered Queer Press office and inventory space, resources and moral support from 1990 to 1998.

An enormous thank you to all the fabulous friends and valued volunteers of Queer Press, especially Jennifer Warren for editorial assistance and marketing, Mordecai Drache for outreach and promotions, and David Christian for design and layout.

Finally, I wish to thank my partner Monique for her love and support and for her many hours of solo parenting as this book progressed to fruition.

The development of this anthology has grown alongside my young son, whose joyful presence has reconnected me spiritually to the wonders and beauty of this world we share.

Catherine Lake, Editor

Queer Press Non-Profit Community Publishing of Toronto.

9 INTRODUCTION

WITNESS

15 **BORSHT**
Harreson T. Cebiliak

21 **LONESOME GIRL**
Jane Inyallie

22 **CONFESSIONS OF A MUSLIM LESBIAN**
Irshad Manji

24 **ON ONE LEG DANCING**
Mordecai Drache

30 **LET THE CHURCH SAY, "AMEN"**
Alaric Wendell Blair

36 **A SPIRITUAL AUTOBIOGRAPHY**
Cynthea Masson

42 **CONVERSION CLASS**
Cynthea Masson

43 **A MORMON PIONEER**
Frank G. Hull

49 **W.W.J.D., OR JESUS GOES TO PRIDE DAY**
Jenn Thiessen

52 **I AM A MUSLIM HOMOSEXUAL**
Sulayman X

56 **MY HUMAN REVOLUTION**
Kate Greco

59 **MA VIE EN BLEU**
Ace

64 **TISHA B'AV 5756**
Eve Lyons

65 **IN MEMORY OF MY RABBI**
Eve Lyons

66 **BLEEDING G-D**
Eve Lyons

68 **ECCE HOMMO: RUMINATIONS ON A THEOLOGY OF MY QUEER BODY**
Connell O'Donovan

72 **GROWING UP RELIGIOUS**
Brian Day

EXILE

77 **NOSING OUR WAY**
Brian Day

78 **A FALLING FROM GRACE**
Pamela Godfree

83 **BEYOND THE SEXUAL REVOLUTION**
Toby Johnson

87	**CENTENNIAL BABY DOLL**	
	Jane Inyallie	
94	**WITH ONE FOOT I RAN FROM THE PLANTATION**	
	Aswad	
97	**JOURNEY**	
	Barbara Brown	
99	**DENIED POSSIBILITIES**	
	Barbara Brown	
100	**O SILENT GOD**	
	Barbara Brown	
101	**LEG OVER LEG**	
	Barbara Brown	
102	**LIFE PRAYER**	
	Barbara Brown	
103	**WHY I AM AN EX-CATHOLIC**	
	Daniel Curzon	
106	**AL FATIHA—THE OPENING**	
	Mohammed Khan	
109	**KISSED BY GOD**	
	Brian P. Frank	
110	**POSITIVE FAITH: CHRISTIANS WITH HIV**	
	Matthew Link	
113	**DECIPHERING THE 'EX-GAY' MOVEMENT**	
	Matthew Link	
115	**(RE)CLAIMING SODOM**	
	Connell O'Donovan	
117	**DECONSTRUCTING LEVITICUS**	
	Avi Rose	

SANCTUARY

127	**DYKE/WARRIOR PRAYERS**	
	Sharon Bridgforth	
130	**CONFESSIONS OF A TANTRIC ANDROGYNE**	
	Ganapati Shivananda Durgadas	
136	**COVENANT**	
	Ari (Arlene) Istar Lev	
140	**MY JOURNEY INTO FAERIE AND WHAT I FOUND THERE**	
	Connell O'Donovan	
143	**BISEXUALITY AND THE SPIRITUAL CONTINUUM**	
	Brian Utter	
147	**WICCA: FROM THE PERSPECTIVE OF A RELIGIOUS TRANSSEXUAL**	
	Mikki Maulsby	
149	**BIRD FLOCK AND BERRIES**	
	Ann Marie Wierzbicki	
150	**CLAIMING CHRISTIANITY**	
	Gloria Knopf Nafziger	

- 153 **MY LIFE AS A JEWISH QUEER PRIESTESS**
  Alina Ever

- 157 **YULETIDE PRAYER**
  Candis Graham

- 158 **FLYING AT A SLANT**
  Candis Graham

- 159 **VOICES**
  Candis Graham

- 160 **WHEN THE SAINTS GO SNEAKING IN**
  Irshad Manji

- 162 **ON BEING GAY (AND NOT STRAIGHT)**
  David Newhouse

- 164 **SWIMMING WITH APOLLO**
  Brian Day

- 165 **MOONRITE**
  Jane Inyallie

- 166 **FIRE**
  Jane Inyallie

- 167 **BUDDHISM'S RAINBOW COLOURS**
  Beverly Glenn and Evelyn Wolff

- 173 **BUDDHIST GRASSROOTS PEACE MOVEMENT IS A POWERFUL VEHICLE FOR SOCIETAL TRANSFORMATION**
  Carroll Holland

- 177 **BACK TO THE GAY GARDEN**
  Brother Christian Spiritus Zinzendorf and
  Brother Johannes Renatus Zinzendorf

- 186 **LETTER TO A LOVED ONE**
  Sulayman X

- 188 **BLOOD PUDDING**
  Sharon Bridgforth

INTRODUCTION

Catherine Lake

I was sixteen. It was the Saturday night of a weekend youth retreat organized by the Anglican Church and I sat quietly meditating on two questions. The participants were to meet with their minister of choice to confidentially discuss any number of issues affecting their lives or to just talk about God.

I was involved with a young man at the time and contemplating that potential sin of premarital sex. This was question number one that I might present to God's representative. My second option was a far more overwhelming concern in my mind and heart. More frightening than the hypothetical of heterosexual intimacy, was the consideration of my very real love and physical desire for my best friend.

After much deliberation, I chose to request from the minister, God's perspective on premarital sex. I knew I'd taken the easier path because I knew that one doesn't get excommunicated for premarital sex. The Anglican Church has been far more lenient on such heterosexual issues, including divorce, than the Catholic Church for many years. (Eighteen years later though, the Anglican Church of Canada has still refused to come to terms with the issue of homosexuality).

As a member of the church's youth group, I was afraid to be honest with myself, with the minister and with God. I was afraid then of Sodom and St. Paul and of society's regulations regarding the 'forbidden love.' I feared the concept of 'evil' being attributed to myself. And I was not prepared at that point in my life to grapple with rejection. In retrospect, I believe that I displaced that question until I was emotionally capable of standing apart from my Christian upbringing and confronting my lesbianism with relief, courage and pain, a few years later.

One of the themes of this book is the conflict between the lives of queer people and the traditional religious structures of our upbringing. Like the cultural and familial influences in our lives, religion has, for many people, played a key role in our socialization, personal belief systems and individual identities. How then do we negotiate our adult or adolescent queer identity within the framework of the religious teachings of our childhoods? What do we keep, abandon, expand upon or long for from our religious heritage and what beliefs from this heritage shape and/or ensnare us? And finally, how do we (re)create ourselves as harmonious, spiritual and queer identified?

In response to these questions, I have chosen writers from a diversity of faiths and experiences. There are writers who have maintained their traditional religious beliefs, some of whom are working towards the queer issues of inclusion and acceptance within their temple, mosque or church. Other contributors write of their experiences in seeking out and finding spiritual paths which create a space for their sexual or gender identities. In addition to the wide array of personal experiences and perspectives, this anthology serves to dispel the myth that we are neither spiritual nor religious. Indeed, as a community, we need reflections of our spiritual and religious selves, if only to combat the vile homophobia which is being spewed from the pulpits of many religious communities under the guise of moral authority.

Some Christian leaders have offered the asinine adage "Love the sinner but hate the sin," as their attempted compromise. But this simply translates to: Homosexual Love Is Sin. And the initial response to AIDS from many religious hierarchies merely highlighted their own hypocrisies, an issue which is evoked in Alaric Wendell Blair's story, *Let the Church Say, "Amen"*. There are a number of religious organizations which continue to staunchly maintain that homosexuality is evil. Pamela Godfree (an ex-Jehovah's Witness) and Frank Hull (a Mormon), both write about growing up under the oppressive thumb of a religious sect which still to date, actively works to deprogram any admitted homosexuals within the flock. In her personal essay, Pamela Godfree writes that "I prayed with all my might that the world would end so that I could be released from my pain." Connell O'Donovan, an ex-Mormon, describes in *Ecce Homo*, how he was offered vomiting aversion therapy as a cure for his homosexuality, from Mormon Church leaders who "spoke in no uncertain terms about the evilness of my 'condition'."

Evil is a powerful societal image and a brutalizing self-image. As moral and spiritual people, we strive to understand our consciences, we strive to be good, in a society which tells us that being homosexual is to be bad, and morally flawed, even of a lesser species. Religion perpetuates both concepts: moral goodness juxtaposed to homosexual desires/sin. This then establishes an anguished dichotomy as we are forced to locate a sense of our selves outside those traditional religious structures. And yet we cannot dispense of our religious learnings any more than we can remove ourselves from our cultural upbringings. It is an imprinting which we must unlearn and unravel and grow from spiritually. When we confront our sexuality in the midst of oppressive religious dogma, we are seeking truth. That journey is borne out from our spiritual selves as much as our sexual selves.

Humans are naturally spiritual just as we are naturally sexual. And just as some selections portray the inherent synergy of sexuality and spirituality, it implicitly follows that a number of pieces would reveal sexual awakenings within a religious framework. Harreson Cebiliak, who writes of the "universal energy of androgyny" in his work *Borsht*, also describes a youthful attraction to a visiting priest. One of the scenes in Mordecai Drache's short story depicts a boy's emulations of his mother dressing for shul, simultaneously evoking ritual and cross-gender yearnings. An even more explicit rendering of this fusion is located in Ari Lev's story *Covenant* in which, in one scene, she depicts the sexual touches of two women who, lying together, are studying the Torah.

When we begin to bridge those worlds that our culture insists on segregating, there is a comfort in finding, acknowledging and revealing our true selves. This concept lends itself to a reversal of that adage, "the spirit is willing but the flesh is weak." For the closeted members of a religious sect, certainly the flesh is willing but the spirit is weak. This statement is not meant to belittle the fact that many closeted individuals live in threat of real harm from their religious communities. But for religious queers, we must begin to perceive and accept our sexuality as an integral part of our spiritual journey.

Our rebellion as sexually marginalized people renders our bodies full of questions. Avi Rose's essay *Deconstructing Leviticus*, reassesses the ancient taboo of "man lying with man as he would with a woman" which continues to be revered as the word of God for many religious denominations. Avi Rose encourages the reader to consider the socio-cultural factors affecting the Israelites during that point in history when these particular laws emerged. And he writes of his impetus to deconstruct Leviticus, stating:

> So, how am I, as a queer, committed Jew, able to live with this text? I cannot simply dismiss it as a piece of homophobic rhetoric, it does, after all, sit within the very heart of my spiritual and religious tradition. Neither am I content to live in it's shadow, accepting its rightness and my wrongness, perpetuating the rift between my Jewish and queer selves.

While queer devotees struggle with various religious laws and parables, there is one basic point that is often overlooked. The antiquity of such text reveals an ancient history of homosexuality. This fact is something we know in an academic sense, that homosexuality has always been part of human life. Think of it this way though: If those religious patriarchs took the time to write a law forbidding homosexual coupling, then damn, we must have been flourishing!

As we seek out and examine these ancient histories, we are inevitably led towards Goddess spirituality and religions. Alina Ever, in working towards a multicultural and inclusive ritual, researched the origin of Jewish holy days. Finding these holy days rooted in pagan ritual encouraged her to create Pardes Rimonim, a "Jewish feminist, earth-based and inclusive ritual community." Society does not present historical images of ourselves; these are censored and hidden. When we take the steps towards learning in defiance of societal silence, we encounter cultures, religious orders and spiritual communities in which we are (or once were) active, accepted and contributing members.

A compelling example of research, religious need and spiritual growth is manifest in Bros. Christian and Johannes' collaborative segment *Back to the Gay Garden*. Through their piece, they share their revelations of an eighteenth-century gay Christian sect on which they initially founded the Hermitage, and the path of their communal and individual journeys that now encompass a pantheistic, earth-based spirituality. Yet another contributor, Mikki Maulsby, recounts the emotional and spiritual pain that she experienced in concert with the realization that "the religion I tried so hard to stay in, truly had no place for me." This state of yearning, combined with strong spiritual beliefs, eventually led her towards Wicca and self-acceptance. No longer content to isolate that queer segment of herself, Maulsby "invented a set of spiritual traditions which blend Wicca sensibility and transsexual activism."

In researching ancient Goddess religions after I came out, I unearthed images of myself. I also recognized pagan rituals inherent in Christianity and was inevitably led to question the authority of the Christian Church and my religious belief system. While reading the contributions I received in response to this anthology, I began to reflect upon the need for queers to incorporate a female sense of 'god' in our lives. As queer people, we tend to allow the expression of both 'feminine' and 'masculine' elements of our inner selves. This necessary refusal to entirely comply with gender roles, informs our ability to (re)create our vision of a deity. More significant however, is the pervasive concept of God the Father. Although deftly programmed into our individual and collective consciousness, the image of God the Father is ultimately disturbing to those of us who are ostracized from our father's house and reviled by our father's society.

Yet despite (or perhaps in virtue of) these distinctions, we continue to need the comfort of ritual in our lives. Ritual which is reflective of our lives: holy unions, blessing ceremonies and a space in which we seek truth and share in the mysteries of life. After the birth of my child I knew that, while I was not prepared to have our son baptized in a church, my partner and I needed a personal ceremony to give thanks to the Great Spirit, for the blessing of our child and to speak our vows to Nigel, to ourselves and to the Creator. I wrote out a ritual which we read on the shores of the ocean under a full moon. This simplicity offered us and those present, a moment to share and marvel in the beauty, wonder and joy of this infant, our son. It gave us the opportunity to express a primal ritual in our own image.

There is much hand-wringing in the halls of religion as individuals and our cultures distance themselves from organized religion. The fact that many of our patriarchal religious communities have refused to even begin to engage in a meaningful discourse on sexuality and gender, is a testament to the stunted spiritual growth of these autocratic religious institutions. While religion attempts to exact order, queerness, within our present societal confines, reflects disorder. This creates a stance of polarity between queerness and religion. Spirituality is unique to the individual and lends itself conceptually to the continuum of moral and religious learning. Thus as a continuum, it naturally includes an intricacy of sexual and gender expressions. Or as Pride members of the Buddhist organization, Soka Gakkai International attest, "from uniformity to diversity." This theme of spiritual journey/self-exploration is prominent throughout the anthology which also reflects the truth that, as we seek God, Goddess, Great Spirit(s), so do we seek ourselves. In seeking a Creator in our own image, we are able to locate a sense of wholeness which then propels us towards a stronger sense of self. Or as Sulayman X writes of Allah in *Letter to a Loved One*, "If you would find Me, find yourself first."

A few months ago, I witnessed a small group of men picketing on the sidewalk out front a high school with signs that read "God Hates Fags" and "Lesbians and Sodomites will burn in Hell." At that moment of intense rage and nausea, I was standing in an office building, half a block from my son's daycare, and was scheduled to go into a meeting. I watched from a third floor window across the street, feeling helpless and victimized as these men would talk to individual students, a few of whom shook their hands before departing for home. I dutifully sat through the meeting, thinking about this anthology, the contributors, my son and myself, eighteen years ago. When the meeting ended an hour later, I rushed back to the window. Yes, those men were still there. But they had lowered their homophobic signs to brace them against their unsteady legs. For they had become surrounded by a large group of angry youth who were yelling and gesturing at them. Some of these students had written messages on paper hastily torn from their school binders which they held up high in compelling reaction. From where I was standing, I could not read the signs nor hear their words but I knew that they were speaking for me, for themselves, for their friends, for their families, and for all of us who believe that hate is not holy.

Peace.

WITNESS

BORSHT
Harreson T. Cebiliak

01.01.01 Dream Work

I remember my birth and slivers of what was before. But, I often ponder over how much has been concocted over the years—a kind of 'nurture versus nature' influence—a tapestry altered with each new wound and each healing of old scars. Yet, there has been an undeniable connection to that which has been eternally present. In times of crisis or extreme serenity, I am guided by silent whispers of self-esteem that re-assure 'we are with you'. This strong link has allowed me to recognize signposts in the form of societal symbols, situations and interpersonal relationships. It has forged a path along which I travel— a path possessing wondrous panoramas and many thorn-covered bridges.

Growing up as an only child in rural north-eastern Alberta was the first of many bridges to cross. There was an expectation to become a farmer like my forefathers. Land was life-blood to be passed on to the next of kin. Cycles of birth, death and each passing season celebrated the cult of family and commemoration of ancestors. Superstitious fears derived from an agricultural community steeped in various Ukrainian Orthodox work ethics only justified the status quo. It was, primarily, a transposed culture contained under glass, guarded by blind faith and fear.

How I yearned to unlock that passion, that essence that longed to be free. But it would only categorize me as somewhat odd and different—even at a very young age. My immediate family perceived it as 'something special' but had no idea how to properly foster it, except, perhaps for that one matriarchal figure who was able to forge a home from all that wilderness—my grandmother, my Baba.

12.07.62

Come een,
Come een,
   To wohrm sohnbed
   Off mehmorhree, cohltoore,
   An soorvivohl.
Come een,
Come een,
   Vhen vee feenish
   Plhanteen gahrdohn
Come een to mine house...
   (The lingering scent of
   Garlic pickles,
   Drying dillweed,
   And cabbage rolls
   For harvest time
   Threshing crews
   Invited reality
   Into my nostrils
   To twirl
   And step dance
   A bit.)

Come een,
Come een,
   To echoes off mehmohreez
   Dat hreezound een soul
Come een,
Come een,
   Vhen vee feenish
   Choppeen vhood,
Come een to mine house.
   (Her lullabies
   Affirmed each new dawn
   Encompassing me
   In a protective shell
   As real
   And inviting
   As the fleshy arms
   That cradled me
   To sleep.)
Come een,
Come een,
   Heer chorch belz hreeng.
   (She sang
   Stories of the stars,
   And the moon,
   And the gifts
   Each season would bring.)
Come een,
Come een,
   Come een to mine house...

When she died, the old ways were no more. All that remained to commemorate her passing was a wood and gold-plated crucifix that hung silently on the living room wall above my father's curling trophies. For a long time, that was all I thought it was—just another trophy, but something vaguely recognizable drew me to and beyond that gold figure again and again.

Since playmates were scarce, an active and rich imagination became my only faithful companion. I could live in worlds of both future or long ago with many make-believe friends, often wise and refined, who revealed to me the marvels of life and living. And my grandmother was there among them. I thought this was normal. I just wanted truth. But when I approached my parents with continuous questions of body, mind and spirit, their answers were fraught with fear and suspicion. Their misguided metaphors didn't gel with what my heart longed to express. So I chose to delve deeper, to explore and feel beyond what was only apparently there.

Kalyna

The spring and summer cycle brought a wealth and variety of ancestral rites that ensured the continuing prosperity of our agricultural community. Family graves were swept clean and re-flowered. Fresh, green saplings hung over doorways of houses built the previous fall and winter and were officially blessed with a housewarming. Once, when I was four or five, a neighbouring family hosted such an all-day, all-night affair. Friends and relatives travelled from far and wide. Fresh garden borsht and potato and cheese pyrohy were among the many dishes the 'ladies' served from the big new stove in the bright new kitchen. Kegs of beer and bottles of vodka flowed freely as the more daring males shot back the odd glass of moonshine out behind the barn. But amid the violin and accordion music, the taste of holubsti and nachnyka, beyond the chatter and laughter of all the revelry, I found myself quietly drawn to his presence. I never knew his name, only that he was visiting our priest from a parish out east. Something in his youthful presence separated him from that of his grey-haired elder. His jet-black vestments sharply cut his towering form, the white of his collar accentuating the glint of his gentle smile. But it was his eyes—those wolf-like eyes, that knowingly penetrated the very core of my being—that made something 'ancient' churn deep inside. He saw right through me, into me, and it felt like I no longer possessed a body. It was as if he knew that I knew that he knew—but what that was, I had no idea back then. The children flocked to him as did every single young maid. When they soon tired and chased off to play other games, it was I who remained faithfully by his side. I remember we took a walk around the farmyard just as the sun set—just the two of us. He pointed to the animals, and the trees, and the stars that began to twinkle against the purple-blue prairie sky. He spoke of God's creation and my responsibility to it. And for a moment, I could feel Baba, my birth and before. Although details of what was said have faded, the comfort of his voice, the electricity of his warm, strong hand in mine, the vision of that familiar crucifix dangling from his neck—and those eyes…which I never saw again…after that day…still remain…

There had always been an attraction towards men—not so much to the superficial libidinous posturing, but to some deeper secret inside. I was puzzled why they wouldn't or couldn't express it as easily as I. Perhaps I possessed more of a healthy indifference to gender. I could play with dolls and skip rope as well as play with mechano sets and toy cars. Role models did not solely lie in action-oriented men of sport and chaos, but also in spiritually-adventurous lone wolves like the Tarzans, the Johnny Appleseeds, and that young priest who visited that day.

Because of this openness and playfulness in evoking both masculine and feminine spirit, the proverbial slings and arrows came fast and hard as I got older. Wounds were deep. It was soon made painfully obvious that I wasn't like the other little boys in school. One on one, a common bond could be struck momentarily, but I quickly became an outcast with larger groups. I began to hang out with the girls. Well, at least they could relate…sort of…for awhile, until puberty set in and I was demoted to "the fairy", "the limp-wrist", "the crazy lady", "the drop-dead, you fucking fag". Abandoned, except for a smattering of brave, but suspicious fellow outcasts, I felt bereft of self-esteem and the capacity to love wholeheartedly. Grief, anger and fear bloated me over time. My life-force, the magical child within, was nearly all but extinguished— somehow perceived as enemy of an out-of-control masculine myth. I purposely plunged into my creativity whether through painting, music or drama. Making art became salvation. Yet, in many ways, I was told I didn't deserve to live and thus, rejection became my initiation.

Grade Ten Itinerary

7:45 a.m.	Get up after Dad leaves for work and before Mom comes off the nightshift at the hospital.
8:00 a.m.	Full breakfast: 1 Diet Pill 2 Valium (chase down with Kahlua and milk). 1 Muscle Relaxer
8:20 a.m.	Feed dog and cats. Smoke joint on route to school bus stop.
8:30 a.m.	Sit with elementary kids because no one else will sit with me.
8:45 a.m.	Arrive at school, hide out from bullies till 1st class.
9:00 a.m.	1st Class Settle down, take out books, try to feel legs which begin to go numb. Take notes and doodle weird pictures on scraps of paper.
10:30 a.m.	2nd Class Ignore humiliating catcalls from class mates. Take notes and compose morbid poetry for doodles of first class.
12:00 p.m.	Lunch 2 Valium Another joint (chase down with can of Coke). Avoid getting pushed up against lockers by grade eleven and twelve boys. Try to strike up conversation with those who care enough to listen about: The new Alice Cooper/Steve Miller/Donna Summer album. What was on T.V. last night. The paranormal, UFOs and getting high in old abandoned graveyards. What's on T.V. tonight. Potential weekend parties which I'll never get to attend.
12:45 p.m.	3rd Class Give teacher forged note excluding me from gym class (especially the shower room!) Hang around anyway just to pine over new gym coach. Doodle his likeness on a scrap piece of paper.
2:15 p.m.	4th Class Argue with art teacher (I want to work with acrylic, not powdered tempera!). Find potential subject matter in doodles and transfer them to canvas. (Not masonite!).
3:45 p.m.	Come home to empty house. Try to find out where Mom is this time by phoning her friends but with little success.

4:00 p.m.	Smoke joint. Play with dog and cats.
4:15 p.m.	Play with myself.
4:30 p.m.	Listen to spacy rock music while drafting the ultimate screenplay (hoping Streisand will direct).
6:00 p.m.	Fix supper for Dad while he rants about me getting a real job.
7:00 p.m.	Watch him polish off a six-pack of beer and pass out in front of the T.V.
7:15 p.m.	Do homework as Mom finally comes home and does her nightly "Woe Is Me" worry dance.
8:00 p.m.	Finally get to watch my T.V. shows as Dad stumbles off to bed.
10:30 p.m.	See Mom off for sixth night shift in a row. (check for booze breath).
10:45 p.m.	Go into her stash and steal more Valium.
11:00 p.m.	Get ready for bed. 2 Valium 1 Muscle Relaxer Another joint (optional)
11:30 p.m.	Cry myself to sleep…

By the end of adolescence, everything became way too hot to handle, yet felt dead in my arms. Leaving home was like leaving a war zone. Alcoholism and denial ran rampant like a wild prairie fire over what was left of my family. I knew if I succumbed to my parents' feeble pleas to stay on the farm, I would soon die along with them. My spirit yearned to find its own, to express itself in venues that could be constructively challenged instead of quashed by fear.

It has taken me many years to honour, not hide, the fact that I am indeed different. I can now appreciate, at a deeper level, my interactions with various sects of society. Negative experiences can be integrated without painful repetition. This doesn't stem from any elitist standpoint. It arrives with playful celebration of a hidden heritage that sashays on a spiraling rainbow spectrum beyond the noisy illusions of duality born of fear.

Remaining true to my soul's evolution has allowed me to magically transform as a dance with the Divine. My sexuality just becomes one of many avenues to touch that bliss instead of harbouring a vampirical beast never fulfilled by its hunt. By accepting heartbreak, the most luminous of my strengths are purified and reborn from the ashes of vulnerability. Yes, occasional anger, fear and pain swell in those nooks and crannies that may still be too tender to touch. Nevertheless, I am seeking wholeness which has become my life-long vision quest. Whether through tapping into creativity, psychotherapy, or a myriad of other techniques, encountering one's soul and understanding its purpose offer empowerment beyond all archetypes that govern this existence.

Whatever the final result of any work I do, 'spirit' is revealed, revered and re-evaluated with a focus on inner healing. Through intuition, initiation and integrity, the masculine and feminine principles converge and bring forth a universal energy of androgyny. Life inevitably becomes a curriculum unhampered by egocentric hierarchy. And as my skills, talents and perceptions are freed up within, I can allow myself to morph into a more authentic role model, not only for the gay community, but for humanity at large.

BIOGRAPHY Harreson T. Cebiliak

Originally born in North-Eastern Alberta, multimedia artist Harreson Cebiliak has criss-crossed the borders of body, mind and soul to currently reside in Ontario. A graduate of Grant McEwan College in Edmonton and York University in Toronto, Harreson has been engaged in numerous art exhibitions and has contributed to several periodicals in the holistic and gay communities.

Since 1990, Harreson collaborated with local artist Michelle Threndyle to create "Inner Light Visions," a specialized visual arts company that transforms working and living spaces into environmental works of art.

The excerpts from *Borsht* derive from a larger evolutionary work entitled *Bread for my Children* which integrates performance, text and visual sources with various modes of storytelling.

LONESOME GIRL
Jane Inyallie

lonesome girl
stands on the edge
of a path
shaped
by the soles
of her feet
solitude brought her
to this spot
she no longer remembers
the way back

turtle woman swims through air
lands on a rock beside her
she breaks away
old bone armour
made to shield a heart

thunderbird woman hovers
lightening strikes
the ground
it shivers and quakes
and crumbles beneath her

lonesome girl
tumbles into dark
she struggles and gasps
air whistles past

turtle woman appears at her side
thunderbird woman on the other
lonesome girl smiles
and reaches
to outstretched hands

BIOGRAPHY Jane Inyallie

I'm a two spirited Sekani woman. I live in Vanderhoof, British Columbia with my partner Gayle and our two donkeys (Chimo and Cruiser), three goats (Willy, Sushi and Rocky) and dog (Sinjin). We spend the summers packing and hiking on the trails with our animal friends. When I think of spirituality or beliefs, I think of women and spirit and that is what I write about.

Jane Inyallie's poems *Centennial Baby Doll*, *Moonrite* and *Fire* also appear in this anthology.

CONFESSIONS OF A MUSLIM LESBIAN
Irshad Manji

Forgive the morbid thought, but I often wonder if, in nervous anticipation of meeting the Divine One, I'll renounce my lesbianism on my death bed.

Granted, right now I'm filled with the requisite irreverence of youth. According to the scripture of the twenty-somethings, if I have worries about explaining myself to my creator, I should save them for the Day of Judgement and get on with the business of being invincible.

Problem is, every day is Judgement Day for the likes of me. As a semi-practicing Muslim and a full-practicing lesbian, I'm constantly asked how I reconcile my spiritual orientation with my sexual one.

The latest burst of curiosity came from someone to whom I had just been introduced. She flipped when I told her I'd be writing a column about what it's like to be a devout dyke with a Muslim god. "Send me a copy," urged the straight but skeptical Catholic. "I can't wait to see how you pull this one off!"

Here's how: My Allah (God) has no problem with my lesbianism. Honest. I asked Allah point blank. I could do that because one of the great Islamic traditions is self inquiry—the duty to grow into faith by constantly revealing yourself to your creator.

"In the philosophy of Islam," writes scholar Ali Shari'ati, "the relation of God and humanity is one of reciprocity, where self knowledge and knowledge of God come to be synonymous." Put bluntly, denying my dykehood could amount to blasphemy. Lord knows that's the last blotch I need on my record.

Nor is blasphemy the driving concern of Toronto-based Salaam, quite possibly North America's only support group for lesbian, gay and bisexual Muslims. (One individual drove up from New Jersey to attend a recent meeting.) What Salaam members are concerned with is finding acceptance of their whole selves, a goal that honours the philosophy of Islam.

But in organized religion, often it's not philosophy that oppresses. It's politics. Of this, Salaam's members are painfully aware. "Growing up as part of a minority has its fair share of challenges, including discrimination and alienation," reads the group's brochure. "For Canadian Muslims who are gay, lesbian or bisexual, the issues of discrimination and alienation are further compounded as these individuals are a minority within a minority, and are more often that not scorned by their birth community because of their sexual orientation. The fact that Islam and its adherents are stigmatized by many only compounds those challenges."

Yup, never mind the bigotry of religious leaders. Western culture's hate for both homosexuality and Islam ain't done me much good either. It's hard to say which hate hurts more. It's also useless: acceptance implies taking the entire package. No conversion expected. No compensation requested.

Salaam's search for acceptance of the whole person should inspire all lesbians and gay men because we're forever being prodded to compensate: "Could you introduce him as your friend?" And if we don't introduce our partners as our pals, we're punished by having to confess the perceived contradictions of out existence: "How can you consider yourself a queer and my son?"

One Salaam member has already replied: "If it's contradictory, I can live with that. Contradiction is human, so I don't think in absolutes."

And why should he have to? Islam's sacred text, the Qur'an, suggests that the richness of humanity is only realized on a life-long journey. Identifying with homosexuality instead of heterosexuality, or vice versa, may be a pitstop en route to knowing the self. The point is we are migrants. We can no more be afraid of new stations than we can be of our own shadows.

I know about changing stations. A few years ago I refused to call myself a Muslim. After all, I'm a lesbian. The way I figured it, to claim both identities is to be severely deluded about the flexibility of faith.

Then Omar, a founder of Salaam, exposed the artificiality of my choices. He convinced me not to let anyone else define who can come close to Allah. These words echoed the Persian poet, Bayazid Bestami:

> For years I sought God and found myself
> Now that I seek myself, I find God.

Which means there's no guarantee that I won't renounce my lesbianism on my deathbed. If I'm true to my migrant, Muslim self, the station-change could reflect growth, not panic. Still, I'm the first to acknowledge that the timing would be a little suspect.

NOTE: This article was previously published in **Xtra!** magazine in September of 1994. The group referred to as "Salaam" was disbanded in 1998. Currently, queer Muslims can contact the Toronto chapter of Al-Fatiha, an international organization of LGBTQ Muslims.

BIOGRAPHY Irshad Manji

Irshad Manji is host and senior producer of Citytv's **The Q-Files**, the first show on mainstream North American television to explore gay, lesbian and other queer cultures. She is also the best-selling author of **Risking Utopia: On the Edge of a New Democracy**, which chronicles how Canadian youth are transforming alienation into hip citizenship. In her community work, Irshad helps lead the "Youth, Media and Politics" program at Toronto's Laidlaw Foundation. **Ms. Magazine** recently named Irshad a "feminist for the 21st Century" and **Maclean's** has chosen her one of "100 Canadians to Watch." The category they listed her under? "Dreamer."

In that spirit, Irshad's answering machine greets callers this way:

> As-Salaam-un-Alaykum. In Conversations with God, Book One, God says "I do not show my goodness by creating only what you call perfection all around you. I do not demonstrate my love by not allowing you to demonstrate yours. And you cannot demonstrate love until you can demonstrate not loving." Clues into why there is hardship, even under a merciful God.

From her refugee roots, Irshad has learned to view hardship as an opportunity to mature. Hence her personal motto: "For all of my so-called minority labels, I've grown up with the greatest privilege of all—self-esteem."

Irshad Manji's essay *When the Saints Go Sneaking In*, also appears in this anthology.

ON ONE LEG DANCING
Mordecai Drache

My mother was very conscientious about her appearance, especially when preparing for shul. Her blonde hair was always tidily brushed, her blazers tailor-made to fit her slender body, while her makeup blended into her delicate features with skilled and adept craftsmanship. She hardly looked glamorous, nor was that her intention. Hers was a dignified and modest beauty, which I felt became a Jewish woman on her way to worship. I would watch her with fascinated ten-year-old eyes, a practice that before my having reached puberty, she thought nothing of.

Her body was fair, almost white, like mine, and she adorned it with only the most particular care. Her favourite shul outfit was a wine red pleaded skirt and matching blazer, under which she wore a simple silk blouse (no frills) and the most exquisite handcrafted porcelain brooch, a gift from and made by her sister, my Aunt Brie.

She also wore clear stockings, black low-heeled shoes and silver hoops in her ears. As she carefully applied only a hint of eyeliner, I watched with eager ten-year-old eyes the careful and deliberate motion of her fingers, knowing that one day I would emulate them.

I wore a navy blue suit, a colour I absolutely despised, and a navy blue tie, both of which my father chose. Though he was an utterly unsophisticated man who rarely wore ties himself, he insisted on my wearing one, out of fear I was becoming too feminine. My father was a math professor, and everyone knows that one of the key requirements of math professors is, above all, complete disregard for fashion sense.

On top of my father's obvious fashion blindness, he was a staunch atheist, who refused to enter a ten-foot distance within any religious setting. As a German Jew who was raised by strongly assimilated parents, and then smuggled to Israel to live on a completely secular kibbutz, he hardly understood the point of worship. Yet because he was my father, he somehow had the right to determine how I should dress for this weekly event.

The first day he tried to put a tie on me, as his hands moved towards my neck, I screamed, cried and violently thrashed at him. To a ten-year-old boy who desperately wanted to be a girl, that tie may as well have been a noose. When my mother appeared, I immediately ran to her for protection. My father started shouting contemptuously in his characteristic German/Hebrew/English dialect about how much she spoiled me and what little respect I had for his authority.

I begged my mother not to make me wear a tie. She sat down and put her arm around me. My father rolled his eyes. She explained to me that all the men and most of the little boys wore ties. Did I wish to be different?

"Yes!"

She gave my father a look of bewildered desperation. He returned it with a scowl. In his opinion I spent far too much time with her, absorbing far too many of her "feminine sentiments." She switched to German, thinking I couldn't understand what she said to my father, making a suggestion, to which he answered with a curt nod.

"I want you to wear a tie until you have your bar mitzvah. Then you can decide for yourself, as long as you continue to dress decently in your suit and good shoes when you go to shul."

I didn't like it, but I agreed. My father taught me how to tie a Windsor knot, but after his first tie-tying lesson, I couldn't resist pulling the hanging end above my head, making my head go limp, bugging out my eyes and crying out, "I'll convert! I'll convert! Christ is my redeemer." I then let out a guttural wheeze. My father shot me such a hateful look that to this day the memory of it gives me shivers.

As my mother finalized dressing in her outfit, placing a burgundy felt hat upon her head, she turned to me and asked, "Jonah, what do you find so fascinating about watching me dress?"

It had never occurred to me that there was anything unusual about wanting to emulate her style and grace. To me it was just a given. I answered her question with a shrug of my shoulders.

"What does this mean?" She emphasized this with an exaggerated shrug of her own shoulders. I nonchalantly shrugged my shoulders in response.

She then put a dab of perfume behind her ears, took my hand and led me to the television room, preparing herself for the battle she knew she was to have with my sister. The sounds of moronic laughter, gunshots and Elmer Fudd echoed into the hallway.

My six-year-old sister, muscular and chunky in her boy's pajamas, sat stubbornly in front of the TV with her arms crossed. My father was watching with her.

"Naomi, you have to get ready for shul," my mother said.

"No!"

"Naomi."

"Dad says I don't have to go."

That was a shock. My parents had agreed that until we reach the age of thirteen, Naomi and I would attend shul regularly, and then make up our own minds as to whether to continue or not.

"Wir haben ein Ubereinstimmung gehabt," my mother said firmly in German. We had an agreement.

My father responded again in his characteristic German/Hebrew/English dialect. "See you yaldah, das will el beit hamikdash to gehen?" which I think translates to "Do you see a girl who wants to go to shul?"

My sister's eyes were locked on the television. She pretended to ignore the conversation that surrounded her.

"Jonah grew to like shul. Naomi isn't even giving it a chance and you're encouraging it. You would rather she watched this crap than learn about her heritage!" she shouted in English.

She went over and turned off the television. My father started to scream something incomprehensible. My mother screamed back in German. Soon they were arguing heatedly, as Naomi's eyes remained glued on the television screen. I can't remember how the argument ended, except that my mother looked at her watch and bit her lip. We were late. An expression of triumph registered on my father's face.

As my mother and I piled into the car, she started muttering angrily, something about attributing Christianity's success to the lack of violent, inane cartoons on Sunday morning.

The argument with my father left my mother in foreboding silence. Judaism was important to her. The very thought of its diminishing from hers and my father's lineage left her in a state of perpetual dread and fear that she failed as a parent. After all, intermarriage was on the rise. Naomi's obvious lack of interest in keeping the faith and my fathers tacit approval pushed her to push me all the more.

My father cared about Judaism too, but in a different way. He was a nationalist, a staunch Zionist who committed himself to continual and unbound support for

Israel as a secular Jewish state. Though he'd lived in Canada for more than half his life, he essentially viewed our home as temporary. He always spoke of Israel with tears in his eyes and of his and my mother's plan to retire there; however, he could never understand my mother's abstract notions of what she referred to as 'Jewish spirituality,' which like most of her ideas, he deemed 'feminine' in principle. Their dual interpretations—one religious, one nationalist—never ceased to build an unscalable wall between them.

It was only as we drew nearer to Beit Avraham, our synagogue, that my mother began to relax. Beit Avraham was, and remains now, a conservative synagogue. Though the politics of a reform temple might have been more compatible with my mother's, she remained loyal to this shul, mainly out of discomfort for non-traditional services and devotion towards our Rabbi.

Beit Avraham's coat room was located directly across from the sanctuary. Upon hanging her things, we ran into Esther Hertz, the matronly wife of our Rabbi.

Esther, in her black skirt and white blouse, walked with a cane, as she supervised her six-year-old granddaughter, Miriam.

"Gut shabbos," my mother greeted her warmly, kissing her on the cheek.

"Gut shabbos, Ruth. How are you today?"

"I'm fine."

Esther turned to me and knelt down. I hugged her. "Gut shabbos, Rebbetzin," I said, calling her by the Yiddish title that refers to a Rabbi's wife.

Esther started laughing. My mother looked mildly embarrassed.

"Call me Esther, Jonah. Rebbetzin is so formal."

I was so disappointed. I just loved the sound of the word 'Rebbetzin.'

"Your hair is growing long, Jonah. You're starting to look like your mother."

I beamed.

"The last time Joel took him to the barber shop, he bit three barbers."

"I only drew blood once."

There was an awkward silence. Then Esther let out a nervous laugh.

"If Jonah wants to grow his hair long, believe me, things could be worse," she said.

Miriam ran over to Esther and smiled at me elfishly from behind her mother's skirt. Esther affectionately caressed the top of her head. "This one's sister just dyed hers pink. Of course, she gets angry when I call it pink. 'Bubby, it's mauve,' she corrects me like I'm a child. I told her that I'm sixty years her senior and thank you very much, I know pink when I see it."

Esther shook her finger menacingly. The sleeve of her blouse fell, exhibiting the numbered tattoo on her arm. Though it was well known she experienced horror in her native Poland, she still emanated life. There was solidity in her plump body and confidence in the way she carried herself. As she smiled at my mother with a set of still intact white teeth, she gave her hand a squeeze before we entered the sanctuary through its large oak doors.

The sanctuary had a somber feel to it. The lights were always kept dim. The two of us found a seat at the back.

My mother was always different when she prayed. She would close her eyes and murmur the prayers almost by heart, her lips moving gently and swiftly as she recited the words. Despite the fact she always held a prayer book, it never occurred to me that she was giving the words anything more than a quick glance. She seemed to know them so well, I believed they were inscribed inside her. While the whole service touched her very deeply, no other part had so much affect on her as the Torah-reading.

The entire congregation watched and sung as the Torah scroll was ceremoniously disrobed of its silver breastplate and velvet coat.

"Barchu at adonai hamvorach," Cantor Lithwick chanted.

"Barchu et adonai hamvorach lolam vaed," the congregation responded.

"Baruch atah adonai, eloheynu melech haolam, asher bachar banu mikol ha'amim, v'anatan lanu et toratoh. Baruch atah adonai noten hatorah."

"Aaaamen."

We all sat down.

Perhaps the Torah-reading meant a great deal to my mother for its content, but for me, it was the wondrously deep and resonant voice of our handsome Cantor Lithwick. Like honey melting in tea, I could never help but feel something unspeakable stir inside, as the steady flow of ancient Hebrew melodies poured forth fervently from his lips.

During the Torah-reading, congregants would be called up to recite certain blessings. This was called aliyah. Traditionally, women weren't allowed to do this; however, we weren't an Orthodox shul, but Conservative, so it was allowed.

For some reason though, my mother never went up, and I've never known why. She was asked to many times, but always declined. I, however, despite being a child, went up many times, before and after my bar mitzvah, and would always come down afterwards to see her eyes welling up with tears and pride. I knew she saw in me what she felt she could never be, which amazed me, because I always thought she could do anything. As her eyes followed me from my seat to the podium, I knew where one day, she hoped I would stand.

When the Torah-reading came to an end, Cantor Lithwick concluded with the appropriate blessings.

"Aaaamen," the congregation responded.

One of the congregants who had been called up for an aliyah, held up the Torah as it was rewrapped in its velvet garments. The entire congregation sung, unified as one, as the Torah was carried down the synagogue aisle, followed by Rabbi Hertz and Cantor Lithwick.

Married men wearing satin prayer shawls kissed the fringes that were hanging on the ends, then touched the Torah with them. Women and children did the same with their prayer books. My mother did it and so did I. The Torah was placed tenderly back in the ark, sheltered again by the hanging curtain. Less than half hour later, the morning service concluded, and the congregation sat silently, awaiting Rabbi Hertz's sermon.

Meanwhile, I had to pee something fierce. My bladder felt like it would explode. I immediately ran to the washroom.

I was only at the urinal for a few moments when Arnie Lithwick, Cantor Lithwick's son, came in and assumed urinating position. However, from what I could tell, he didn't seem to be urinating. He started talking to me and I found myself a little embarrassed. He was a few years older than me, amiable and chatty.

He asked me to follow him outside. I wasn't sure if I should. Although a lot of kids spent most of the service outside the sanctuary, my mother was strict, and musaf services would begin after the Rabbi's sermon.

"I have to go back in."

"It'll only be a minute. Trust me."

"Why do you want to go outside?"
"There's something I want to show you."
"You can't show me here?"
"It's not a good idea."
I had the distinct sense something forbidden was involved.
"What do you want to show me?"
"I have to show you outside."
My heart started pounding.
"It has to be quick," I warned him.

An adult came in and went to the urinal. Arnie nodded his head towards the door and I followed him. It was a warm fall day. As I walked behind Arnie, I was getting more and more anxious, partially wanting to turn back, but knowing I could not. At that moment I felt like Eve in the Garden of Eden, drawn to the fruit of knowledge. He took me to the back of the building, where a large hedge shielded us from the street. We tucked ourselves into a corner between the hedge and the synagogue.

He instructed me to stand a few feet away, perfectly still. He unzipped his pants and started violently yanking his penis. He started moaning, panting and groaning. He was yanking so vigorously, I was scared he would pull it off. At first I wanted to run, but my feet felt cemented to the ground. Then I felt embarrassed, and finally confused as to what my purpose was in being there. After all, I wasn't really doing anything except watching, but soon I found I just could not stop watching. I was hooked on the sight of him furiously yanking himself to the point his little dinky was turning red. I just stared and stared and stared until finally, white goo spurted out. His moans became softer, his yanking less vigorous. His breathing that had been fractured and short, was slowing down, becoming normal. He zipped up, wiped his hand on the handkerchief that he usually used for cleaning his glasses, and shook my hand.

"Don't worry. You'll be able to do that in a few years."

Then he was gone.

I stood there in shock. For some reason I felt good and tingly, but strangely like I'd done something wrong. I wondered why that made it feel all the more tingly. I wondered if I should tell my mother.

I entered the sanctuary and made my way back to my seat.

"I was wondering if you fell in," my mother remarked. "What's this?"

I didn't realize that Arnie left a huge stain on my knee. My mother touched it with her fingertips. Her eyes opened wide. "Jonah, is there something you wish to tell me?"

I frantically shook my head.

My mother's eyes grew dark and serious. "Did anyone do anything to you, you didn't want him to do?" Rabbi Hertz was still talking. Luckily, the seats surrounding us were empty. I looked up at her. I told her no.

"Are you sure?"

"Yes," I looked at her straight in the eyes.

After a moment, she said, "I'm glad, Jonah. Now I want you to know there is nothing to be ashamed of, but there's a time and a—"my mother stopped herself. As if to punctuate or finish her sentence, she slammed her open prayer book over the cum stain on my knee.

"You don't mind if we join you for the remainder of services, do you?" Esther and Miriam appeared.

"Not at all." My mother flipped to another prayer book to the correct page, as I religiously held the one she had been using, over my knee.

Miriam sat beside me. She covered her face playfully with an open prayer book. "Peekaboo," she whispered, peering above the open pages.

"Peekaboo," I whispered back.

Giving me the same elfish smile as before, her eyes danced with mischief.

NOTE: This story is the first chapter of a novel in progress.

BIOGRAPHY Mordecai Drache

I have my Bachelors in English Literature and a Human Services Administration Diploma and presently work in television. I have not as of yet found a synagogue that suits my needs though I am a regular attendee as well as a board member for Congregation Keshet Shalom, Toronto's Jewish gay, lesbian and bisexual worship/social group.

My third proudest moment was helping lead a pro-choice march, captured forever on a videotape advocating an anti-choice stance. My second proudest moment was reading from The Men with the Pink Triangle at Trent University's Holocaust memorial Day ceremony. My first is getting published in this anthology: **ReCREATIONS**.

LET THE CHURCH SAY "AMEN"
Alaric Wendell Blair

"Get up," Ma called from down the hall.

Sunday morning, and she and my sister were already up preparing to leave for church services. I'd only been asleep a few short hours and wasn't ready to get up. That day didn't feel like a normal Sunday for me. I felt a foreboding—like something awful and enlightening was about to take place. It was a feeling I'd had only before visits to the doctor.

"I'm not going today, Ma," I called back.

"As long as you are in this house, you're going to church, so you might as well get up. Maybe you shouldn't stay out so late on Saturday nights."

It was clear that Ma was making it more and more inconvenient for me to spend time out on the weekends. There were Saturday nights when she found little household jobs for me to do that would keep me busy until late. She probably hoped that I would be too tired to go out, but I always found the strength to go out whenever I wanted.

I didn't feel like arguing, so I got up, showered and got dressed. My stomach was still churning from the night of drinking so I skipped breakfast. On the way to church, Ma and Ray were going over the Sunday school lesson and quizzing us. She always wanted to be sure that we'd read our Bibles during the week and since she and Ray were Christian educators, she wanted us to be prepared. Of course, I'd never had any problems responding to their questions because I'd been in Sunday school so long I knew that the lessons were all recycled from previous quarters and years.

I usually enjoyed going to church, but it soon became a drudgery—a type of prison with hymnals. I still liked going and experiencing the spiritual sensations I once had, but the sermons all seemed to point out that people were not doing enough to please God. I guess we all knew that none of us were doing enough, particularly the gay population in the congregation.

Since I'd been going out, my senses were sharper, especially when it came to finding other gay men in the church. I noticed them more often now but not in a purely sexual way. And I watched how they acted around women and men in order to get some idea of how I was to act in similar situations. On the one hand I felt as though I had to be honest with myself regarding my sexual attraction to men, but I also knew that the church was not the environment where sexual attraction was a particular interest or priority.

Everybody knew those heterosexual members who were involved in extra-marital affairs and those who were blatant fornicators. The drinkers and smokers were also fairly obvious. Pastor Goodman had enough material to preach about without ever mentioning homosexuality. Still, he eventually breezed over these issues on his way to this more 'life threatening' issue. Those sermons became very popular after the advent of the virus that causes AIDS. In that day, every religious demagogue had medical proof that God wasn't pleased with the gay community. They called it the "plague".

"Saints, God is not pleased today."

Amen!

"Satan is loose and he is plaguing the nation with a deadly virus for which there is no known cure. I know that some of you have heard about AIDS and HIV. It's killing our young men."

Lord have mercy, today!
"They say that this virus can live in your body for years before it starts to kill you—breaking down your immune system. I've read accounts where men have suffered horrific deaths at the hands of this virus."
Have mercy, Lord!
"Children of God, no one deserves to die a death the likes of what I've heard, but God is trying to tell us something. If we don't straighten out our lives, He'll destroy us and raise up a nation of people that will obey His commandments."
That's right, Reverend!
"Now, they say that this virus came over from Africa—contracted from a green monkey, but somehow a flight attendant got it and brought it back over to the States. He was homosexual..."
Lord, have mercy!
"...and when he did what it is they do together with other men...y'all don't hear me."
Speak, Pastor!
"When he started burning in his lust for another man and actually laid with another of his own kind, he gave the virus to that man. You all know the story. Before long, homosexuals all over the country were dying of this mysterious virus. Now, it's an epidemic. I tell you. God's not pleased. Just like in the days of Sodom and Gomorrah, He is purging the city of wickedness and He's looking for a righteous man. The Bible speaks of God cursing those that rebel against Him."
Amen!

The sermon went on and on about how AIDS was a curse from God against gay America. I couldn't believe my ears. Pastor Goodman had been one of the most intelligent non-academic types that I'd known. He was articulate and insightful with regard to the scriptures, a community leader and a role model. After that sermon, my opinion of him plummeted. I don't know if it was because I was gay that I took exception to everything he said, or if it was the fact that he dared to substantiate his homophobia with the Holy Bible. During the sermon, I wanted so badly to rise up from my seat and challenge him, but I would have been lynched. Those people were riled up—their righteous indignation stirred.

Throughout the services, I saw people give Paul and a few other choir members menacing glances—almost accusing them of bringing HIV to our community. I decided that I'd had enough, so right in the middle of pastor's sermon I went outside to have a smoke. I went around to the back of the church—where all the smokers gathered—and I found several other young guys back there who'd decided to have a smoke as well. Paul was among them.

"Why didn't you sing with us today," Paul playfully chastised.

"Well, I'm only here for the summer, and I didn't attend choir rehearsals."

"As you can tell, we haven't learned any new songs. Pastor has been coming to choir rehearsals and teaching the Word."

"He what?"

"Uh Huh. He says that we all need to know and understand what we're singing about so he is teaching us instead of us learning new songs."

"How long has this been going on?"

"For about two or three weeks. Some of the other guys in the choir have already left. They joined the choir over at Rev. Eliot's church—Liberty Temple."

"That choir can *sang*," I said.

Paul lit up another cigarette and stared straight out over the back parking lot—thinking. I thought that it would be a good opportunity to talk to Paul about the sermon.

"When did the pastor start harping on AIDS and homosexuality?"

The question caught Paul off guard and just when he had inhaled from his cigarette. He exhaled the remainder of the smoke and looked at me. It was a look of sadness and despair.

"You're grown now, Fitzgerald. I remember when you were just a little boy—running around here and shouting. I think you know why Pastor is saying these things. There are a few of us left here who were born and raised in this church—long before Pastor Goodman came—and we're not leaving. Let me tell you something, Fitzgerald..." I noticed the resolution in Paul's voice as he squared his shoulders.

"Listen, you don't have to make any confessions to me or anything like that," I began. "I've known that you and some of the others were gay for years, but what I want to know is how you all can sit here Sunday after Sunday and be humiliated—all in the name of religion. Pastor may as well start naming names and pointing fingers over the pulpit."

"I don't think that would be a wise thing to do. He just might find that he has a lot of company in the crowded closet of this church. Honey, most of these people don't pick up their Bibles until it's time to go to church," Paul said. "And a whole lot of them are carrying on with 'their own kind'."

Paul took another long drag from his cigarette. He looked wise and tired. He was no longer the young man I remembered. Though only in his thirties, Paul's face and attitude were mute testimony of how oppression can age a gay black man.

"When we were young, people called us sissies and fags on a daily basis because they were ignorant; they really didn't know any better. Now, as adults, people are still calling us fags and sissies—only now they use nicer words and their calling us perverts and psychos is backed up by the government, schools, the medical profession, our families, and even God himself," Paul said.

In those few moments, Paul had relived his entire life of rejection and prejudice, especially within his own family and in the church. I never knew that he was so unhappy, but how could I have? Anger stirred in me as I tried to persuade Paul to do something about being lambasted in Sunday services. I used all my militant vocabulary and evocative skills to no avail. Paul only looked at me, half smiling.

"Baby, you sound like those white boys in Washington, DC—fighting for gay rights. The only right you do have, honey, is to keep your mouth shut about the certainty of your homosexuality and to not make any waves in the community. If you think there was a riot here in '68, these niggas will tear up Chicago looking for the 'children'."

"That is so depressing and hopeless, Paul."

"It's reality, honey. Don't get me wrong, I think you have great ideas, but they are only ideas. People will never accept gays—especially black gays—as equals in society."

"But can't the revolution start here in this church and in this neighborhood? You just can't co-sign your own death warrant, and if you remain under Pastor's ministry, that's just what you'd be doing."

"Don't worry about Pastor and this "gay" thing, honey. It's like anything else, baby. Eventually, this AIDS thing will blow over and there will be other issues for the black church to address—like welfare and the miseducation of its youth. I don't see any real need to get alarmed."

"But don't you feel injustice is being served to the black gay community and that we are allowing this injustice to prevail by our silence?"

"It doesn't matter, Fitzgerald. Even if we speak out, what will we say? All that would do is give them yet more reasons to hate us and exclude us. They outnumber us. Hell, they got God on their side. The best we can hope for is to be left alone and to catch some of the leftover Holy Ghost that falls from the Welcome Table." Paul motioned for one or two of the others to walk back to the front of the church and gave me a wink as he walked away.

I was stunned by Paul's attitude. After finishing my cigarette I returned to my seat in the back of the church. By then Pastor was wrapping up his sermon and inviting people to join the church. Just when it seemed that no one would accept the invitation to discipleship, a young man rose from his seat and slowly, and with great difficulty, walked down the aisle. He was a mess—crying and raising his arms. The congregation of mostly women and children roared with applause. They were always excited when men joined the church, especially with the current shortage of "good, God-fearing" men around.

The pastor welcomed this young man and introduced him to the congregation. His name was Mickey and he was new to the neighborhood. Still weeping and "praising God," Mickey managed to confess that he had already been baptized and had backslid from the church. He had a real testimony and the sisters in the congregation were shouting up a storm. Hell, I felt like doing a jig myself. As Mickey continued in his testimony, I noticed him getting a little shaky and he had to be assisted to a chair facing the congregation. It was then that he confessed to the church that he had recently been delivered from a homosexual lifestyle and that he was afflicted with the virus that causes AIDS.

Silence.

Even the babies stopped crying. Pastor slowly released his grip of Mickey's shoulders and suggested that the two of them meet later that week for counseling. No one ever saw him again.

The ride home was a quiet one, but (being the instigator that I am) I decided to break the silence. I knew that Ma feared me bringing up the subject of Pastor's sermon and that she probably wished that I could have found another way home. I could almost hear her teeth grinding nervously.

"Boy. That was some sermon today. Wasn't it?" I began.

No one answered. I hadn't expected that they would. Deep down inside, I didn't think that Ma and Ray really agreed with Pastor on the direction of his ministry, but they would never tell us kids that. Finally, Tina (who normally slept during the sermons) asked what Pastor meant by God cursing "at" people. Ma tried to explain:

"It's not like cursing when you say a bad word or anything like that, Tina. God becomes angry with rebellious and disobedient people and He punishes them."

"Does He kill 'em, too?" she asked.

"Yes. Sometimes he does kill them—like in the story of Noah's Ark and the Ten Commandments."

"I think that's pretty mean...to kill someone just because you don't like 'em."

"It's not that God doesn't like them." Ma continued. "He doesn't like the things that they do."

"Why does God care what people do as long as they love Him? It shouldn't matter."

Out of the mouths of babes.

I gave Tina's knee a squeeze in approval. Ma had been watching me through the passenger-side mirror and she looked worried.

"But it does matter, Tina," Ma said.

Things continued to be tense—with the family speaking as little as possible about anything at all. I sometimes loved it when Ma and them were silent about something or other. It usually meant that they were thinking, and thinking was a good thing. While everyone escaped to their rooms to take their afternoon naps before dinner, I decided to sit in the kitchen and talk to Ma. I had grown up enough not to fear her as much as I once had. Though I always knew how far to go with certain subjects, I could always rely on Ma to challenge my beliefs as I challenged hers. That day, however, she didn't feel much like talking.

"What's wrong with everybody? Everybody is acting like someone has died," I asked.

Ma continued preparing dinner—never even looking in my direction or acknowledging my comments. Now, I was worried. After several moments of silence between the two of us, she said, "I hope you haven't been going around here telling your sister that you're that way. She doesn't need to know."

"As a matter of fact, I haven't told her a thing; I don't think she'd understand."

Ma looked relieved, and then she just stood at the stove staring at me as if she'd never seen me before.

"You know, I sent a perfectly fine boy off to college and after one year you come back into my house telling me that you like guys, you drink, you smoke, and God knows what else you do. I don't know what will come out of your mouth next, Fitzgerald. And I don't need this frustration. You strut through here like you have the answers to everything in your shirt pocket and the rest of us are damned idiots. You've got a lot to learn, Fitzgerald T. Washington. Just keep living."

Ma was telling me exactly how she felt and I got the feeling that soon I wouldn't be welcomed home with the same enthusiasm as before. The chasm between us was growing and I had no earthly idea as to how I could bridge it. I couldn't tell Ma that inside I was just a little boy craving his mother's approval and support. While I sat there, realizing that Ma was at the point of washing her hands of me and the whole 'gay' issue, I felt as though I was truly alone in the world.

"I'm sorry, Ma."

"For what, Fitzgerald?"

"I'm sorry that I have caused you so much pain over the years. I'm sorry that I'm gay. I just have these feelings that I can't ignore. I don't know how to cope with them because there are too many to deal with. I'm doing my best to remain sane, you know? I would pray about them, but I don't think God will listen to a homosexual's prayer unless it's one of repentance for being gay."

"I can't imagine what you're going through, Fitzgerald, but I do know that God still cares. He's patient. He'll keep knocking at the door of your heart until you hear Him and let Him in."

"Can't we talk like friends and not like church-goers for a change? I know the scriptures, too. All of that stuff is fine on the onion-skin pages of our deluxe, leather-bound Bibles, but how does it translate into real life experience?"

"That's just it. Until you really experience life, scriptures won't mean a thing. In the meantime, could you tone it down just a little for your sister's and my sakes. I may not know a lot about being homosexual, but I don't think that's the way you want to live your life—a life of rejection and condemnation. Why would you want to do that to yourself?"

A storm raged in my brain as I listened to my mother's voice that knelled the first few rocky years of my adulthood. How right she was. The last thing I wanted out of life was to not be accepted, but what was I supposed to do? Who, on earth, did I have to turn to for support? I guess Paul was right: a queen's life can be grand, but ain't nothing grand about being alone.

Amen to that.

BIOGRAPHY Alaric Wendell Blair

The author of **The End of Innocence: a journey into the life**, Alaric Wendell Blair is best known for his scholarly and critical voice in **The Harvard Gay and Lesbian Reviews, Lambda Book Report**, and **Venus** magazine. A critical work of the Chicago native also appears in the best-selling anthology **Back 2 Back**—which features the works of James Earl Hardy.

Alaric has also worked as an educator, journalist, and activist. He is working on a number or scholarly papers for publication and a series to his debut novel. This excerpt from his novel appears courtesy of Mirage Publishing Company.

Like the protagonist in this story, Alaric was raised in a strict Black Baptist Church that forbade his disclosure of his homosexuality. The story describes a young man's desire for spiritual equality and freedom from the oppression of the church.

MEIRA JAEL BAT AVRAHAM V'SARA: A Spiritual Autobiography
Cynthea Masson

This essay was originally written as the answer to "Question Four" of the Jewish Information Class Take Home Examination in March of 1997: "Write a spiritual autobiography." The essay covers part of the process and some of the issues involved with my conversion to Judaism. It was directed to the Reform rabbi who was supervising my conversion. The title of this piece includes my chosen Hebrew name, "Meira Jael." Hebrew names incorporate the names of one's Jewish parents; people who have converted to Judaism conventionally add "bat Avraham v'Sara," daughter of Abraham and Sarah.

I begin with the assumption that my spiritual autobiography is different from that of most Jewish Information Class students. This is not to say that it is better or worse or that no one else, in the history of JIC, has followed a similar path to mine. Nonetheless, I know that most of the students in my JIC class are planning to marry a Jewish partner (of the opposite sex) and are choosing Judaism, at least in part, as a necessary step toward a Jewish wedding and family. I realize that no one's journey toward Judaism is that simple; everyone has slightly different reasons beyond marriage for choosing Judaism. Yet I also know that the introductory remarks in the first JIC class were almost all variations on the following theme: "Hello, I am here with my fiancé(e), and we are taking this class because we are getting married next year." I was seated at the opposite end of a very long table from the couple chosen to begin the introductions; thus, by the time my turn came around, expectations had already been set. My words did not meet those expectations: "Hello, my name is Cynthea. I am here with my partner, Tracy. I am taking this course because I am interested in learning more about Judaism."

I have always been a very spiritual person. By "spiritual" I mean that I have always believed in the Divine; I have always believed that we are more than just our biological bodies, that we are connected to the Divine, and that, through the Divine, we are connected to each other. However, until recently, I was not religious. As a child I went to church infrequently. I think that I was baptized Anglican, but I am not certain. If I was baptized, the ceremony likely was done as a matter of protocol rather than of unwavering faith. My parents were not religious at all. Occasionally my grandmother would take me to a Palm Sunday service—I only remember this because I liked the small crosses, made of palm fronds, that I held during the service. Other than gift-giving at Christmas and candy baskets at Easter, that was the beginning and end of my Christianity.

As I grew older, I became interested in spiritual visualization and meditation. I joined a meditation group during my undergraduate years at the University of Guelph. We would focus on opening ourselves to the Divine, on sensing and using the energies that flow around and through us. This particular practice was an extension of the other major source of learning and growth for me at that time: feminism. Although I had known that I was a lesbian since the age of fourteen, I had never met any other lesbians or women who thought positively, from a feminist perspective, about being lesbians.

My growing circle of friends, whom I met at the University of Guelph in the mid to late 1980s, were all self-identified feminist lesbians. Most of these women were also vegetarians; they were concerned for the environment and for animal rights. They strove for freedom from all types of oppression and worked toward equality for all people at the grass roots level. Over the course of my undergraduate years, my understanding of the world—both physically and spiritually—was greatly influenced by these women.

Of course, most of these women spoke stridently against the 'patriarchy' and, consequently, against the so-called 'patriarchal' Judeo-Christian religions. The thought of joining a Christian church repelled me at that time; the thought of becoming Jewish never entered my mind. Instead, I was swept up willingly into the Women's Spirituality Movement. This 'movement' does not have one leader; moreover, it is not organized in any formal way. Yet, wherever I would go, women were gathering into small groups to perform rituals, form healing circles, and participate in spiral dances. Such activities were prominent at women's festivals and, in particular, at the Michigan Womyn's Music Festival[1] in the mid to late 1980s.

I vividly remember one night at Michigan when hundreds of women gathered in a field around a huge tree for a full moon ritual and dance. The woman facilitating this ritual celebration broke us into four groups, according to our elemental signs; earth, air, water, fire. Each group had to develop a dance to represent that particular sign. I was in the water group; we just danced around in a waving motion while making swishing noises. But the earth group had us all place our hands on the earth; they then began to pound the earth with their fists. Because hundreds of 'earth' women were doing this, I could feel the vibration move from the earth up through my arms. I could see the moon through the branches of that tree. For the first time in my life I felt connected to the sky, the people, the earth—the life above, beside, and below me. To me, this was an experience of the Divine Presence in the world.

Despite the power of this night and many other positive experiences at women's rituals throughout the years, I gradually felt a growing dissatisfaction with what I perceived as a lack of organization and spiritual sincerity at some of the rituals. One particular full-moon ritual, which I attended three years ago, consisted of a bunch of women running around howling at the sky and each other. I left early with some of my equally dismayed friends. What had once appealed to me began to feel surprisingly trite. I also found myself getting annoyed at women who claimed that they worked for everyone's equality and then proceeded to make negative comments about people who followed 'patriarchal' religions such as Christianity and Judaism. I believe, even today, that women's spirituality and ritual has a valuable role to play in the world and, in particular, in women's communities. However, my personal understanding of spirituality and religion had begun to shift by the early to mid-1990s.

This change of attitude was caused, in part, by the new and more informed understanding of Christianity that I gained from my work as a graduate student. My Ph.D. dissertation, *Crossing the Chasm: The Rhetoric of the Ineffable in Margery Kempe and Julian of Norwich*,[2] discusses the methods by which two medieval women rhetorically construct their mystical experiences or, for lack of a better term, divine encounters. Using theories of negative theology (which maintain that God cannot be known or explained in human terms) in combination with rhetorical theories of figures such as chiasmus (which posit ineffable points of crossing between opposites), I argue that Julian of Norwich and Margery Kempe rhetorically structure their texts to point or gesture toward that which can never fully be explained in words. Although these particular mystics are Christian, my work on female mystics, mysticism in general, and negative theology in particular helped me to realize that (just as 'lesbian' does not mean one thing) 'Christian' has many connotations beyond its God-the-Father, Christ-the-Son 'patriarchal' theology. Julian of Norwich, for one brief example, discusses God as "Father" and Jesus as "Mother" who nurtures and protects her children.

Although the subject of Christian mysticism fascinated me, it remained just that: a subject for study. Despite the numerous books and articles I read on various aspects of Christianity during the course of my M.A. and Ph.D., I was not swayed to attend Christian services. The thought of actually believing in Christ as Saviour held no appeal for me. Indeed, the most personally appealing aspect of all my academic study was the idea that God cannot be described in human terms at all—or, to put in another way, that the Divine is beyond all language and even all thought. As Vincent Gillespie and Maggie Ross contend, "(God) can only be loved, not thought".[3] Arguably, the iconography of Christ—an apparently divine being—hanging on a cross contradicts the idea of an ineffable God.

By the time I met my partner in January 1995, I was in my last full year as a graduate student at McMaster University. Because my partner was Jewish I decided, out of respect for her and her background, to read a few books and gain some knowledge on Judaism. To my surprise, much of what I read about Jewish belief in God corresponded to what had already come to be my own belief. In particular, I was drawn to the Jewish faith in God's existence and Oneness and, at the same time, Jewish rejection of physical representations of God. Indeed, I discovered that, to Jews, even God's name is ineffable. This initial appeal spurred me to read more and eventually, to join the JIC class.

Ironically, or perhaps inevitably, the first Shabbat service I attended was at the Michigan Womyn's Music Festival (in August 1995). Although I had not noticed it before, the Jewish lesbians at the festival had, over the early 1990s, organized themselves to such an extent that by 1995 they had their own tent and program of events. Earlier that year I had observed Passover with my partner, but from the point of the Michigan Shabbat (and, in particular, of Havdalah) onward, Judaism was something that I would pursue for my own sake (rather than simply out of respect for my partner). In my dissertation, I had spoken about the crossing of opposites as the point where the human and the divine theoretically meet—a point beyond all thought and language, and, thus, beyond memory. At Michigan I attended the Havdalah service and, when the words were read in English (after the Hebrew) I felt moved to tears. To me, this service marked my point of crossing. Like the rhetoric of the mystics who attempt to recount their understanding of the Divine, the words of the Havdalah service gesture toward Divine presence at the moment of crossing between opposites: "Holy One of Blessing, Your Presence Fills Creation. You separate the holy from the not-yet-holy, light from darkness, Israel from the other people, Shabbat from the six other days. Holy One of Blessing, You separate the holy from the not-yet-holy".[4] When I returned from Michigan I began to keep my journal and record my journey towards Judaism from that point forward.

Through the remainder of 1995 and into 1996, I continued reading about Judaism. Although I was preparing for my dissertation defense and teaching a third-year course for the first time, I managed to read through several books. I was, however, worried that I could not attend services because I did not have the money to become a member. Fortunately, I had a student in my Chaucer class who told me about the Reform congregation to which he belonged. He explained that he and his wife had attended services for a few years before becoming members. Thus, I attended my first Shabbat in early 1996.

At the 1996 Michigan festival I again attended many of the services and events organized by the Jewish women. One of the most interesting workshops in which I participated focused on tefillin. A woman showed other women (most of whom, being women, had never worn tefillin) how to put them on, what prayers to say, et cetera. I thought at the time that, quite likely, this would be one of the few opportunities I would ever have to learn about tefillin. I also bought a Star of David at Michigan—one which I will begin to wear after mikvah. I wanted to buy this pendant at that time because the Jewish lesbians at this festival were influential in helping me to reconcile feminism with Judaism.

As opposed to some of the non-Jewish feminists who speak out against the so-called 'patriarchal' aspects of Judeo-Christian religions, the Jewish women at Michigan helped me to realize that such generalized accusations were unfounded and based, primarily, on a lack of knowledge about Judaism. Most non-Jews, for instance, do not realize that there are different movements within Judaism (Orthodox, Conservative, Reform, et cetera). Clearly, many feminist women and lesbians find spiritual fulfillment within the various traditions of Judaism. Indeed, one lesbian couple had their daughter recite her Torah portion for her upcoming Bat Mitzvah in front of a circle of supportive, mostly lesbian, women. Although I believe that lesbians can and should become members of mainstream Jewish congregations, this type of support within the Jewish lesbian community is essential to combat the isolation many lesbians feel within primarily heterosexual Jewish organizations.

By September of 1996 I was enrolled in the Jewish Information Class. As time moves forward, Judaism is becoming more and more a part of my everyday life. The rhythm of the Jewish calendar feels right to me. I enjoy the observance of mitzvot and holidays, especially Shabbat, Yom Kippur, and Passover. Judaism reinforces the belief I have always had in God and provides the formal organization and religious sincerity for which I have always longed. Becoming 'officially' Jewish is important to me because I will then be able to publicly validate the choice I have already made in my mind and spirit.

The second part of the 'spiritual autobiography' question on the JIC examination asks, "What changes do you anticipate in your life?" I find this to be a difficult question to answer. I do not know what changes to anticipate; I know only what changes I have experienced thus far. Presumably, my Judaism will result in a life-long process of making Jewish choices for myself and my children (should I be blessed with them). Thus far, the changes have been gradual rather than sudden and, therefore, have not been immediately obvious. Indeed, they feel like natural progressions within my growing faith. I have noticed, for example, that I am much more aware of North America's Christian-focused attitude. Although I have, for many years, made it a habit to wish people "Happy Holidays" rather than mention any particular holiday, I now find that store clerks who wish me "Merry Christmas" annoy me more than ever before. I realize that they are attempting to be friendly, but they annoy me in the same way that straight people annoy me when they assume that I must have a boyfriend. How does a store clerk know what my faith is? Why do they presume that I celebrate Christmas?

Likewise, I have noticed that I am more sensitive to issues of anti-Semitism. Although I was already aware of issues surrounding various types of prejudice and oppression (through my feminist theory background) and have, for many years, integrated discussions of these issues into my teaching, I now make conscious efforts to raise awareness specifically of anti-Semitism. I also pay more attention to news about Israel. I organize my schedule around Jewish holidays. I think daily about my relationship with God and other people.

Generally, when I am planning a trip somewhere, I worry if there will be any lesbians there. This is especially true when I venture to relatively isolated places. Now, when I think about spending eight weeks in North Bay this summer to teach, I ask myself, will there be any Jews there? If a small congregation does exist, will the people accept someone who has not yet officially converted? Will there be any Jews who accept lesbians? Will there be any Jewish lesbians? I find, in other words, that my identity and my day-to-day concerns are being reshaped by my expanding faith in God and knowledge of Judaism.

The last part of Question Four asks about the challenges encountered in the process of becoming Jewish. All of the challenges I have met in this process stem from my identity as a lesbian—or, more accurately, from attitudes of other people toward that identity. Some of my lesbian acquaintances initially questioned my interest in what they still perceive to be a misogynist religion. Most often, however, I have remedied this problem by explaining the diversity within Judaism (and, in particular, the value Reform Judaism places on equality of men and women at services and the increased use of gender-neutral language in updated siddurim) and by emphasizing my desire that my friends respect my choice. I find, more and more, that feminist lesbians are recognizing the need to respect difference within the lesbian community. Many feminists of the 1990s (as opposed to those of the 1980s) have received extensive education (both formal and informal) on issues of anti-racism and appreciation of difference. Unfortunately, an equivalent education appears to be rare within the general, heterosexual, Jewish population.

I realize that efforts are being made within the Jewish community to begin this process of education. In November, for instance, the Temple hosted a full-day conference on ethnic diversity, multiculturalism, and racism. Nonetheless, the only 'ism' covered in the JIC class is anti-Semitism and, though certainly a crucial topic to cover, this is not the only 'ism' affecting the cohesiveness of the Jewish community. I believe that educated instructors who are trained to lead workshops on anti-heterosexism, anti-racism, and appreciation of difference should be integrated into at least one three-hour class of the JIC program. This will, in turn, promote understanding and support for all Jews by people who are about to join the Jewish community. Certainly, we cannot expect others to eliminate anti-Semitism from their communities if we make little effort to rid heterosexism and racism from our own. As many of us realize, as long as any form of oppression continues to exist, the door remains open for others to flourish.

My lesbianism cannot be separated from my Judaism anymore than Judaism can be separated from any choice any Jew ever makes. This is something that heterosexual people, in general, tend to ignore or make no effort to understand. "Why have a gay and lesbian synagogue?" straight people often ask. "You people are welcome here!" This may be true. However, people who make such comments neither fully realize the importance of a lesbian community to lesbians nor fully recognize how isolating it can be to be one of a very small number of lesbians in a predominantly heterosexual congregation. This has been the greatest challenge to me thus far. The quoted statement above is, in effect, analogous to a Christian saying to a Jew, "Why have synagogues? Why not attend services at our Ecumenical Church? We worship God here!"

Yes, my partner and I have been welcomed by most people at the Temple. We have met some very good friends and are thankful that we were accepted into the JIC class as a couple. However, certain people have made us feel very uncomfortable. One congregant, in particular, has made my partner feel so uncomfortable that she dreads attending Shabbat services! (She has been constantly harassed by one man who insists that she should get married and that he would marry her himself if he were younger.) We realize that this is just part of being lesbian in a predominantly heterosexual world. We often feel that we have no right to expect people to change. However, as human beings, no matter where we are, we simultaneously hold out the hope that someday people will stop assuming that we are straight, stop asking us (individually) when we plan to marry a man, stop assuming that we are not really family, that we cannot really get married, that we are not planning to have children, that we have chosen to be lesbians. We hold onto the hope that someday Jewish gays and lesbians will not be a controversy, an 'issue' in need of discussion and resolution, but will be valued by all as a legitimate part of the fabric of the Jewish people.

Endnotes

1. The Michigan Womyn's Music Festival (also known simply as "Michigan") is a women-only, lesbian-positive festival held each year in August.
2. McMaster University, 1995.
3. Gillespie, Vincent and Maggie Ross. *The Apophatic Image: The Poetics of Effacement in Julian of Norwich*. **The Medieval Mystical Tradition in England.** Ed. Marion Glasscoe. Cambridge, England: D.S. Brewer, 1992. 53-77; 55.
4. Diamant, Anita and Howard Cooper. **Living a Jewish Life: A Guide for Starting, Learning, Celebrating, and Parenting**. New York: Harper Perennial, 1991, 63.

BIOGRAPHY Cynthea Masson

In the Fall of 1997, I formally converted to Judaism through Bet Din and Mikvah. My commitment to Judaism and study of Torah continues today. I am currently enrolled in a course on Jewish Feminist Theology through which I not only have been exposed to the experiences, theories, and theologies of other Jewish feminists but have also met some incredible women and wonderful friends. My academic work on medieval mysticism and, more recently, on medieval alchemical literature, continues on a postdoctoral fellowship.

CONVERSION CLASS
Cynthea Masson

Shema Israel: Adonai Ehloheinu, Adonai Echad!
Hear, O Israel: the Eternal is our God, the Eternal is One!

I am a lesbian not yet Jewish.
My mind and spirit are in transition
Learning to rewrite the past in a room
Full of heterosexual couples
Anticipating huppah. My partner
Breathes in patience as I sound my Hebrew
Letters, returning to aleph, voiced from
Silence.
If I were to scream would you hear
Me? Could you hear a sound formed without words?
You say nothing against us. No one quotes
Leviticus. No one says we are an
Abomination. No one asks us to
Leave. We explain we are partners; like you,
One is Jewish; one awaits the mikvah.
You tolerate, but can you understand?

Shema Israel, hear us, we have a voice!
Hear our prayers as we light the Shabbat lights.
Hear our faith as we read the Haggadah.
Hear our strength as we blow Shofar. Do we
Not worship the God who is One? Do we
Not understand persecution? Do we
Not deserve our names in the Book of Life?

Shema Israel! God is One and we two
Are one in partnership, founded in love
Made in the image of God.

NOTES:
Shema Israel	The Jewish prayer that declares God's Oneness (Deuteronomy 6:4).
Huppah	The traditional canopy under which a Jewish couple is wed.
Aleph	The first (and silent) letter of the Hebrew alphabet.
Mikvah	The ritual bath taken as the last step of conversion.
Shabbat	The Hebrew word for the Sabbath, the day of rest.
Haggadah	The book containing the liturgy of the Passover seder (meal).
Shofar	A ram's horn, blown on Rosh Hashanah (the Jewish New Year).

MORMON PIONEER: Facing My Truths - My Own Story
Frank G. Hull

I remember my Baptism.

I was eight years old and one of the first to be baptized in our new baptismal font. Brother Ryan* baptized me. The chapel had just been completed. The Halifax branch of The Church of Jesus Christ of Latter-day Saints was born. How befitting that my rebirth would happen at such an exciting time. Frank George Hull is now a Latter-day Saint. From that day forward I knew that I would now be accountable for all my sins, and that I would do my best to choose the right.

In primary class, my teacher gave me my Choose The Right ring. I was seven years old and I remember Sister Smithe's* words, "Frankie, you are such a righteous little boy. You are a shining example to your mom and dad. I want you to have this C.T.R. ring. It will help you to remember to always choose the right." Later in my life, Sister Smithe and I would become very close.

I spent a lot of time during my summers at Brother and Sister Smithes' house. My parents were often fighting. Home was a very unhappy place for me. The church became my everything at an early age. I was a child and everything had an answer. Right and wrong was very clear.

I started speaking in church at nine years old. I was the little boy with the strong testimony. Sundays were my escape from home. I wanted what everyone at church had. A Mommy and Daddy who got married in the Temple for time and eternity. Family home evening on Monday nights. Daddy would give a lesson out of the Book of Mormon. No coffee, no cigarettes, no tea, no alcohol, and because this tranquility did not exist in my home life, I looked down on my parents: Dad for fighting and hitting Mom, Mom for getting drunk and hitting me. I figured that the church was the answer for my family. As I got older, I realized that it was not. The child in me was fading fast and at twelve years old, reality would hit. Little Frankie would be all grown up in just four short years.

The beginning of 1985 was an exciting time for me. My birthday was coming up on January second and I was going to be twelve years old. Brother Ryan would ordain me into the Aaronic Priesthood as a Deacon. All worthy Latter-day Saint boys of twelve years of age receive the Aaronic Priesthood. That same year I would also discover my crushes on men.

Summertime came and I was going swimming almost every day at Sister Smithe's apartment building. I was also spending a lot of time with the missionaries. I had a secret crush on Elder Scott*. Before I continue, let me explain what an Elder is. At eighteen years old, the church ordains men into the Melchizedek Priesthood. You then have the title of Elder. At nineteen, you serve a Mission to teach and baptize others into the church. Missionaries travel and live together in pairs. As a Deacon, I could tract door to door with the missionaries to seek out new converts for the church.

I met a missionary who I became close to. His name was Elder Morris*. I talked to him over the phone every night. I told him about my home life. He made promises to me. One promise that stands out clearly in my mind, was his promise to take me back to California after he was finished serving his mission for the church. He told me not to talk to people about our phone calls. During one of our conversations, I asked Elder Morris if I could go dooring with him and his companion Elder Hanson*. He went one step further and received my mother's permission to stay with him for the month of August. I was so excited. I was going to be the youngest person ever to live with missionaries. Elder Morris told me not to tell anyone at church. I had no idea that my stay with the missionaries would take away my childhood, tear down my trust, and take away my faith in the Church of Jesus Christ of Latter-day Saints.

This is the first time I have ever written a record of my stay with the missionaries in so much detail. I feel like I am jumping off a high diving board with my eyes closed. So here it goes.

I remember looking through the picture window in the living room waiting for the missionaries to arrive. My suitcases were packed at the front door of the house. When the white K-car pulled up the driveway I felt this surge of excitement through my whole body. "Mom they're here! They're here!" I shouted. My mom gives me a kiss goodbye. She says, "Now be a good boy Frankie."

My mom was happy for me. She always trusted people from the church. I think that she knew it made me happy. I think she also believed that the church could provide for me in ways that she could not. My mother had joined the church shortly after I was born, when she was sixteen or seventeen. She had always allowed members to take me in the past. So giving me up to the missionaries was no different then seeing me off to Brother Ryan or Sister Smithe's home.

It was a basement apartment in Lower Sackville, Nova Scotia that would become my temporary home. I was picked up on a P-Day, Preparation Day for the missionaries, which was every Monday. On that day, missionaries have to prepare for the week, do housework, discuss new converts, make lesson plans and send in statistical data for the church. I remember the musty smell. The entrance was on the side of the house and Elder Morris assisted me down the cement stairs. His companion, Elder Hanson, followed behind with my suitcases. The entranceway was through the kitchen. The small living room was off to the side. There was a separate bedroom with two single beds, two dressers, and a small bathroom with a bathtub, shower and of course a toilet.

After supper, we went over our plans for the next day. There was a challenge. How was I going to walk the long distances? Walking door to door would be difficult for me because I have cerebral palsy. We had that white K-car, but missionary work was mainly knocking on doors finding new converts. I could walk short distances, but missionaries walk long distances. Elder Morris decided that he and Elder Handson could take turns carrying me on their shoulder.

I enjoyed the days in the hot summer sun. Most people would welcome us with refreshments. We'd introduce them to the church in the hopes that eventually they'd be baptized. (There were two baptisms during my stay with the missionaries). My first week with the missionaries was wonderful. I slept on the couch in the living room. We were in by 10 p.m., to bed by 10:30 p.m. and had to arise by 6:30 a.m. Elder Morris would often drop Elder Hanson off at home and take me to McDonalds or Dairy Queen for a treat. We had many long talks. I told him things like, "I don't want to go home," and "I wish you could be my dad."

Everything to me was fun and best of all it was better than home. Elder Morris represented everything I wanted. I thought: He'll take me away from home. I'll live in California with him. He'll get married in the Temple with a nice Latter-day Saint girl. We'll be the family I always wanted.

I remember it started at the end of my first week with the missionaries. Saturday night we went on a split. Elder Hanson was with Elder Scott and Elder Morris was with me. We had an appointment that finished early. Elder Morris and I went back to the apartment alone. Elder Morris was complimenting me on my work, saying, "You are such a good little missionary."

I remember telling him that I was not such a good missionary. I had a secret. Tears were in my eyes, as I confessed myself to Elder Morris. Finally, after beating around the bush, I just said it directly. "I think I like Elder Scott. I have these feelings." I thought for sure that he would be mad at me. I would never use the word 'gay'. That was a bad word and the thought that I might be gay was terrifying to me.

Elder Morris led the conversation from there. He asked me questions that were very difficult to answer. Two questions that stand out in my mind clearly were, "Have your privates ever got bigger down there?" and "Have you ever had dreams about Elder Scott?" After I answered yes to these questions I knew he understood exactly what I was talking about. He knew that I was scared. I told him that I felt alone. He assured me that I was not alone. He invited me to sleep in the same bed with him that night. We shared his bed for the rest of my stay.

To this day I still feel some guilt for accepting his offer to share his bed.

My memories of my nights in the same bed with Elder Morris come back to me in flashes. He'd cuddle me in the night. If he placed my body on top of his I knew that, this meant he'd be touching me sexually. He'd place his hands on my backside. He'd stimulate my genitals from behind. Sometimes he would kiss me. I kept quiet. Sometimes when he'd take down my pajama pants I'd shake my head "no." To this day, I wonder if Elder Hanson knew what going on in the very same room that he was sleeping in.

August passed. I'd never speak of the abuse. Or so I thought. Late September of 1985 I went swimming at Sister Smithe's indoor pool. The missionaries from Sackville also went swimming. Elder Hanson was the first to leave the pool to go up upstairs to the apartment. Sister Smithe, Elder Morris and I remained. We were playing and having fun together. When it was time for us to leave Sister Smithe witnessed Elder Morris touching my backside as we entered the male change room. While driving me home that evening she asked me a direct question. "Does Elder Morris touch you in your privates?" I was trembling and I just nodded my head "yes." The following Sunday, I was brought into the Bishop's office. Soon after, I met with the Mission President. The main concern of the church leaders was to keep me quiet. I was told not to tell my parents or anyone else. Elder Morris was transferred away. That was the last I saw of him. The church always taught us to obey our leaders. And I was going to do the right thing. Later in my life, I realized that doing the right thing for me would be more important then doing the right thing for the church.

It was 1991 and I had just got my apartment in Richmond Hill, Ontario. I was still an active member of the church. I was now an Elder and a year away from going on my Mission. However I would never go. I had a close friend Brian. I told him about Elder Morris and in 1992 he helped me scribe a report to the R.C.M.P. The outcome was a warrant for Elder Morris's arrest in Canada. The American authorities never forced him to come to Canada to face charges. During that year, I'd also come out as a gay man. In coming out, I realized that I would have to exile myself from the church, and just like the Mormon Pioneers who travelled to Salt Lake City to escape persecution from the others, I had to escape persecution from them.

After I came out, I had to go to the Church Court to be judged for excommunication. There were twelve church leaders in the room. This included the Stake President who is the leader for all the churches in the local area. Before entering the court, I met with the Stake President. I was told not to mention anything about the sexual abuse and the R.C.M.P. report or he would stop the court. This angered me and I told him that I will tell the truth. I was determined not to let any church leader scare me into hiding. I told them that I was gay. I told them about my abuse. The court was not stopped and for the first time I saw the church leaders as human beings who make mistakes, like all of us. I was equal to them. They decided not to excommunicate me. Instead I was sent to Church Social Services for help. I only attended two sessions. They wanted me to go through some kind of treatment. They were not specific. I prayed about this and I had a bad feeling. Something was not right. I had heard of the torture other gay men had to go through in the past. Things like shock treatments to your genitals, or brainwashing using guilt. It was time for me get away while I still had some sense of who I really was.

With no support system and my spiritual world in an upheaval, I discovered an organization by the name of Affirmation. I was reading a book I found at the library called **Out Of the Bishops Closet**. The book had mentioned Affirmation Los Angeles, an organization for Gay Lesbian, Bi and Transgendered Latter-day Saints.

My first contact with Affirmation was when I was still active in the church. I spoke with a man named Angel who really was my angel. Yes, Angel was his real name. (Years later, I found out that he died from an AIDS-related illness). I was around twenty-one or twenty-two at the time. I was feeling suicidal. I needed help. I found the phone number for Affirmation through directory assistance in Los Angeles, California. Affirmation gave me the help I needed to see that I had the freedom to find my own spirituality. Not from the church, the bible or the Book of Mormon but from within myself. I discovered that the wisdom and strength I needed to go on did not come from a book. I just had to look within me.

When I moved from Richmond Hill to Toronto I did not tell anyone at church. And I have not looked back since. I moved downtown from the suburbs because I wanted to be closer to the gay community and wheeltrans (a transportation service for the disabled).

However I still found myself missing the church. About five years ago, in 1994, I met a man while I was dancing on my knees at a bar called Colbys. He thought it strange to see a man on his knees dancing. At first he thought I was drunk. I assured him that I just couldn't dance standing. To my surprise he didn't ask me about my disability. He just said, "Dance on my feet." Later, he walked me home (well I drove in my electric scooter) and we took our time so we could talk. He told me he was HIV positive and I replied, "So, I have brain damage. Sounds like a good beginning to me."

So began a new journey for me.

Enrico Franchella, breaking every rule. Always shape shifting, changing, not fitting a mould. Loved for his courage, strength, his ability to see others and not through others. New journeys and new beginnings are never ending. Remembering we aren't here to see through each other, but here to see each other through.

I was with him and stayed at the hospital by his side the whole time. There was a five year waiting list to get into the subsidized housing in Toronto, and I needed to be close to Enrico to look after him. I prayed sincerely and received an apartment in two months. He passed away in my arms on May 16 at 11:30 p.m. 1996. I wish I could have married him in the Temple. I still find that thought strange because gay marriage in a Latter-Saint Temple is considered sacrilegious, yet the thought is comforting because a Temple marriage is for time and all eternity.

In 1997 I went to my first Affirmation conference in Salt Lake City. I met lots of other gay Latter-day Saints. We shared stories and I even talked to others who had also experienced sexual abuse. There were workshops on relationships, homophobia, and there was even a gay group of students from Brigham Young University, a Latter-day Saint University in Provo, Utah. I felt like I was back home again and being with all those queer Saints made me see that I could apply my value system to who I was. Being gay only forced me to become more open minded. So being gay was a blessing. Meeting gay and lesbian couples excited me the most. Some had been together for more than twenty years. I figured that there was hope for myself to find a stable relationship. (This is still a challenge to date). I even dated while I was at the conference. I met a man named Travis who took me to see the Mormon Tabernacle Choir. He was a gentleman. He showed me the same affections that straight couples show in public. He had his arm around me as we were sitting in our seats. An usher approached. I just told him that, "Everything is fine Elder. We are hoping the boys in the tenor section of the choir will notice." In confronting that usher, I now realize how that moment was very healing for me. I had no guilt about my sexual orientation. The truth had set me free and in spite of my conflicts with the church I learned to accept the Mormon in me and the gay man in me.

My next challenge would be sex. Oh I am full of a lot of stories when it comes to sex. But the reality was that I never really enjoyed it. Because of my experience with sexual abuse and the church, I felt guilty and dirty. I found it hard to feel safe with any man until I finally allowed myself to communicate my sexual needs and my fears with others. To my surprise good sex came during a very recent one-night stand. (He even told me that he had a boyfriend, so say good-bye value system). It was not my ideal romance. He was not going to be my eternal husband. But he was a part of my first steps to healthy sex. The details are explicit.

My sex life in the past consisted of blowing my partner off or jacking him off in a dark room at the bath house, theatre, etc. They got off. I did not. When I got tired of this kind of sex, I just became asexual. My hand was safer.

I met Patrick like I did Enrico, on my knees. He told me he found me delicious. I asked him if he would assist me off my knees to my chair so we could chat. I found him extremely sexy. I wanted sex and said to him, "I don't care if you have a boyfriend. I don't want to know. I just want to have sex with you. I want to take you home and have sex." He laughed and said, "YES."

I am used to driving the twenty-minute drive to my home in my chair. It was cold so we tried to get a cab. Most would not take a wheelchair and no wheelchair taxis were running. So Patrick figured how to get my electric chair into the trunk of a regular cab. We made it home. It took an hour to get a cab willing to take us. He did not give up.

Here is the hard part. I got really got excited during our kissing and petting. I went into a spasm. I lost complete motor control. I could not talk or walk. He remained calm. He said, "If you are okay, give me a signal." I looked at him and blinked. He managed to find my straws in the kitchen and got me some water. Then he just held me until it was over.

When I could talk, I proceeded to explain how my body works. He said he could already tell I had cerebral palsy. That it was okay. He understood. I told him that I had never cum with another man. He said, "Well, we are going to change that." He was gentle and he started touching me again and kissing. When my legs would stiffen he massaged them. We kept kissing. Sometimes I would laugh in pleasure. But the moment that stands out in my mind was when I started to cry after I had my orgasm. My biggest fear was spasming during sex and feeling safe. Now I know that it can be okay. I feel I also lucked out. Not very many gay men have knowledge of cerebral palsy like Patrick did. I feel that, in the future, I will have to communicate with other partners before I have sex with them, and tell them what could happen if I spasm. I feel this is my next challenge. One I am sure I will learn to face.

As for religion, I feel that it is like cars. Everyone is driving a different model trying to get to the same place. I believe I am finding my peace of mind through being my own kind of beautiful. I know it sounds churchy. But that Mormon churchiness is just another part of me. I have learned to apply my belief system to myself. Heck, maybe that gay Mormon man is waiting for me somewhere out there. Heck, any healthy relationship will do. It all starts with me. I would not change a thing. Good or bad, I have learned from each experience. I have earned my peace of mind and I plan to keep it. So it is okay to suffer. It is okay to hurt. Because through it all I have found some of my greatest joys.

*Names have been changed.

BIOGRAPHY Frank G. Hull

Writing this down has been very healing for me. This is the first time I have ever been published and the first time I have ever shared my personal story so publicly. Currently, I am not an active member of The Church of Jesus Christ of Latter-day Saints and to my knowledge I am still not ex-communicated. I do check in with the church through the general conference over the internet which is broadcast on the church's L.D.S radio network. I also listen to the Mormon Tabernacle Choir and I still enjoy the music from the church.

The church rejects me for wanting to have sex with men. I can not change for them. So I turn to myself for my spiritual needs and that has given me more freedom to grow and learn. I now have a safe home. I am single and I plan to choose my relationships wisely. I have never had a fancy job. My pension supports my temporal needs. I have a grade eleven education. As for my future, I will wait and see. It is not status that concerns me. It's being a part of the journey and what a ride it has been so far.

W.W.J.D. OR JESUS GOES TO PRIDE DAY
Jenn Thiessen

I am talking with my friend, Liw, about the upcoming Conference of Mennonites in Canada meetings. Liw and I are members of the Brethren & Mennonite Council for LGBT Concerns (BMC). Since BMC is not allowed inside the conference, we are going to set up an information table outside the gates of the convention site. Liw tells me she is planning to hang a sign near our information table with the four letters "W.W.J.D.?" Liw tells me that in the current fundamentalist Christian scene, W.W.J.D. has become a code for the question, "What would Jesus do?" Being a recovering fundamentalist myself, I started wondering, "What exactly would Jesus do if he was around today?"

Later, I am in dialogue with a woman from my church. She has seen a brief TV news clip about BMC's participation in the Toronto Pride Parade. In the clip, I am filmed reading my Bible and talking about my faith inside the church building. She wants to know why she wasn't asked before our church was outed as being gay positive on the local news. She is concerned about affiliating our church with some of the more fringe elements of the queer community. She wants to know, "Do I actually support Pride Day?" Now, I know that she has never actually been to Pride Day. She has no idea that much of the crowd is just as boring-looking as I am. She is picturing the entire crowd of 700,000 as outrageous drag queens, punk bull-dykes and naked leathermen. My misinformed friend wonders, "Do I want myself and our church associated with those people?" And again I wonder, "Would Jesus?"

I know that I could reassure this woman by telling her that the queer Mennonites in the BMC always keep our clothes on in public, usually exhibit gender-appropriate clothing and have few visible piercings, but instead I tell her that a crowd of 700,000 is going to include a bit of diversity. And I tell her that although I am not a member of the groups she is concerned with, I don't think that Pride should be only limited to those who look as bland as a bunch of queer Mennonites. How can I, as someone who experiences rejection for being queer, reject others because they are queerer than I am? What would Jesus do?

Would Jesus go to Pride Day? I think he would. Jesus loved a party. (Remember the wedding reception at Cana?) I picture a modern-day Jesus having a great time at Pride Day. First, I imagine him sitting in the PFLAG beer garden. Somebody's mother comes up and tells him that they are running out of beer; he turns some tap water into Canadian Lager. Later, he shares a few cold pints with Mary Magdalene. I picture Mary with six rainbow coloured earrings adorning the outer edge of her left ear. She is wearing black leather shorts with suspenders. There's a pack of Marlborough Lights rolled into her right sleeve revealing a black tattoo of thorns around her bicep. Jesus is wearing cut-off jeans, sandals (of course) and a white t-shirt that says, "Hate is Not a Family Value." The two friends laugh and reminisce about past adventures and their travels together.

After Mary leaves to go hear Carole Pope sing, Jesus decides to take a walk beside the AIDS Memorial in Cawthra Park. I see him begin to cry as he reads the seemingly endless list of names. Maybe he stops to place some flowers by a friend's name. When he reaches the section of new names for 1998, there is another man standing there, staring at his partner's nameplate. Jesus gently puts his arms around the grieving man and holds him while his body shakes.

When the time comes around for the Pride Parade itself, would Jesus be asked to be the parade's grand marshal? Would he even accept this prominent, prestigious role? Probably not. This is after all the same man who chose to make his grand entry as the Messiah, riding a donkey, not a stallion. Jesus didn't go for much pomp or prestige. If he's not the grand marshal, who would Jesus spend the parade with? Jesus was pretty flamboyant. Maybe he would go-go dance on the trendy Oz Hair Salon float. Or maybe not. Maybe he would just sit as a passenger on the Toronto Transit Commission's Pride Bus. Or is this too much like hiding your light under your bushel?

Would he march with queer Jews, or with BMC, or the queer Anglicans, or the queer Mormons? The Metropolitan Community Church? The Buddhists? Taoists? How would he choose? I suppose that since this is a 90's Jesus, he could don rollerblades and scoot back and forth between all the groups. He could give each group a few minutes, shake hands, pose for pictures and then move on like a politician. But—Jesus was a lousy politician. He never chose the actions that would make him popular—he chose the actions that felt right to him. He did what seemed fun and fulfilling for himself, while still being helpful for others—not what was expected or popular. Look at his life. When he was hungry, he invited himself for dinner with the despised tax collector Zacchaeus. When he was thirsty, he asked a Samaritan woman, who was considered unclean, for water. For disciples, he commissioned fishermen. He honoured tax collectors. One of his best friends was a woman previously possessed by seven demons. His career was introduced by a wild desert man, and he regularly mocked and showed belligerence to the religious leaders who could have helped his career. No, Jesus wouldn't schmooze from group to group just to keep everybody happy.

Jesus probably wouldn't even choose a group. (In the Bible, groups chose him. He ran away from the multitudes.) I think Jesus' preference would have been getting to know one person. Jesus sought out individuals who valued him and whose company he enjoyed—often these were the most marginalized and least understood people in the crowd.

I picture Jesus standing anonymously along Yonge Street watching the beginning of the parade. Eventually he sees someone dancing alone down the street. She's tall and quite feminine, but femininity has not come easily to her. Her tall stature and uncommonly large hands betray a split identity. She is clearly in the parade, but none of the groups marching nearby seem to be associated with her. Jesus looks into her eyes seeing pain, rejection, anger. There is also exceptional courage. Jesus looks deeper, past the bravado to a wounded soul with a fighting spirit. He sees beyond acts of both kindness and belligerence. He sees cherished friendships, victories and relationships. She meets Jesus' eyes and looks into his loving heart. He leaves the crowd and saunters over to her. She beckons him closer with one bright red-tipped finger. Laughing, he places one hand on her waist just as "I am what I am" begins to blare from the approaching sound truck. As Jesus dances with her down Yonge Street, will he be recognized? Could this be the Christ, the Son of God, dancing and celebrating life with a person proudly portraying gender-fuck in all its revolutionary confusion?

"They who have eyes to see, let them see."

BIOGRAPHY Jenn Thiessen

Jenn Thiessen is a Mennonite from Waterloo County. Although her life has always been urban (including electricity, plumbing, automobiles and not horses or barn-raising), her childhood was deeply segregated from voices of dissension. As an adult, she has chosen to walk away from the Mennonite voices concerned with binary ideas of fundamentalism and instead found community among other Mennonite people who share her devotion to the Christ-like ideas of community, dialogue, simplicity and the pursuit of peace, justice and understanding. As an out butch Toronto lesbian, Jenn is an active member of Danforth Mennonite Church, an employee of the Brethren and Mennonite council for LGBT concerns, and a member of the 1999 Toronto Pride Week Committee.

To contact the Brethren and Mennonite Council for LGBT concerns, write:
P.O. Box 43031 Eastwood Square, Kitchener, Ontario, N2H 6S9.
E-mail: BMCouncil@aol.com. Home page: http://webcom/bmc/

I AM A MUSLIM HOMOSEXUAL
Sulayman X

The Islamic Penal Law Against Homosexuals in Iran, approved by the Islamic Consultancy Parliament (30.07.1991) and finally ratified by the High Expediency Council on (28.11.1991) calls for the following:
> Article 110: Punishment for sodomy is killing; the Sharia judge decides on how to carry out the killing. Article 129: Punishment for lesbianism is one hundred (100) lashes for each party. Article 131: If the act of lesbianism is repeated three times and punishment is enforced each time, the death sentence will be issued the fourth time.

FROM HOMAN, the Iranian group which has dedicated itself to defending the rights of Iranian gays and lesbians, and which maintains a website at: http://www-pp.hogia.net/iran.homan/intro.html.

I am a homosexual. I have always been a homosexual. There has never been a time when I wasn't. It would be dishonest to say otherwise.

I am also a Muslim, and, inshalla, God willing, shall die a Muslim proclaiming my belief that there is no god but Allah, and that Muhammad is His Prophet.

It is not an easy matter to bridge these two worlds of Islamic spirituality and homosexuality, for Islam is fiercely homophobic, and what I am is an affront to Muslims all over the world. In some Muslim countries, I could be put to death, beheaded, burned, or thrown off the top of a high building. An intense hatred burns in the hearts of many Muslim fundamentalists, for who and what I am. I've lost track of how many times a Muslim brother said he wanted nothing more than to kill me, to crush the life out of me, to silence me forever.

In November of 1997, I started a modest Web site on the Internet called Queer Jihad. It was meant to be a place where gay and lesbian Muslims could find some consolation in a world which despises them, where they could share their stories, discuss homosexuality, come to terms with their sexual identity. Instead, I found myself buried in hate mail, death threats, slander and derision. Few of my homosexual brothers and sisters in Allah would not even so much as leave a message, for fear of their identity somehow being disclosed. But the haters and fag-bashers came full on. I would wake in the morning to discover my e-mail box stuffed with thousands of hate messages. My site was hacked. A protest was initiated to get my web page service provider—GeoCities—to kick me off their server. I was accused of a vast number of things: of being a Jewish conspirator trying to destroy Islam; of being paid by governments to undermine the image of Islam; of being immoral, promiscuous, immature and much, much more.

While other religions are coming to grips with homosexuality, or at least making an effort, Islam has yet to even begin. With an estimated 1.2 billion Muslims all over the globe, the number of Muslim homosexuals must be in the range of about 60 million and the needs of those 60 million men, women and children will have to be addressed.

The human rights group Homan, quoted above, says that since 1980, more than 4,000 homosexual men and women have been executed by the Iranian government. A recent report from Reuters said two homosexual men were executed by the fundamentalist regime Taleban by having a wall collapsed over top of them. OutRage, in the UK, says Muslim militia groups on the Philippines island of Mindanao have been terrorizing homosexuals, threatening them with castration in an effort to drive them elsewhere. They add that homosexual relationships are banned in many Islamic countries including Algeria, Bahrain, Bangladesh, Bosnia, Iran, Jordan, Kuwait, Lebanon, Malaysia, Oman, Saudi Arabia, Syria and the UAE. Homosexuality is punishable by death in Iran, Mauritania, Saudi Arabia, Sudan and Yemen. In Malaysia, the homosexual can be put in prison for twenty years.

Because of the oppression and fear, Muslim homosexuals have kept silent, myself included. We have every reason to be concerned as to what might happen to us if we break that silence. And yet, if there is ever to be a time when the Muslim homosexual can live in peace and be guaranteed basic human rights, the silence must be broken, the battle must be engaged. I have written a book, available on my internet site, called *A Guide for Gay Muslims*, which is my own breaking of the silence. It is offered to other Muslim homosexuals as one Muslim to another, addressing our common concerns and questions. In particular, I would call on Muslim homosexuals to remain true to their Islam, and to lead lives of decency pleasing to Allah despite the very real temptation to do otherwise.

My book is not an attempt to engage the Muslim world at large in a debate on homosexuality, for that is beyond my talents, and is, I suspect, time and effort not well spent. The more enlightened Muslims among us will already have discovered the truth about homosexuality; the less enlightened will continue to hate regardless.

> As Muslims, we have a responsibility that goes beyond ourselves, our
> community, and the ummah to the world as a whole. Concern for
> humanity, for suffering and ailment, for famines and disaster, for cruelty
> and hunger is only the first step towards this awareness.
> FUTURE OF MUSLIM CIVILIZATION, Ziauddin Sardar, p 228

Like homosexuals the world over, I know a great deal about hate. As homosexuals, we are, from our earliest years, the object of scorn and ridicule, carrying as we do our fearful, terrible secret. We read about ourselves in the straight man's books as being perverted, unnatural, given over to animal lusts. We are called sodomites, faggots, queers, reprobates, shaitan (satan). We are not like others; while friends talk endlessly about sexual interests, we keep our mouths shut. We don't dare be honest.

There is no solace to be had in the religion of our youth. This religion, we discover, condemns us. If you are Muslim, you are told the story of the Prophet Lut; if you are Christian or Jewish, you hear about Sodom and Gomorrah. You are attacked with scriptural passages like "men working with men that which is unseemly" or "surely you are exceeding the bounds." Like so many before us, we may spend years tormented by doubt and uncertainty. We are often well aware of our sexual identity; we may have read all about it in the secular press; we may even have homosexual friends and be leading the so-called 'homosexual lifestyle'. But still, those doubts remain. Are we pleasing to Allah? Will we go to Paradise when we die? Are we, because of our homosexuality, sinning? Are we mentally ill, spiritually unfit, given over to our lusts? Did we abandon Islam because we could not live up to its demands?

The fear of damnation is very real, one that can torture and torment endlessly. Such fear is actively promoted among the more hard-core religious fundamentalists, who hasten, at every opportunity, to assure us that we are on the path to perdition. They confuse us with endless prattle about 'choice' and 'lifestyle', how we have 'chosen' to be homosexual, and how we could, if we really wished to be pleasing to God, un-choose our homosexuality and be 'normal' like everyone else.

When I attend Friday Prayers at the local Mosque, I usually get there just before the prayer starts and vanish just as soon as it is finished. I would enjoy going earlier, making friends, participating in the Muslim community. But they don't want my participation. They are willing to extend friendship based on the assumption that I am a heterosexual, that I am part of the straight man and his straight world. If I were to blurt out that I was homosexual, the good will would vanish, and I would find myself the object of scorn and derision. I have heard many stories from homosexuals—both men and women—who have been driven from their Mosques for being honest about their sexuality.

During prayers, I try not to look at anyone. I don't want them to see my eyes, or take too much notice of me. I don't want to be found out—unveiled, outed, confronted. Still, is it me or are there whispers behind my back? Are there questions? Do I walk in such a way as to betray myself as an effeminate man? Was there something about the tone of my voice that set off alarm bells in the minds of those around me? Did I make a gesture with my hands that might characterize me as limp-wristed?

There are periods in my life when I don't go to Friday Prayers. While I would like to participate in the life of the Muslim community, I find myself angry at the treatment I receive from those around me, by the hypocrisy and transparency of those who would have nothing to do with me were I to be honest about my sexual identity. There are other times when I am just plain afraid—afraid of their anger, of what they might do to me should they discover my secret. There are times when I feel like a fraud, when I think that the prayers of those around me are sweet in the sight of Allah, but mine are a perversion, a travesty, a mockery. I remind myself that Allah does not base the worthiness of my prayer on my sexuality—that just because a man is heterosexual does not mean his prayers are worthy—but still I am troubled by doubts. What if Allah really does despise me?

Could it be that Allah truly detests the sight of me, that my prayers and my efforts to be just and righteous are a sham? Could it be that I am so totally deluded, so given over to a life of sin and reprobation that my every breath is an affront to Allah? Could my reason and judgement be so clouded and skewed that I am unable to tell the difference between right and wrong in such a fundamental matter as sex?

Homosexuality is natural for me: I have always been homosexual and I have never known anything else. Heterosexuality would be unnatural—not what I am inside and no matter how many times I've tried to put on that cloak, it doesn't fit. I am not interested in members of the opposite sex. No amount of trying, not even a failed marriage, has made a difference.

My soul tells me that I am homosexual, and to accept that, to move on. It does not condemn me; it does not haunt me. When I pray or talk inwardly with Allah, I feel no condemnation, no recrimination, no cause for guilt. My conscience is clean. It does not accuse me of doing wrong. Homosexuality is just a fact of life. It is not a rebellion against Allah or society. It is not a choice. It is not an attempt to stick out, to be different, to be obstinate in an illicit sin, to be any sort of exception to any sort of rule. It is not a political statement, not a fad, not a passing whim. It's not even something that I wanted to be but it is what I am.

The imam at the local mosque once compared me to a lustful animal bent on satisfying unnatural desires, as being unable to resist the temptation to depravity, as being no better than a dog in heat. Although he does not know me, he says I am depraved. He hands down his judgement upon me and never questions whether it is a fair judgement or not. He has probably not heard my side of the story. He would probably not care to listen if given the chance.

I would never be asked to serve as an imam, just as openly homosexual young men are not allowed to become priests in the Catholic Church. My homosexuality is somehow, in a way that is never clearly spelled out, an indication of spiritual confusion and unworthiness. Just the very fact that I am a homosexual somehow means that I am misguided, that my moral sense and moral judgement are skewed, that there is no possibility that I could be in possession of valid spirituality or have anything worth offering in the realm of spiritual matters.

This is the world that we inherit, the world that awaits each and every young soul that discovers it is a Muslim homosexual. Some of us believe that Islam can do better, that it has the strength to develop a compassionate, pragmatic response to homosexuality, and that the needs of 60 million hurting brothers and sisters—who want nothing more than to be members of their communities and to be honest about themselves—must no longer be ignored. Driving them away, misleading them with false information, killing them—surely this is not what Muhammad meant when he said that, "believers are not believers until they wish for others what they wish for themselves."

It was the eloquent Krisnamurti who once said:
> It is easy to hate, and hate brings people together after a fashion; it creates all kinds of fantasies, it brings about various types of co-operation, as in war. But love is much more difficult. You cannot learn how to love, but what you can do is to observe hate for what it is and let it drop away; brush it aside, it is not important.
> KRISNAMURTI 100 YEARS, p. 175

BIOGRAPHY Sulayman X

Sulayman X is a journalist and writer based in the Far East whose work has appeared in numerous Asian newspapers and magazines. He is also the founder of the Queer Jihad website and a member of the executive board of Al-Fatiha, a queer Muslim group based in the U.S. Sulayman X writes that, "The X in my name does not mean I'm a member of the Nation of Islam. Rather, my Muslim name was Sulayman Muhammad but in protest against the Islamic treatment of homosexuals, I dropped the Muhammad and replaced it with an X."

Contact: Al-Fatiha Foundation; P.O. Box 300, Astor Station, Boston, MA, 02123.
Tel: (617) 685 - 4175
Queer Jihad: www.geocities.com/westhollywood/heights/8977

Sulayman X's *Letter to a Loved One* also appears in this anthology.

MY HUMAN REVOLUTION
Kate Greco

I had one foot in the convent when I started university. Having been raised in a very devout Catholic family, with two aunts who are nuns, the thought of entering the convent seemed quite natural to me. My mother, a WASP who converted to Catholicism when she married my Italian Catholic father, was quite upset. She thought the nuns were 'influencing' me.

In my second year of university, I began dating a very nice law student. As our relationship progressed, I abandoned my 'vocation' and accepted his proposal of marriage. Not only was he a respectable person, but I knew it would please my parents if I married a lawyer. His profession represented financial security, which was very important to me.

As a twenty-year old newlywed, I moved to Parry Sound, Ontario where my husband was opening his own law practice. I attended the Catholic Church where there was a lone organist and no choir. Having sung in church and school choirs since my youth, I organized a choir, and led it for the next seven years—and what a seven years it was.

Four years into our marriage, while my husband and I were on a weekend boat trip with our best friends, I had an unexpected sexual awakening. The four of us were sleeping in close proximity in the boat, with the two husbands on the outside, and the two women side by side in the middle. For the first time, I felt an extremely powerful attraction to my woman friend. We talked about it the next day, and found that the feeling was mutual. This was the beginning of my 'coming out'. This newfound love had serious implications for my job at the local Children's Aid Society, where the director was an ultra-conservative Baptist. It had drastic implications in terms of my faith. I felt very guilty about knowingly committing adultery as I carried on a clandestine affair with my lesbian lover, while both of us continued to live with our husbands. Yet I lacked the courage to do anything differently. We both felt that we had too much at stake in terms of our jobs and our respectability in a small town. My lover and I frequently travelled to Toronto for 'shopping weekends'. Although we thought that we were being very discreet, we later learned that other younger lesbians in town were very aware of our affair. We were their role models!

After four years, my husband and I separated amicably, without my ever coming out to him. In a discussion years later, he said he never really knew I had a woman lover, although he had his suspicions. As a part of my coming out process, I stopped attending church for the first time in my life. It seemed hypocritical to be leading the choir in a church that did not accept homosexuality. I knew that people in the congregation would not want me leading their choir if they knew I was lesbian. My departure from the church left a spiritual gap in my life.

My lover and I decided to leave Parry Sound—her home town. She began applying for transfers, and successfully landed a job in my home town. It was at this point that she separated from her husband and set out on her own. Within six months, before I had the opportunity to relocate to live with her, she met another woman and left me heartbroken. She reasoned that her guilt about her sexuality and her marriage break-up was linked to me, and that our separation was a step away from this guilt. Shortly afterwards, I began dating a woman who lived in Toronto. It was through friends of hers that I was introduced to the Buddhism of Nichiren Daishonin.

All of us were visiting Toronto from our homes in cottage country and staying together in my lover's home. I heard chanting coming from the guest bedroom. Because of my choir history, I was intrigued by the sound, wondering what the music looked like. How did they know when to chant quickly or slowly, alone or together? Despite my curiosity, I didn't ask any questions. It was too weird for me, and I wasn't really interested in taking it up in my own life. It was not until two years later that I found myself at my first Buddhist meeting.

I decided to try chanting while driving from Ottawa to Parry Sound at the end of a two week vacation. I chanted for hours, to the music on the radio, with the goal in mind that my Buddhist friends would be home when I dropped in to visit on my way home. I arrived at their home and kiddingly asked, "Here I am, were you expecting me?" They replied, "We have been phoning you for three days to invite you to a meeting we're hosting, to introduce people to Buddhism."

Fourteen years later, I continue to be seriously and happily chanting Nam-Myoho-Renge-Kyo, and participating in the activities of the SGI—Soka Gakkai International, the lay organization dedicated to world peace through the propagation of this Buddhist practice.

Initially, I asked myself the question, "Is it the actual practice that brings about results, or is it faith in the practice?" As a Catholic, I have recited the rosary with the whole family, so I understood chanting. And as Catholics, we have candles and incense and beads. So, I thought I could just be a better Catholic and work to strengthen my faith. I understood that well enough, but the lesbian part still didn't fit. The main difference for me was the fact that I was introduced to this practice by an out lesbian couple. As a Buddhist, it was okay to be my True Self. The major difference between my experience within the Catholic Church and the SGI is the basic premise— all beings are equal, and you can attain enlightenment just as you are.

In studying the Buddhist teachings I have discovered that it is my karma, my 'mission' in this life to be an out lesbian, so I can help change people's negative attitudes towards lesbians through the example of my life. I can be a role model to other women and men who do not have the courage or the supportive environment to come out. And I can be a role model to my nieces and nephews and other youth that I encounter in my work and social activities. I am fortunate that I am living in a time when society's views are broadening. It makes all this so much easier.

The Buddha has four characteristics: Eternity, Purity, True Self and Happiness. We are encouraged in this practice to be our True Selves, to use our life experiences to grow, and to encourage others who are experiencing similar difficulties.

The most important element of this Buddhism is actual proof. Through chanting, you tap into universal life energy and draw to yourself the things that will contribute to your happiness. I've been chanting for fourteen years. And five years ago, I met my partner and her two sons who were then ten and seventeen years old. I have lived with her and her younger son since that time. Although they do not share my enthusiasm for this Buddhist practice, because I spend a great deal of time participating in Buddhist meetings and activities which take me away from home, they recognize that it is important to me. They recognize its value in my life. Balancing family life and Buddhist activities has been very challenging. It has from time to time been a source of some conflict in our relationship. Fortunately, we have been able to compromise and find resolve. I try to develop wisdom through my chanting, so I can make healthy choices in my life. I chant for a harmonious family. I have found that when I hold up my end of the household responsibilities and take care to nurture our relationship, then things at home run much more smoothly. This harmony was manifested clearly last Mother's Day, when my partner's two sons and ex-husband prepared a dinner for their father's wife and my partner and I.

One of the most important lessons I have learned through my past relationships, which is supported in Buddhist philosophy, is that I alone am responsible for my own happiness. When I take responsibility for my own happiness, then my environment mirrors my internal experience. My life and my environment are connected. When I run into difficulties, I acknowledge that I, through my own past actions, have created the cause which leads to this experience. Likewise, through chanting, I can expiate that karma, and focus my life in a more positive direction. Difficulties motivate us to chant, and are the springboard for our growth.

Catholicism says that homosexuality is a sin. Buddhism says that every being can attain enlightenment just as they are. So, although we may encounter some homophobic attitudes within our organization from time to time, we are all dedicated to peace, to "limitless self-improvement," and to mutual respect.

Through the years of my practice, my life has changed dramatically. I now live and work in Toronto. I am able to be completely out at work, with my family, and with the people in our Buddhist organization. I feel I can be my True Self and my life continues to improve steadily.

I know that chanting Nam-Myoho-Renge-Kyo is the tool for achieving a happy life and overcoming difficulties. Like any other tool, it doesn't work by itself, but rather with the power that I exert to make it work. Unlike Christianity, in which a powerless individual prays to an omnipotent God for assistance, mercy, forgiveness; as a Buddhist, through chanting, I summon up from within myself the power to change my situation. Based on a deep appreciation for my life, I fuse my life energy with universal life energy through the sound of Nam-Myoho-Renge-Kyo.

Most importantly, it has been the concrete proof—the actual results that I have experienced over the years—that has made it very easy for me to embrace and continue with this faith.

BIOGRAPHY Kate Greco

Kate Greco is a 46-year-old lesbian who migrated to Toronto from Northern Ontario as part of her coming out process, which began in 1977. In 1982, she left the Catholic Church, and in 1984, began practicing the Buddhism of Nichiren Daishonin. She lives in Toronto with her partner of six years and her sixteen-year-old son. Kate is actively involved in Sokka Gakkai International of Canada (SGI), a lay organization dedicated to achieving world peace through individual growth. SGI has fifteen million members in 126 countries. Canada was the first to form Pride Groups—in Vancouver, Montreal, Ottawa and Toronto—for gay, lesbian, bisexual and transgendered people and their friends to learn about and practice the Buddhism of Nichiren Daishonin.

MA VIE EN BLUE
Ace

I consider myself a no-op FTM, because that's the way I was born. I was born in New York City in 1946. My mom named me Azar, which is Farsi for "holy flame". While pregnant, Mom knitted everything blue because she "just knew it was going to be a boy".

I was raised a Roman Catholic (in the 50's and 60's that meant strict!), and was so afraid that I would go to hell because of my thoughts and because I liked to wear pants, boy's shoes, play baseball, and swagger. I could obey all the church's regulations, (except the ones about having 'impure thoughts') but when I heard the pastor railing against "women who wear pants," I cried bitter tears because of who/what I was. I knew I couldn't change, and had no one to talk to. Being an Italian-American (the first in my immigrant family to be born in the U.S.) compounded the matter because my family had imported their own brand of Italian morals, ritual and 'pecking order', and adhered to this as their norm.

I never knew what it meant to live a 'normal' family life, nor did I know what options I had as an individual growing up in this world—family life was not a nurturing one. My father was terrified of Mom, and would stay out at nights on the weekend—Mom would accuse him of being a homosexual. Every time she'd scream that at him, I'd cringe, and pray that I wouldn't be discovered. My favorite childhood idol was Mowgli, the jungle boy, and I imagined myself to be him, surrounded by loving women and lots of horses, cats and dogs and jungle animals. I loved watching cowboy movies, and I used my little sister for Roy Rogers lasso practice; I even tried to pee standing up whenever my dad took me fishing. As a five-year-old, I proudly announced that I would grow up to be a cowboy and all my relatives would say, "No, you mean a cowgirl." Hell no I didn't!

I wrestled with my gender identity and preference. I knew I had a man's soul in a woman's body, but was laughed at by everyone I told this to. As you can guess, I received no support whatsoever, and all kinds of threats. Mom and Grandma noticed at a very early age that I was quite boyish. Mom would scream at me and say in a belittling manner, "What are you—a man?" Nonna (grandma) would (usually) gently laugh and say "Maschione!" which means "tomboy" in Italian.

Then came 1959—a turning point in my life, and a very pleasant one indeed! I was twelve, going on thirteen and suddenly, life opened up to me! I knew that the world had been handed to me, in all its glory and wonder and beauty, and because of that I wanted a Bar Mitzvah (not a Bat Mitzvah—that was for girls!). Of course, my stern Catholic mother refused! I still have hope that maybe one day...(Later in life, I dropped out of religion for ten years until a sweet Jewish girlfriend started taking me to Mass (Dignity). For that may she be canonized! I read recently that she has, unfortunately, passed away.)

I was really happy, and very much proud of the fact that I was a 'tomboy'. What a life! The world was mine! I discovered Brigitte Bardot, whose movies were quite popular at that time, and the thought of her curvaceous body and ripe lips made me tingle and smile as never before. Brenda Lee singing *Sweet Nothin's* ("Mama turned on the front porch light, said, come in honey, that's enough for tonight!") turned me on in a warm-chocolate-milk-before-bed way. I was still trying to be the Good Catholic kid, so going to Bardot's movies was out of the question, although I would sneak a peek at the magazines the boys would pass around in class.

As this was the era of the classic '59 Cadillac and other bombastic Detroit machines, I became totally turned on to cars. What a lark! Walking down Pelham Parkway on a sunny breezy day with these gorgeous machines going by, ragtops down, 50's music blaring and tinkling from radios, wayward notes hanging in the air and expanding in the bright sunshine! This turned into a life-long love affair. I now own and customize my car, work on others, talk shop with the guys (whose wives realize right off the bat that I am no threat) and teach women (and some men) about automotive maintenance.

So there I was—life in the Bronx, cars, pretty women, songs in my heart, a smile on my face. I even found someone to love me—a tiny kitten I brought home, raised on a doll's bottle and taught to sit on command. We were both wild and wild about each other. Mom, in her inimitable style, would always threaten to "get rid of the cat" if I misbehaved. As I got older, I worked with and supported many animal rescue leagues, because there is just too much brutal treatment of cats, dogs and other animal companions out there—we all resonate with life, and what is done to animals (who have souls and feelings, in their own right) is felt by all of us alike.

After graduation, I took a crummy job selling towels, (still falling in unrequited love here and there), and went to art school. I worked in that store for two years, and enjoyed most of my fellow employees, including one little old Italian lady, Mrs. Rodello. She was so much like the little old Italian ladies from the Bronx, that it was easy relating to her. One day, (in 1965!), out of the blue, she said to me, matter-of-factly, "You know, why don't you just get one of those sex changes?" I was so shocked, I don't remember what I told her. She may never know how much she boosted my ego!

Then I started to hear my mother say things to our neighbors. "You know, when my daughter passes by the young girls, I see them admiring her because they think she's a guy—how disappointed they look when they realize she's female!" Wow, thank-you Mom for that surprising compliment! I got my driver's license, started cruising around in Mom's 1968 Camaro (which I made sure had performance parts installed). How free I once again felt! The real Ace was beginning to emerge from the long-dormant egg.

At this point, I was in the 'hippie' stage of my life. But I was still going to church, being the good Catholic kid. I don't disparage it because it gave me a sense of order and ethics, but its dogma and its writings about homosexuality cramped my sexuality something awful. Sometimes my friends would come along with me to Mass, and we'd put oregano joints in the collection basket.

Then in 1969, something happened that changed my life forever. Stonewall. Even though I loved Andy and Chris, the two wonderful creatures I worked with at the towel store, I still perceived gay men as being swishy, weak and effeminate, and gay women (I did not know any gay women personally) as being tough and hardened butches, which I did not identify with. When the TV news and the Village Voice carried the Christopher Street coverage, I was all eyes, ears, heart and soul. Hey Ace, those are your people! There's nothing wrong with them, or with who you are, what you feel!

Even with all of these 'prods', I still did not quite come out. One more thing had to happen, and it did—a most unexpected 'sign'. While in DC one day, I didn't have enough bus fare. So I walked three miles to the Pentagon, hailed a bus, showed the driver my money and said "Is that enough?" He waved me on, and I sat in my usual spot, the back of the bus. Wait a minute, what's this wedged between the seat and the window? With great effort, I pulled out a thick paperback, Gordon Merrick's novel **The Lord Won't Mind**. The book basically states that all people are loved by God, even homosexuals. The novel dealt with a gay man whose kindly aunt innocently and unwittingly encouraged his friendship with another man, a friendship which turns into a deep relationship, even though the central character marries a woman. I read the first few pages, and could not put the book down. Although it was about gay men, this book's message was directed to me too. When I got home, I stayed up until 1 a.m. reading this book. Even though it contained passages dealing with wife-beating, the rest of the book caressed my soul with loving acceptance and now I knew beyond a doubt that I was gay. I was relieved, happy, ecstatic—gay! (I kept the book as a memento for a long time, but when my stepfather started brutally beating my mother, I threw it out—the author seemed to be condoning the main character's wife-beating and exalting this character's love for his boyfriend in one and the same breath. I could not keep this book knowing how terribly bloody, bruised and broken my mother was after the beating that my stepfather gave her.)

I came out apprehensively to my Mom the next day. You know what she said? She, who had made fun of me when I was thirteen, said something like, "Gee, if you had said that to me earlier, it would have solved a lot of your problems when you were younger! I knew you were different!" In fact, she even told me that she'd had crushes on some of the nuns who taught her when she was a kid, and that she probably never should have been married because if she was not gay, then she was asexual.

Once again, I became the carefree thirteen-year-old who had sashayed and strutted down the streets of the Bronx in macho arrogance. On Friday evenings, with a song in my heart, I'd leave work and walk thirty blocks to Georgetown, where, at Grace Episcopal Church, I met up with other homosexuals (all men) to share our coming-out experiences. I was warmly welcomed the first day, and felt very much a part of this 'family'. We all had common threads of "thinking I was the only one" and being put down by parents and friends. But here we were, with each other, ecstatic—we had finally come out, we had found each other and our lives were finally full! I identified with the men very much, had no trouble relating to them. But if I could only find a woman to have a requited love relationship with!

I was now working as a display trimmer, and had lots of gay friends (all male, many of them drag performers). One of the men I worked with, Dan, was a bisexual Warlock. From him I learned a lot about alternative religions and Paganism—the doctrines, discipline and ritual all made a lot of sense from a primal and evolutionary perspective. It was not at all scary, confusing or misidentified, as Mom used to tell me. The ancient religious practices (Egyptian, Mystery Religions, Zoroastrianism, Astrology, Buddhism) were a fascinating study. In them, I could see the way thought and ritual evolved (yet in many ways stayed the same) into today's religious disciplines, universal thought and dogma. Even the martial arts and Eastern philosophy held me spellbound. The sense of order and ritual and power inherent in these philosophies complemented, meshed with and sometimes exceeded the concurrent ancient religions from the other side of the world. Not everyone has to be Catholic, I began to realize.

I started incorporating these different yet intertwined religious philosophies into my own way of thinking and worship. My life was once again beginning to expand. Even Mom (who could sometimes be my best buddy when she was in a better mental state) now began to take notice. With Dan, we'd discuss these philosophies well into the night. I read about the Tarot, Alchemy, Sufi-ism, Witches and Warlocks, and Lost Civilizations; I began to realize the worth and power of the human consciousness (and subconscious), and understand that the universe is within me as well as around me ("As above, so below," an ancient Alchemic philosophy). I began to identify as a "soul-incarnate" clothed with humanity, and the gender of my choice, which was not necessarily the gender of my birth. One of Mom's favorite philosophies involved the proposal that humanity was multi-gendered/hermaphroditic in ancient times. My asexual self could very well identify with that philosophy. I continued (and still do today) to visit different churches—Unity, Science of Mind, Catholic Mass (Dignity), Unitarian and Episcopal, as well as attending Jewish, Buddhist, and Wiccan ceremonies. I have also studied mythology and pagan philosophy. Regarding the matter of religion in my life now, I consider myself to be Omni-religious.

Attending the True Spirit conferences of 1997 and '98 brought me closer to my true self, and was a wonderful male-bonding experience. The workshops I attended there brought me into closer contact with those of my 'tribe', and helped me appreciate and understand more fully the varied efforts and life-paths that all have taken to achieve their FTM quest. I see in all my friends the beautiful variety of gender-forms and realize that I am in the presence of very brave people, who are in the vanguard of tolerance and acceptance.

We are all connected. We are spokes on the Wheel of Life and as such, we touch the Wheel, which represents our existence (and I include animals on this Wheel, because they are souls incarnate, just as we are, and are much more in touch with the whole picture of existence than most humans are). In addition, we, the spokes, are all connected to the Hub, which is God/Higher Power/Source of the Universal Existence—whatever you feel comfortable calling this Power. I feel so connected to animals, because, 1) if the Bible is correct, Adam and Eve were not thrown out of the Garden of Eden for anything that the animals had done 2) if, "Man...was created a little less than the angels," then perhaps it is the animals themselves, who are angels in their own right, and 3) we resonate with all of creation and animals/fish/birds can teach us so much about love, communication, interspecies friendship and connectedness.

What have I learned/gleaned from my experiences? That we are all inheritors of supreme goodness and kindness and love—we all share in this, although there are so many out there who are not yet aware of this. That there is a supreme Love (not mushy, but powerful yet almost shy in its respect for our individuality) that permeates the whole of creation that we tap into and use. That, as the Bible says, "The Kingdom of Heaven is within you"—i.e. each and every one of us has the use of tremendous power for good that comes from within us.

The next time you are stuck in traffic, or in a large gathering, think thoughts of peace/love/kindness, and imagine those thoughts springing forth from your heart or mind or soul, and descending on all around you. I like to picture it as a colorful cloud (pink? the color of love) filled with gold flakes that float down and gently cover all those around me. If this sounds corny, then feel free to choose your own imagery. Whether or not those folks around you at that moment are spiritually or psychically aware of what you are doing, be assured that it will surely help to comfort, heal and awaken some of those around you.

The next step for me as a member of the Trans community (and a feeling I have embraced since I was about five years old) is to learn about the lore and initiations of Native American communities. This to me will round out the real reason I came to this earth. However, I will say that even if I had a million lifetimes to live, I still wouldn't be able to do, experience, learn and enjoy all that there is out there.

We must learn to generate peace. We are all souls having a human experience, and it is up to all of us to help make this world a better place for everyone, no matter how much we feel we are being persecuted. This is part of our strength.

Peace to all. A.

BIOGRAPHY Ace

Ace was born a biological female in NY City, in 1946. S/he is a Taurus with Gemini Rising and Scorpio moon. S/he enjoys working with animals and loves the outdoors, gardening, fishing, hiking, camping, working on, customizing and showing custom cars. S/he practices martial arts and teaches courses. S/he is also involved in shooting sports, and used to be friends with Sitting Bull's great-grandson (before he went to the happy hunting grounds at 76.) Ace always knew from the start (sometimes painfully so) that s/he was different, and nowadays is ecstatic that there are so many other like-minded, friendly souls in this world. Because of all the hatred/non-acceptance/ridicule s/he received when seeking God in church, Ace is now Omni-religious. Although still a Catholic (attending Dignity), s/he now also attends Science of Mind, Episcopal, Wiccan (animal-friendly!), Unitarian (a bit too dry), Unity (love them) services, studied Buddhism, Sufi-ism, the Egyptian Book of the Dead (incredible insights), ancient Alchemy (as above, so below). By pursuing these varied interests, s/he has come to the conclusion that the SAME undercurrent of truth runs through every religion and dogma/creed. We are "souls incarnate having a bodily experience in a world that consists of vastly more than just the three dimensions which surround us daily." And, the logical conclusion from that is, "Why, when there is such valuable and wonderful diversity of expression and existence, must those (trans-folks and others) who exist as they are, be considered unacceptable?"

TISHA B'AV 5756
Eve Lyons

Two thousand years ago we prayed together
under constant threat from the Romans.
Before them, the Greeks, and before
them, the Assyrians.
Today we only fear the car accident
on our way to synagogue,
or that when they are done
burning Black churches
we will be next.
Or our fear comes from
inside these stained-glass windows,
these staunch-backed pews.
We fear the rabbi's condemnation
of our desires.
We fear judgment by people
we thought were our family
only to find ourselves
shrunk down to a tinier minority.
Two thousand years ago the Second glorious Temple
loomed in our peripheral hindsight.
We cursed ourselves bitterly
for fighting amongst ourselves,
vowing "never again."

NOTE: Tisha B'Av is the Jewish holiday commemorating the destruction of the First and Second Temples. It is also the day in history of the Bar Kochba Revolt and the expulsion of the Jews from Spain. One of the ways Jews are expected to observe it is by fasting.

IN MEMORY OF MY RABBI
Eve Lyons

Because I never liked you much
I never let your
overbearing whine of a mind
trample mine.
Now I can't help but crawl back
to that place I used to know
like an elementary school swing set.
Board meetings and
you taking offense
at rewrites of Friday night services.
Smoking and fucking
when we should be praying.
That's what youth group was all about—
but at least we were dating Jews.
Too bad your stomach
couldn't take it.
Too bad that might have been a lie.
Too bad you couldn't have been
a role model.
You weren't out
and neither was I.
Raking the ashes,
the dead, crunchy leaves.
You're keeping Jason
Hilary and Laura
company now.
The dead are making coffee
pulling all-nighters
to watch over me.

BLEEDING G-D
Eve Lyons

There are lots of people
bleeding god on Amtrak
maybe it's
being so close to the earth
after trying to reach heaven
where we're deluded
into believing
G-d lives.

This one man
thick beard and thicker opinions
tried to convince a younger man
thin sideburns and
light enough to float above
these false borders
that it is better to sacrifice yourself
for the world than to
save yourself
for a better fight.

I left, went and
ate breakfast with
a woman whose
baby bled dead
from between her legs.
My other meal companion
told her smoothly that
now she has an angel.
It seems like a flimsy reward
for blood never regained.

I found a third woman
fleeing men's advances
and America's as well.
We bonded over
coffee and pizza,
me thinking I had been
led by G-d to take off
my headphones
let this one in.

Tourists clamour on this
rickety silver beast
thinking they've found
the real thing
the real G-d or

America or their own
soul.
I trudge my way
out of the country
thinking I'll find the same thing.

"It does come back to theology
and how you look at it," the
thick man says
he's now beginning to
piss me off
in his righteous casual assertions that
my Amtrak soulmate and I
have missed
the boat the messiah
the word of his god.

With faith
I head toward
the land he believes
will be destroyed.

BIOGRAPHY Eve Lyons

I am a twenty-five-year old Reed College graduate working in Portland, Oregon, with emotionally disturbed, abused children. I also devote a great deal of energy to being president of my local union. My work has appeared in **Women's Words** (short story) and in **Labyrinth** (poetry). I am an unaffiliated, somewhat observant Jew who studied in Israel and travelled the Middle East in 1995.

ECCE HOMO: Ruminations on a Theory of my Queer Body
Connell O'Donovan

One day in March 1977, as a fifteen-year-old Mormon boy confused by and fearful of my sexuality, I walked into my high school religion teacher's office in Clearfield, Utah and tried to explain to him the depth of what I then perceived as my sinfulness. Overwhelmed by guilt and confusion, there were no words with which I could speak my crimes. When words failed me, Brother Wood cautiously asked, "Do you think you might be homosexual?" Relieved and grateful that he had spoken what I could not, I only nodded in humiliation. And thus began my ten year journey through the belly of the beast; ten years of negotiating my way through the Mormon Church's torturous experimental programs for reorienting me into a heterosexual.

During those ten years, church leaders supplied me with many anti-gay books and pamphlets published by the church. I personally attended many addresses given by high-ranking church leaders who spoke in no uncertain terms about the evilness of my 'condition'. I spent years in humiliating weekly interviews with various church leaders in which I was required to give graphic details about my thoughts, dreams, actions, desires. In 1978 I was counselled by a church leader to go to Brigham Young University to experiment with vomiting aversion therapy (but somehow I had the sense to refuse this torturous cure). On at least four occasions (perhaps more—I don't recall for sure), I had Mormon leaders try to cast demons out of me through emotionally and mentally crippling priesthood exorcism rituals. I went to a Mormon psychologist for hypnotherapy in which he had me visualize myself split into Straight Connell and Gay Connell and then had Jesus come down through the ceiling to trample Gay Connell to death. I frequently spent hour after hour in total fasting, prayer, and scripture reading, begging for answers, begging God (who is quite literally a white, heterosexual male in Mormon dogma) with every ounce of my being to validate my piety and faithfulness by curing me, changing me into a heterosexual. I frequented the secret rituals of the Salt Lake Mormon Temple—always feeling too unworthy to be in such a holy place but too afraid to be elsewhere. I developed and maintained a profoundly personal relationship with Jesus Christ. And in 1984, having been ordered to do so by a high Mormon official, I married a woman in the Salt Lake Temple in order to experience 'normal' sex. We struggled together for a year of anger and pain before I asked to leave the marriage, for through all of this, I remained distinctly and completely queer.

I struggled within Mormonism for several more years after our divorce, but finally left in 1989 over its fundamental sexism—I had watched my mother, sister, many female friends, and my wife get hurt too deeply, too often by a patriarchal dogma that invalidated them on just about every level. It wasn't until much later that I was able to relate feminist criticisms of Mormon patriarchy to my own plight as a queer man. Not surprisingly, denial runs deep in Mormon culture.

Some two weeks after my church court in 1989 (I was tried for excommunication on the grounds of my homosexuality but was ultimately only put on probation), I had an intense dream: I entered a Mormon chapel for a congregation-wide dinner, to find a huge table almost breaking under the weight of all the food displayed upon it, yet every single person in the dining hall sat with nearly empty and still untouched plates in front of them, emaciated and glassy-eyed from starvation, while a Mormon bishop droned on and on in some irrelevant sermon, and no one dared eat until he finished. I was ravenous and refused to wait for the sermon to end.

Regardless of the visible horror of everyone present, I heaped food on my plate and began to satiate my hunger, partaking noisily of the huge feast laid out before us. Upon awakening from this dream, I knew that I had to leave—Mormonism was spiritually starving me to death.

Several years after my painful departure from Mormonism, I finally realized two vital things about my relationship to religion. First, my feelings of profound but obsessive intimacy with Jesus Christ were clearly and overtly of a homoerotic nature. I had carefully masked my homosexuality by deflecting my love and desire for other men onto the suffering body of Christ. Jesus had become for me the Ultimate Lover—masculine but gentle, patient, godly, all-loving, and best of all absent, unavailable. In coming out (and thus finally accepting the physical realities of sex and the presence of the body), my desperate intimacy with Christ ended. Secondly, I discovered that while I had been carefully taught that I was not worthy of any spirituality because of my queerness, in reality I had a spiritual nature that was completely independent of (and perhaps even antithetical to?) religion. The sense of holiness that always overwhelmed me whenever I entered the Salt Lake Temple was not because of any intrinsic holiness that could be attributed to the edifice itself, but because I had made it holy. I now understand that the presence of my queer body in the Mormon Temple had sanctified that place for me. As my queer Quaker predecessor, Walt Whitman, wrote, "Divine am I, inside and out, and I make holy whatever I touch or am touched from" (from *Song of Myself*, stanza 24, **Leaves of Grass**).

My spirituality and my (homo)sexuality became reconcilable (indeed, inextricably so) at last. Because of my queerness, I was profoundly wounded by the homophobia of my family, my religion, my government, my culture, my society. But I have now chosen to see that wounding as a site for rebirth and renewal. Those gaping wounds have become openings, entrances into the mystical Silence. For me, that Silence is God. And there, in that Silence I have found Voice. In that Silence I have found ways to articulate and speak my body—this body of a gay, white, bourgeois, able-bodied, North American male. In that Silence I have found ways to articulate my difference(s), my queerness(es). And there in that Silence I have found the beauty of other queer men's bodies.

In the past, I referred to these articulations, these musings as a gaialogy[1]. While theology is the study of theos (the male god), gaialogy is the study of Gaia, the Greek Earth Goddess. For me, gaialogy emphasizes earth, connectedness, bodies, cycles of life and death, fluidity, chthonian tensions, joy, the lack of opposites. Gaialogy celebrates what is.

It is upon the basis of my body and my sense of connectedness with earth and matter that I have found so much of my healing. I recently spent two and a half years living in the desert of southeastern Utah. It was there that I first discovered that I really even had a body. And it was there that I learned to love that body, for I would look at a ruddy sandstone canyon and know the beauty thereof. And then I would look at my body and see similar ruddy canyons there. In treading gently upon the earth, that far country of desert sandstone, I found the beauty of my own canyons, my owns fens, cliffs, buttes, mesas, alcoves. Right there, in and upon my body! It was an exciting time of growth for me.

That was also the beginning of my return journey into subjectivity; subjectivity in that I am truly seeing that of God (the I am) in everyone and everything. And this is a return journey because I remember as a child feeling no sense of being able to objectify people and things around me. It seems that objectification came much later on. My queer self as a child came naturally with the ability to relate as subject with subject, not as subject to object.

At the end of 1995, during a Quaker Meeting for Worship in Santa Cruz, California, I had a vision of the immanence of God, in which we danced together naked in the center of the Silence of Meeting, swirling, twirling around each other ecstatically, holding hands, our eyes laughing in bliss. And although I am usually skeptical of such mystical phenomena, I somehow knew that this god with whom I danced in vision was the Faggot-God. So beautiful, so male, and so very, very gay! Moved by this experience, a couple of weeks later I painted a large mural on my bedroom wall of this Faggot-God, dancing naked with a lit candle at His feet. As I contemplated that experience and meditated while sitting before that mural, I found myself cycling back toward a theology (in that this God of my devotion is male), although it is now more of a homotheology, into which I incorporate gaialogy as well.

When I make love with another man, I dwell upon the mysteries of his sameness rather than his otherness. With my lips I brush the nape of his neck and I find God there. Then I ruminate on the unblurred similarities and symmetries of our beautiful bodies; on the tension of muscle, bone, sinew; on the choreographies of our desire. I cry out from all my skin and hear my own voice echoing from the warmth of his body. And the vibrations of the echoes last for hours and days, filling me from my in to my out. I relish my concavity to his convexity and his concavity to my convexity. With the newest of tongues we begin to speak that he and I are paradox incarnate: two whole and perfect subjects and objects of desire—not subject to object, but subject with subject and object to object—without loss of identity, both of us still able to clearly and queerly speak our names. Simultaneously embracing, collapsing, and transcending our subjectivities and objectivities into meaningful meaninglessness. From the edge of my skin, I follow the geographies and topographies of his body and I see and know that his body is my body is his body. Subtle differences contained within Sameness. Through the grace that is Desire, I carefully trace my name upon his skin so that I can remember how to fable the ineffable; and to remind us until the very end that no longer is it that I want him, need him, or love him, but that I AM HIM.

Endnote
1. Lesbian poet and cultural anthropologist Judy Grahn, has theorized that we Gay folk are named after the goddess Gaia. However, I am far more inclined to think that the word originated with the pre-Christian, itinerant, and mendicant transgendered (and homoerotic?) priest/esses of the mother goddess Cybele, called the galli in Latin.

BIOGRAPHY   Connell O'Donovan

While I grew up a Mormon, I am now both a radical faerie and a member of the religious Society of Friends (Quakers), and this essay reflects my journey out of Mormonism and onto those different, but compatible, spiritual paths.

I have also published the following essays in other anthologies:

(Re)claiming Sodom in **(Re)claiming Sodom**, edited by Jonathan Goldberg, Routledge Press, New York & London, 1994.

The Abominable and Detestable Crime Against Nature: A Brief History of Homosexuality and Mormonism, 1840-1980, in **Multiply and Replenish: Essays on Mormon Sex and Family**, edited by Brent Corcoron, Signature Books, Salt Lake City, Utah, 1994.

Connell O'Donovan's essays *(Re)claiming Sodom* and *My Journey into Faerie and What I Found There* also appear in this anthology.

GROWING UP RELIGIOUS
Brian Day

    All
the essential scenes of our lives
took place beyond our telling,
in realms we could only
imagine. From the church we had the glass
of a text, the grace
of language. For that other
there was no writing we knew.
Fag jokes were a relief
from the burden of silence, the blank
pages that kept us closed.
We passed from altars to
city bookstores, reached
for resemblances, found paperback
epiphanies, accounts
of men whose hungers confirmed our own:
our first reflection of ourselves
in print
troubled by the bitter mouths of men,
the absence of all we took
for love. This was not
the future we'd been promised: we wanted
a washed, sacramental life.
    Flesh
intervened with demands of its own;
the one Christ candle
of our skin was ignited.
We gave ourselves over to unloving men
who used our bodies as we used theirs:
as a screen for fictions
we soon learned to keep silent. We left
the church, or watched unmoved
as it faded behind us. We prayed the way
we always had, lending our minds
to the world we advanced to,
as we layered our sex
on remembered religion.
    Poems
of our elders fell into our hands,
gave us a place among literate men
whose wrestling extracts the blessings
of angels. No longer living
as hermits in our histories,
we gathered the scattered
pages of our prophets, making multiple books
the font of our faith. We'd found a succession

that was our own, heard a strain of the song
of our songs. We'd run our fingers
down lines that were lit
with our own revelation, pages of
carnal, incarnate love.

BIOGRAPHY Brian Day

Brian Day grew up as a Christian in Mission, B.C. A few years after coming out and moving to Toronto, he became interested in Pagan perspectives and rituals. He now participates in a ritual group which celebrates Pagan shabbats as well as significant days from other religious traditions. His current spiritual practice combines embodiment work and centering prayer with writing, and physical exercise.

Brian Day's poems *Nosing Our Way* and *Swimming With Apollo* appear elsewhere in this anthology.

EXILE

NOSING OUR WAY
Brian Day

When our mouths open
we don't know where
our prayers might lead,
and we follow in darkness
until the pictures appear.

Jesus, half clad in green,
is playing his pipes
among the sheep,
his quick eyes watching
over the flock,
and when he leaps
his feet are cloven.

The Goddess
in her virgin form
is counting out gold
to the innkeeper's hand
and walking down
by the shore of the sea,
her body a bell
ringing out in fog.

Our mouths, our skins
of wine pour prayers
before these figures
who may yet be our parents,
and we begin
to draw them together,
nosing our way
to the nipples of the world.

Brian Day's Biography appears on page 72.

A FALLING FROM GRACE
Pamela Godfree

I always liked the idea that we were brothers and sisters, part of some eternal secret society. Aunt Louise persisted in calling it The Order. She openly resented that she couldn't intelligibly discuss any details of her sister's faith without acquainting herself with our dialectical explanations of the Bible's teachings. You couldn't blame her. The idiom we used as members of our Christian society sounded like a foreign language to one not yet a convert.

Once I felt a vague sense of superiority having almost been born into this brotherhood, and therefore didn't have to understand it from the viewpoint of an outsider. The outsiders, one quickly learned if you were on the inside, were lamentable souls; either rich pompous figures exerting evil power over one another, or one of the ignorant heathen masses who had not yet chanced hearing our message. When I saw from a dim point in my world all the turmoil and confusion in the outside world, I believed that my reality was better.

My mother became a Jehovah's Witness when I was five. She raised me to believe that if a person didn't have the sole guiding force of Jehovah God in their life they would always remain an unfulfilled, struggling individual who could never be happy. (Jehovah was their translation of the Hebrew name for God.) This gave me a purpose for my life; we were all part of the divine plan. She had tried various fundamentalist beliefs on for size, had found a suitable fit in Jehovah's Witnesses and then tried to fill what she felt to be a tremendous spiritual void in her life.

As a child of six I remember her reading about the promised paradise to come for all believers in Jehovah and I was thrilled at the prospect of bliss shown in the pictures accompanying the text. It was the first study book we had, bright orange in colour with big print for us kids to read more easily. That was my second reader and it created impressions in my mind that were not soon to leave me. Mother and I would read over the "Bible stories" together, discussing how we used to be perfect before Adam and Eve sinned and then we all began to die.

As I grew older at school I took pride in being different. I refused to stand for the national anthem and was silent during the Lord's Prayer. Any embarrassment I suffered was worth it because I belonged to a radical religion, one that considered itself no part of the world and therefore nationless. That appealed to me. I still see patriotism as nothing more than a divisive, fruitless gesture of so-called love of country. I wanted no part of mouthing an empty prayer. That sense of radicalism ran contrary to normal society's rules, and as far as I could see, not many out there knew what to believe in. I, however, assured myself that my devotion would lead me to The Truth. It was my passport to the future where all survivors would enjoy perfect peace and happiness.

Our Bible Study meetings (held three times a week) were rigorous to help us firmly acquaint ourselves with the Scriptures; it was our guidebook and constant point of reference. I read it ravenously. The "powerhouse of wisdom," as my mother called it, was not quite like any other book I'd come across. It used beautiful mythical language to create mystical answers for almost any question I had. I was carried away. My reverent fear of God and impressionability convinced me it was gospel. The Bible itself has the supreme knack of convincing its readers of its authenticity. To question any point of doctrine was to question the authority of Jehovah, himself and one could only question if they were seeing things through their imperfect human judgement.

We were constantly told that we were half-human, deficient until we loved our Creator with all of our being and were made whole. Who were we to judge The Truth without the divine wisdom of God?

Kingdom Hall, where our meetings were held, was a simple, unassuming brick building usually built by the brothers themselves. Sisters were never assigned to such a task. If they wanted to participate they could serve refreshments to the industrious male workers afterwards. However, we all participated in practice talks given to each other in front of the congregation to prepare us to bear witness in service. Service was an integral part of our worship, where we would share the "Good News" by door to door proselytizing. Saturday and Sunday mornings we knocked at people's doors, giving them the message that the world was on its way to destruction and that a better existence was drawing near. All they had to do was embrace the faith, becoming dedicated followers of Jehovah. Our handbooks, *The Watchtower* and *Awake* were left for ten cents a copy—an assurance there was no profit motive.

Modesty was big on the list of Christian attributes. We preached our message modestly and dressed in a manner befitting Christian-minded people. Special emphasis was placed on female modesty. If your hemline didn't reach your knees while seated, you were inviting temptation and stumbling your brother. I considered the possibility that if any man looked at my legs as anything other than appendages of my body that was his weakness, not mine. But the upholding of chastity was the primary duty of women, as everyone knew it was more difficult for a man to control his carnal instincts. I cooperated in giving more mystique to the female form by hiding it from view. I had already learned that woman's role was to be caretaker of men's emotions. Women were subordinate both inside the organization and out, so I guessed I was obliged to accept it as a natural fact.

Every spare minute of our social lives was taken up with activities revolving around association with other Witnesses, whether it be an afternoon at the swimming pool or an evening at the movies. Dating was prohibited unless one was considering marriage; needless to say many married quite young.

As I entered high school, I began to realize that "worldly" people were not despicably wicked or ignorant as I had been led to believe. I met people who were likeable, intelligent and interesting. My mother would call school a den of iniquity and she was successful in persuading me into business and the girlish pursuits of typing and shorthand, where minimal thinking was involved. I had wanted to focus on academics but, as a witness of Jehovah, I was warned against the danger of pursuing higher learning. I would need some practical skills later on in order to make a living while serving as a pioneer. (Pioneers devoted many extra hours in the converting work.) Higher education would only lead to investment in the "old system of things" and high-headed ideas.

It was perplexing to me how God could be such a composite deity: merciful, loving benefactor and vengeful warrior who would slaughter all non-believers at Armageddon. The paradox seemed impossible, but with God, I was told all things were possible.

I kept finding evidence of an overwhelming part of the world that had ritual, colour and an unrelenting energy. My indoctrination did not prove to be complete. I had a spirit that was growing restless.

Why did three-quarters of the world's population not practice Christianity? Were they doomed just because they grew up in a culture that worshiped differently?

Why was sexuality so distasteful, and was it natural to despise my own flesh as weak and filled with desperate sinful desires? I have a distinct memory of one of my spoken queries (queeries?) about homosexuality. The Society's Watchtower Bible & Tract Society (the official arm which publishes the Witnesses' materials) often had articles on sexual matters. The one that so interested but confused me was on homosexuality and The Society's stance towards it. I must have been about fourteen. Questioning my mother about this article, I asked what was wrong with men being with other men (I don't know if it even mentioned lesbianism). After all, they were alike and I thought their coupling seemed natural, right. Flustered, she replied that it was an "abomination in the eyes of Jehovah." So, I guessed that that meant it was very bad. I don't think I ever asked her about sexuality again.

Rather than talk to me about such matters, she gave me the article, *A Mother Talks to Her Daughter*. It outlined the necessary topics like menstruation but it also addressed masturbation. Preparing one's body for something it can't have, i.e., premarital sex, it was therefore a dangerous activity that would make you unchaste. Did my mother have me read the article because I was spending to much time in my room? I would guiltily think. I didn't want to wage constant war with my body and my mind.

I felt grossly dissatisfied with my isolation, yet terrified of what might happen if I rejected my religion. I asked more questions, sometimes audibly, and was told it was not my place to overstep the God-given authority of the elders (spiritual leaders) of The Society. I was given counsel and spiritual advice to dissolve my doubts, but they would just become stronger, tormenting me until I let them rise in my consciousness. Acknowledging my doubts was far easier than feeling guiltier when I was pretending they didn't exist.

I continually wondered why, if my religion was the only true one, our numbers weren't greater. After all the preaching day in and day out, surely some of it should have paid off by now. The power of false religion is great, I was told. We fostered a hatred for Catholicism, as it was the bulwark of Christendom. Since ours was the true religion, the powers that be under the direction of Satan would do their utmost to suppress and even destroy it. Persecution was the sign of a true follower of God. So when thousands of Witnesses were incarcerated, tortured or killed under fascist regimes, this was supposed to prove that we alone had the true religion.

Every calamity in the world around us was seen as a "sign of the time of the end." Earthquakes, famines, juvenile delinquency, divorce—all were seen as pointers to the end of the world. I was taught to look fervently for calamity as an indication that these were indeed troubled times. The world was to be shunned at all costs. Comfort and warmth were only to be found inside the ark of God's organization. Any desire to be a part of the world meant a weakening of the flesh and giving in to Satan's temptation.

Exercising my rebellious feelings, I began to seek out worldly companions. My real desires flowed, but only when I was out of sight of the watchful eyes of those who were waiting for me to fall. In order to keep my sanity I developed a dual nature. One side of me maintained a sort of Christian calm and an acceptable level of religiosity. I prayed with all my might that the world would end so that I could be released from my pain. When there was a particularly violent storm and the elements acted up, I would be filled with dread, wondering if this was the long-anticipated end of the world.

Another part of me screamed loudly for expression. I wanted to be able to develop free associations without fear of reproach, to get rid of the strict conventions governing my behavior, to make my own dreams even if they, too, proved an illusion.

I knew that emerging into the real world would be a sharp slap in the face. But being a worldling and dealing with the struggle of living among the blemishes had to be better than the stark, artificial reality of my monochromatic vision. I felt locked in a straightjacket of fixed dogma, and being a non-participant in my own life was becoming unbearable. I wanted to live in the present, instead of viewing the world around me as a "dying old system of things." Lying awake at night, I would think about walking out the door, never to return. Even if I was destroyed with all the rest, I would have achieved something I could call my own before I perished. I still anticipated being cut off while still in my youth, but after weighing everything, I decided to risk obliteration.

I was sixteen and had already been warned about my insurgent behavior and bad associations. I committed minor offenses punishable by The Society and was given a probationary period to realign myself. Now overtly defiant, I searched out forbidden contacts and proceeded to explore my wakening sexuality. Still hesitant to go all the way, I dabbled enough to be considered a whore by the church. As we were trained to spy on one another, it wasn't hard to make certain that I was squealed on. I was subsequently brought before a judiciary committee of elders who would decide my fate. They questioned me in elaborate detail about my wrongdoing. Listening intently to the sordid account of my illicit encounters, this tribunal regarded me with distaste, as one who had erred severely, and required strong punitive measures. Sitting around me in the living room of my parents' home, they quoted scripture and asked for my repentance. I remained silent while they used every psychological weapon they knew of to break down my resistance. They, along with my parents, tried to browbeat me into submission, but I refused to comply saying that I didn't see anything wrong with what I had done. Eventually, they saw that they could make no headway with me whatsoever and so concluded that there was no other choice but to "disfellowship" me. Their malediction was pronounced upon me in hushed tones, reeking of self-righteousness. I was now considered excommunicated and none of my former friends were permitted to talk to me. My family was also expected to ostracize me.

My parents entertained a faint glimmer of hope that I would succumb to the pressures of being an outcast with nowhere to go, see the error of my ways and repent. They didn't seriously think I had the gumption to leave. My father caught me red-handed looking through the newspaper ads for somewhere else to live. He grew enraged and flew into a tirade of abuse. The sharp missiles hit hard and I grew terrified of his anger. Then the words bounced off me; I had prepared my suit of armor for just this occasion. He ordered me to leave. Barely having time to throw some clothes into a suitcase, I called a friend from school to tell her to expect me.

I could feel my mother's stony presence—she was sitting stiffly, resolutely on her bed, immovable as granite. I left without saying goodbye. My pride would not allow her to see my face, clouded with grief, the undressed wounds that were my eyes. As I closed the door behind me, the floodgates opened and the tears began to fall. Depleted, my spirits dashed, I just made it to my friend's house before I collapsed, giving way to the tremendous strain of those last few weeks. It was the night before school was to start. That previous summer, due to excessive pressure from my parents, I had agreed to quit high school and attend a business college. Now that I was out of their jurisdiction, I triumphantly reversed that decision and bleary-eyed, I accompanied my friend to school the next morning.

I was grateful to them for only one thing—my freedom. Their expelling me made it much easier to beat a hasty retreat. I was left with a dogged fighting will to go forward without looking back. For once in my life I felt uncertain of my future—and so pleased to be part of the real struggle of living.

BIOGRAPHY Pamela Godfree

These days my attitude towards spirituality is in a state of flux. For many years access to my spiritual self was blocked; through a process of equal parts experimentation and deprogramming my channels of thought, I have now reached a point where I can find solace in spirituality. My relationship with my family remains highly problematic. My mother died a year and a half ago. That has meant a shift in my relationship to the family, especially my connection with my father (who has never become a baptized member of the church). We are (re)creating a father/daughter bond. As far as my three siblings are concerned, they continue to follow (in varying degrees) the edicts of the Witnesses who disallow any unnecessary contact with me. My love for them remains, but as we grow older we move further and further apart. I have no relationship with my two nieces and nephew who are now teenagers and twenty-something, respectively.

I salute the editor of this important volume of creative work. It has greatly helped the healing process for me. To contact me and/or other lesbian/gay/bisexual ex-Jehovah's Witnesses, please write: c/o Gays & Lesbians Out of the Watchtower (GLOW), P.O. Box 279, Station B, Toronto, Ontario M5T 2W2.

E-mail: xjw@geocities.com. We also have a website: http://www.com/westhollywood/heights/2321

BEYOND THE SEXUAL REVOLUTION
A Spiritual View of Gay Identity and Planetary Transformation
Toby Johnson

The lesbian and gay rights movement is popularly thought of as an extremist faction of the 'Sexual Revolution.' This conception has been reinforced by the peculiar anti-sexual obsession of Western Christianity and the political strategizing of so-called 'conservatives' who know 'other people's' sexual behavior is a hot button with which to stir up voters—along with the defensive pro-sex reactions of many gay political activists who end up inadvertently stirring up the wrong voters with that same hot button. But I believe, interpreting lesbian/gay culture as primarily sexual and its issues as exclusively sexual libertarian completely misunderstands the big picture.

I am, of course, in sympathy with the gay activists (and count myself among their number) and not the old-time religionists (though I was, like many of us in North America, raised as a Christian and attribute my ethical and mystical sensibilities to that upbringing). But I think it is time we reevaluate what the gay rights movement is about and how we ought to be working to change culture. Rather than in the context of the Sexual Revolution, the development of lesbian and gay consciousness makes much more sense in that of eco-consciousness and so-called New Age, new paradigm thinking.

The movement is, certainly, about stopping the victimization of lesbians and gay men out of simple justice, fair-play, and compassion. But it is also—and even more importantly—about recognizing and honoring sexually diverse, non-reproducing individuals' participation in and contribution to the spiritual evolution of human consciousness.

For Jesuit paleontologist Pierre Teilhard de Chardin, his successor, ex-Dominican Matthew Fox, and under the rubric *Gaia* for a whole generation of 'new paradigm' thinkers, planet Earth itself is a living organism. We human beings, along with all the plants and animals with which we share the biosphere, are the 'organs' of this organism. And, according to this new paradigm thinking, it is not doomsday or dystopia that awaits planet Earth in the near future, but a dramatic leap into a new kind of consciousness.

Teilhard proposed that in this transformed consciousness, individual persons will directly experience themselves connected to the collective, perhaps through a heightened experience of compassion and sensitivity to others, with roles to play in the life of the planet. Gaia is awakening. Such a spiritual vision of history, which sees God's plan being continually carried out as evolution in new and sometimes surprising ways, would naturally look carefully at the current day manifestation of homosexual behavior to understand how the transformation of gay culture demonstrates natural processes in the life of Gaia.

Part of that transformation of culture has permitted gay historians to treat gay issues in history. Such gay-sensitive research (by anthropologist Walter L. Williams and by classicist John Boswell respectively) has revealed that non-Western cultures, specifically Native American, honored sexual variance as a sign of divine election and recognized sexually variant people as community leaders and spiritual guides.

The rampant anti-homosexual sentiment in Western civilization, that is thought to be so basic to human nature, actually arose in Europe as late as the fourteenth century. Before that time, the so-called anti-homosexual references in the Bible, for instance, were generally given different interpretations. The condemnations of non-reproductive sex, given such authority today, were based in repopulation imperatives following the Hundred Years War and the Black Death.

As we approach the future, we need to learn to look beyond ourselves, to look for the big picture. It has been my experience and my perception that homosexuals are often broader thinkers, who understand with a less clouded vision what's really going on. Certainly it's true that understanding *anything* is difficult: we are all so apt to have our vision clouded by the unconscious forces of personality that so influence our perceptions and understandings. Maleness and femaleness are major among those forces. The less polarized we are in these traits, the less distorted will be our vision.

Perhaps, since as gay and lesbian people we don't fit in, we've been forced out of the assumptions about what's normal. This gives us a perspective on things. We don't have such automatic answers about how things are supposed to be, because we're not the way we are supposed to be.

We have had to learn to be perceptive and sensitive toward other people because, at least as we were coming out as young people, we felt so different from them and feared their derision if we exposed the truth about ourselves. We quickly discovered that acknowledgement of what's sexually and emotionally pleasing to us brought verbal and emotional abuse. We had to keep an eye on the big picture, lest we make a mistake in perceiving how different the others' worlds were from ours.

We certainly suffer more than our fair share of neuroses and psychological buttons that get pushed—especially in matters of sex, sexual relationships and sexual self-image. But by and large, homosexually-oriented people are conscientious, responsible, law-abiding—if a bit libertine about certain victimless crimes—and unusually courteous, caring, and kind. We make good citizens and good teachers of citizens.

The goal isn't to convert more people to homosexual orientation. Though as the world gets more and more crowded, a larger percentage of homosexuals may be needed to get things back in balance. Rather, gay men and lesbians are the exemplars. We tend to demonstrate the blending of masculinity and femininity. We give witness that individual human beings contribute to the planetary being by more than just reproducing their genes—an especially important message in these times of overpopulation. We contribute to the cultural evolution of the planet. Our virtues tend to be those needed for the modern secular, non-patriarchal society. Our struggles for justice and acceptance break down the old archetypes of male and female so that a new equality of men and women can develop.

That partnership of male and female has clear implications for public morality. Most laws are biased in favor of men's domination of women. Child-rearing practices are biased by men's hegemony. Notions of virtue and success are biased toward masculine traits: excellence and competitiveness are intrinsically male ideas founded in hierarchical perceptions of the world. A partnership society which equally values men's and women's ways of being is likely to be more cooperative, less violent, more life-affirming, less judgmental, more concerned with being good and less with being 'right.'

As children, lesbians and gay men sense that we don't belong, we aren't wanted (as gay), we are different, we are outsiders. We learn to be observers rather than participants. That sense of being excluded, alienated, and seeking admission to a circle that we feel does not really want us may be the source both of most of our sufferings (low self-esteem, dissatisfaction, sexual restlessness, compulsiveness, etc.) and of our specialness (sensitivity, awareness, compassion, artisticness, taste, etc.). Indeed, it may be that, irrespective of the hostility of the Scribes and Pharisees of the modern-day church, it is this sense of being outside and wanting more that leaves us dissatisfied with conventional religion and open to something new and motivated to seek something better.

World religions scholar and mythographer Joseph Campbell observed that the potent spiritual/mythic image of today is the view of Earth seen from the moon. It symbolizes that, for the first time in history, human beings are able to achieve a perspective from which to view the whole of the human universe. Campbell noted that this parallels the psychological experience of viewing one's self and one's culture from over and above. And this changes everything. No longer can a person imagine his or her beliefs and opinions obvious and universal. No longer can any one culture claim its 'truth' to be superior. No longer can anybody actually believe (except out of reactionary defensiveness and insecurity) that their god is the only true god, their precious savior the only savior, and the millions of other human beings who worship differently totally deluded and doomed to eternal punishment. Religion has to be understood as myth and metaphor.

The stance of being outside and above the content of individual religions is the only honest approach to religious truth today. This is, of course, the attitude of Buddhism in its purest form, and Buddhism—non-theistic, tolerant, peaceful—is by far the most spiritual of the religions: no one has ever been murdered in the name of Buddha.

This is also the attitude of cultural relativism imposed on modern consciousness by worldwide communication, easy travel, cultural exchange, and scientific objectivity. In a world in which every country has myths of its own precious savior, no one god or savior can be accorded primacy. Thus comparative religion forces students of religious anthropology into a kind of meta-religion in which it is not the content of religion, but the fact of religious questing which provides inspiration and enlightenment. This is the natural evolution of the mythic consciousness. Gay people are naturals for such meta-religion. For, by our gayness, we are propelled into the critical perspective. And—not surprisingly—gay people and our issues are in the vanguard of the transformation of religion, demanding the old traditions widen their scope and recognize that planetary evolution has necessarily changed human nature.

In the big picture, it seems, a new sexual identity has developed among human beings in the last hundred years. While people obviously had homosexual sex in the past, until recently, nobody's identified themselves thereby or experienced that identity as a source of distinctive and positive personality traits. This is something new. It's like the human species is evolving a new sex.

Isn't this a potentially momentous event in human evolution? Shouldn't this phenomenon be of major interest to anthropologists and sociologists and futurists and philosophers of all sorts? If human beings were beginning to develop a new organ in their bodies, wouldn't everybody be interested in learning what it is and what it is for, not trying to deny it and wishing it would go away? Well, in homosexuals, the planet is growing a new kind of human being, a new organ of the collective. Everybody should be interested and supportive. This is what the lesbian and gay rights movement is really about.

BIOGRAPHY Toby Johnson

Toby Johnson, PhD, is a Lammy-winning author of three books about modern cultural and social issues (including variant sexuality) from a mythic perspective and of three novels about gay spiritual consciousness. He is editor of **White Crane: A Quarterly Journal of Gay Men's Spirituality**. With Kip Dollar, his lover of fifteen years, Johnson operates The House at Peregrine's Perspective, a B&B-style country retreat in the Rocky Mountains.

Johnson, a former Roman Catholic monk, was a student and friend of renowned mythologist Joseph Campbell and formerly a Director of the Campbell Archives and Library in Santa Barbara, CA. His website address is: www.whitecranejournal.com.

CENTENNIAL BABY DOLL
Jane Inyallie
Dedicated to Antoinette

oh, where have you gone
Centennial Baby Doll?

trickster incarnate
embodiment of
a wizened crone

you showed up
at the village
one day
flashy dress and all
no one remembers
where you came from or
where you've gone
only that you've
always looked the same

a century-old harlot
boldly brazen
with lips painted red
rouged cheeks
and dolled up hair

your dress crossed
the boundaries
into an area
called bad taste
over your shoulder slung
a harlot bag
to carry
your harlot things

you challenged the
status quo
of self-proclaimed
morally upstanding citizens

you defied rules
of social etiquette
making your own
along the way
and dared to speak
of outrageous acts
laced with
sexual innuendo

you forced everyone
to look at parts
of themselves
they chose to ignore

at first
they tried to hide
behind mask
and other disguise
but they could not hide
from the look
in your eyes

you appeared to men
a lusty young wench
seeking the throes
of passion
a feast for
sexual appetite

the trickster
mirrored images
of fantasy
caught
in tangled webs
of tangled minds

women despised you
for showing them
their fears
of sagging breasts
of losing their men
of becoming useless

they looked at fear
afraid of how it might
be used against them

they did not see
the beauty of
their womanness
this you showed them
in different ways

you made yourself
a target for arrows
fashioned from words
tipped with barbs

of jealousy
aimed at your heart

your laughter
a throaty cackle
shattered them mid-air
with breath
you blew them away
useless against
the skills of trickster

you showed them
visions of immortality
the strength
they innately possess
the core of trickster
that is centre of all

you walked through
illusion
created from words
breaking barriers
of hardened reserve
redefined the meaning
of natural law

for this
they loved you
as much as
they feared you
no one had the courage
to tell you

oh, where have you gone
Centennial Baby Doll?

no one forgot
the nights at the lake
everyone knew when
it was going to happen
they waited and
followed with anticipation

you went by boat
to your chosen spot
started a fire
arranged your things
no one knew why
you were there

or what you were doing

you dressed with ceremony
your painted face
an ancient ceremonial mask
calling upon spirit
from ancestral past

you can be seen
in the dead of night
your spirit spinning
circles of fire
pulsing with luminosity

your shawl threw
iridescence
into the night
leaving a mark
in the form
of northern lights

flames licked the
fringes of your shawl
sending shivers
up and down
tickling the spine
of night

the scent of
your deerskin dress
mingled with the
smell of fire
they danced
leaving a trail
of misty tracks

your slippered feet
touched the ground
shooting sparks
into the air
burning holes
in the curtain of night

sparkles speak
invitingly
whispering secrets
of wonder
beyond
the veil of mystery

on aged legs
you danced the night
leaping and twisting
onto tops of trees

you caught
moonbeam arms
swung
glided and dipped
into the midnight sky
talking and laughing
with your partner
the moon

she smiled and danced
to the peak of her time
and retired till her next
full moon shine

young people could
no longer sit as spectators
the beat of the dance
pulled them in
they had a time
trying to keep up
with you

you egged them on
pushing them
beyond their limit
and howled
with laughter

one day
you were gone
no one knows
where you went
it was as though
you were never there
everyone saw you
but no one really
got to know you

oh, where have you gone
Centennial Baby Doll?

rumours and speculation
were rampant

stories were colourful
you were seen many places
doing many things

your laughter still echoes
across the lake
playing with water
blowing through trees
teasing the ears of children

when you left
everyone missed you
there was no one to blame
no one to make the brunt
of their lewd joke

after awhile
they realized
there was more to you
than they thought

something was missing
the magic
the spontaneity
the village
has been quiet
there are no more
fiery dances
on the lake

barley's
was never the same
without you
you were the first one there
the last to leave
your chair still sits
in a corner

the legacy
you left
is carried to
the next generation
they stare in wonder
and amazement
when stories are told of
Centennial Baby Doll

trickster stirs
the air with curiosity

wonder and excitement
they feel the magic
of your presence

will you present yourself
to the next generation?
how will you be seen?
do people of another time
live through you
as we did and still do?

oh, where have you gone
Centennial Baby Doll?

what universe do you travel?
what dimension are you in?
what form have you taken?

oh, where have you gone
Centennial Baby Doll?

Jane Inyallie's biography appears on page 20.

WITH ONE FOOT I RAN FROM THE PLANTATION
Aswad

When I was in my teens, they ran the mini-series **Roots** on TV for the first time. The part that really struck me was when the elder Kunte Kinte tried to run away from the plantation. When they caught him, they chopped off his right foot to see to it that he couldn't do it again.

Before the black man ever laid eyes on a white man, he had religion. It didn't take place in big shiny buildings with crosses on the top. It didn't even take place in buildings at all. And it was about real spirituality. It was not a 'just on Sunday' religion.

The religions were about the earth, the sky, the wind and waters. They were quite similar to the way the Native Americans of this continent worshiped. That too was before the white man.

But then he came. The white man came to Africa in search of slaves, people with dark skin to pick his cotton, clean his house, slop his hogs and kiss his ass—these being occupations that would continue for generations.

So when the African arrived in America, his drums, his talismans, his juju bags, were all taken away from him. They were burned, the ashes buried. The language, clothing, an entire way of life was destroyed. Perhaps forever.

Then he did it. During slavery, the white man taught that his religion was better, that he, the white man, was better, and the African was made to believe him. It was believe or be whipped. Believe or be bludgeoned to death.

I was born in 1963, virtually 100 years after the signing of the Emancipation Proclamation. My mother raised me as a Southern Baptist. My first recollection of my revulsion for Christianity was from the preacher-man's "fire and brimstone" proclamations about sex, how "whore mongers" and "fornicators" will "burn in hell." There were special rules for homosexuals. I was only seven years old when my mother started taking me to church, so I had no idea what a homosexual was. I didn't know at the time that he meant me.

When I was around sixteen, I realized I hated church. Oh, I liked the music alright. You can't beat the black church for a good old-fashioned, bone-shaking worship session. I guess you can take the drum away from the African, but you can't keep the African away from the drum. I hated church because there was never anybody who would answer my questions like Why is God white? Why does God hate Blacks? and, Why does God hate gays?

Nobody seemed to have answers for what I felt were very simple questions. I would be told, "It's God's way." It was at that point that I realized I didn't like the white man's version of God.

My mother, to this day, refers to me as her "mistake." She told me once that I wanted to be a woman. My mother's a good church-goin' woman. I left her house, my own plantation, when I was seventeen or eighteen. I decided at that point that I didn't have to follow the white man's God since I was no longer in my mother's house.

I had heard about Malcolm X and the Black Muslims through his books. Since I was Black, I decided I'd be a Muslim, but people neglected to tell me that some Muslims hate faggots, Islam being as paternalistic a religion as Christianity.

I then looked into Witchcraft, which seemed as white as any Christian church on any given Sunday morning. It wasn't worth it to me to try to push past another white brick wall, so I gave up on religion and spirituality for a time. Trying to be a good American, I delved into the only church that was open seven days a week and always there for those with the wherewithal to do the penance: THE MALL! This didn't work either. As a black, gay, motherless, fatherless child in the wilds of Southern California, I did not have the money.

I moved to San Francisco in 1995, and then, became removed from the white gay community. I hadn't the money to be part of that scene either. White gay racism hurts more than white straight racism. I expected it from the straights, but I thought white gay men were supposed to be better. I was wrong.

I joined a group for Black gay men. Unfortunately, that didn't work out either. I had recently started studying Shamanism and traditional African religion. But all they seemed to want to do was sit around and cry and moan about being kicked out of the Black church; and clawing their hands bloody, trying to get back in through that mahogany paneled door that had long ago been slammed in their faces by the preachers, the choirs and their mothers. I left that group. I have never understood why Black people who were put into slavery by Christianity would take it up themselves, and even less so when Black gay men do it.

I then began to study Yoruba traditions. Most African-Americans are descended from the Yoruba people of West Africa. Most African-Americans don't know that and most African-Americans don't care. Yoruba tradition was more welcoming to me than any other. Voodoo, Mocumba, Santeria: these all stem from the original Ifa religion of the Yoruba people.

I studied relentlessly for almost a year and had every intention of becoming a fully initiated Priest of Oshun. There were some Yoruba houses that were very welcoming and some that weren't. Some were actually run by gays, but it still didn't feel quite right, so I stopped. It dawned on me that I was doing it again. I never got the approval of my mother because I'm gay. I never got the approval of the white man because I'm Black. I ran hard and fast after the title "Reverend", because I figured that finally, someone would respect me. But the truth was I needed to respect myself. It was my own approval I needed. Not my mother's. Not the white man's. And not any churches, white or African.

Recently, I've taken down my altar. It was a major move for me. I realized that I just don't need it anymore, almost as if the energy, the power, if you will, has moved within me. I no longer need to pray to an outside deity for help or answers. I see my spirituality now as something that no longer needs a name or a title, structure or rules. I just let the energy flow and the goddess protect me. Part of my spirituality is expressed through the traditional African clothes that I make myself, which I wear every day and not just on special occasions. I feel spirits around me all the time, not just on Sunday. As well, I don't discuss my religious practices anymore. I do not share them, especially with white people or Christianized Blacks. White people have proven what little respect they have for the traditional religious practices of people of colour and Native Americans. Also, today's white youth are so desperate to be cool that they brand African religions as 'cool,' until they get tired of being 'ethnic' and drop the whole thing like last season's fashions. This is disrespectful and unacceptable. On the other hand, Christianized Blacks are so fervently adhered to the white man's Christianity, that such a discussion is usually a waste of time.

My religion is just that: mine. I won't have it defiled, debased or insulted. I don't need to ram it down someone's throat to make it real. I don't need to stand on street corners screaming and preaching at people to get my point across. It just is.

I ran away from the plantation hopping on one foot and I'll keep hopping away from this very country—this racist, homophobic country, which is nothing more than a large plantation soaked with the blood of Africans, Natives, gays and witches.

This slave has freed himself and I'll live free or die.

BIOGRAPHY Aswad

Aswad is a 35-year-old self-publishing author living in Berkeley, California. Raised Southern Baptist in Northern Virginia, Aswad was disenchanted with Christianity at a very early age. Aswad studied Islam, Witchcraft and traditional African religion and was dissatisfied with them all for various reasons, including issues of race and homosexuality. After a year of study to become an initiated priest of the Oshun in the Yoruba tradition, Aswad realized that true spirituality comes from a long, intense search. That search can be short or life-long, but must be made to reach inner strength and peace. Aswad continues his religious life in intense privacy, while writing African-American fiction and running his own publishing firm from his home in Berkeley.

JOURNEY
Barbara Brown

Journey. My life image. The only image I have found that can hold the complex truths of my life, of this world. I have longed to have a place to belong, one place, ready made that I could just fit in. But it hasn't worked. I've left many places disillusioned, angry or disappointed, having expected to discover home. But as I began to understand that home was this journey, I experienced a settling I never imagined. I have found resting places and companions for parts of the journey. I have discovered places I will revisit and people who nourish my soul. This journey led me to creating my own understanding of spirituality—one that could hold the experiences of trauma and of joy, one that did not say spirituality is about feeling good or being not of this world/my body. I have searched for an understanding of the divine that could help me make sense of the reality of violence in this world and in my life. Informed significantly by Nelle Morton's and Marjorie Procter Smith's writing, I have discovered that I cannot separate spirituality from my everyday living, that in fact, *how I am in the world is my spirituality*. For me, that includes being a lesbian and being a sexual abuse survivor. It includes having been raised in a Christian family, with white and middle class privileges, while becoming increasingly aware of racism and classism. This includes finding many words to describe the divine—energy, goddess, tree of life, holy. It includes celebrating my desire and love for women and fighting the oppression propagated through sexism and heterosexism.

I believe that an understanding of 'god' as 'other than', allows for the patriarchal splits of spirit/body, male/female, white/non white, straight/gay, with one being superior to the other, closer to god. These splits permeate North American culture and (most) established religions today. It allows people to create judgement of what is right and good and what is evil based on identity rather than harm. It encourages us to deposit evil in some source other than ourselves—in women or people of colour or single moms on welfare. It also permits silence. A spirituality of dualisms and divisions, a spirituality that is disembodied, frees people to believe 'it's not my responsibility because the injustice appears to have nothing to do with me.' Injustice becomes a women's issue or a gay issue, and if I am not this (woman or gay) or don't recognize the injustice even if I am this, then why should I care? Ultimately, however, through this abdication of responsibility for a more just world, children continue to be abused, gay men bashed, people of colour harassed and beaten, women raped.

If our spirituality is about how we are in the world, then our everyday choices become significant. It also means each person, each creature and creation matters. Thus, no one is closer to god or more spiritual than another. We are not better than or more deserving than another. Nor are we worse than or less deserving than another. We all carry the divine within us, we carry the possibility of bringing the divine into being.

And what of evil? I understand evil to be harm done to another, to creation. We all have the capacity to hurt and to bring healing. However, many in this world choose to propagate evil in individual action and by supporting structures that uphold oppression. Those who have experiences of oppression, of violence, know of human capacity to harm—to create evil. I learned this all too well in my experiences of abuse as a child, in being dehumanized as my body, my spirit was violated—an object for another's use. I am reminded of this when I recognize my own fear of identifying as a lesbian. I know the potential loss of family, of employability, of personal safety, as I am reduced by others to a splinter of who I am and become a potential target for the heterosexist cruelty of this world. However, I also need to face the harm I do to myself in not being true to who I am, or the evil I participate in through the ways I uphold systems of oppression. I struggle to name these places in not wanting to be one of them, one of the perpetrators, one of the people who spew hate into the world. To hold myself responsible for who I am and how I am in the world requires an honesty and self awareness that is difficult to maintain in this world of extreme dualities—all evil or all good. I also know that there are differences in severity of harm done, some people actively choose to abuse, to do violence to others. As I attempt to refine my own understanding of 'severity of harm', the blurring begins. As I engage in making judgement (based on harm, not identity), a necessary and appropriate response to the realities of violence and oppression, the measures for doing so are often unclear. Continually, I have to push myself to accurately name how I am subjected to harm and how I participate in ending or propagating harm—how I participate in the incarnation of the divine or of evil.

Similarly, we must all (individually and corporately) be held responsible for our actions. Not confronting evil actions/systems condones them. There must be accountability for how we are in the world. Remembering that I need not confront injustice alone is vital, nor can I leave others to confront alone. Injustice often happens in isolation or creates a sense of isolation. Community in the face of this becomes essential. We do not walk this journey alone, we cannot. If we try to, we participate in the patriarchal notion of 'it's all about me' or 'it has nothing to do with me' which maintains isolation. Change cannot occur in this separation. Relationship (with self, others, creation) is essential. To change systems of oppression requires confrontation in an ongoing way, by people and communities committed to a new way of being.

A new way of being for me is in saying, "I am a lesbian." I only recently came out as part of my journey of searching. As I began trying on the words, "I am a lesbian," something shifted in my world. I continue to settle into these words, into this living of loving women, one that makes more sense to me than anything else I have experienced. As I am able to live in my body, to speak and act on my desire, I discover sacred moments. In these moments, the divine becomes a lived experience.

This understanding of spirituality has encouraged me to mark these moments in words and action and ritual. Doing so requires honouring my own words rather than those given or forced upon me from external sources. It requires transforming and creating images that bring meaning into my life. These words and images become tangible when I act and speak out. They become a part of my lived reality, and open possibilities of finding places of mutual exchange and growth.

I have included here a series of poems, one way I have of marking, that touches on this understanding and comes from a different time in my life. I recognize the use of the word 'god' holds hurt for many and is representative of a patriarchal religious belief system. I offer the poems the way they were written as representative of the movement of my life.

I continue to struggle with how to live a life, to live a spirituality, that integrates my understanding of justice, for I believe they cannot be separate. I stumble over my own heterosexism and racism and classism. I hope that in this stumbling I will do the least amount of damage possible to others and myself. I hope there will be those who can help me understand such places within me, to see what I cannot see. And I hope there will be times when I can do the same for others. The journey continues.

DENIED POSSIBILITIES
Barbara Brown

you stir within me
and disrupt my settled world
arising in me such a
strong, unsatiated hunger
that I will not let you
satisfy
whose cruel hand
holds back my own
from caressing
your body?
what forces drive me to
ignore
avoid
those stirrings
presenting a front of decision?
perhaps propriety
good christian propriety
I do not know fully
I only know it is within me
relentless and unmerciful
in its denial

O SILENT GOD
Barbara Brown

O Silent God
You anger me
where is your voice
in this hurting world?

O Silent God
You scare me
will you forever
be mute to me?

O Silent God
You awe me
as you push me to
call on my own strength from within

O Silent God
where is your voice?

I only hear the cries of
the ones beaten
the ones frightened
the ones lonely
the ones silenced

O Silent God
perhaps you are not so silent

LEG OVER LEG
Barbara Brown

leg over leg
spread
open in invitation

glistening waters
an ocean flows from her

plunging in
tossed by waves
of her heat
immersed in her loving

tastes of sweet saltiness
fill me
filling her
inside

entering
safe in
the darkness
of her internal recesses

safe in her loving
i find
i am home

LIFE PRAYER
Barbara Brown

tree of life
sustain me
shade me
clothe me
feed me
hold me
tree of life
sustain me

BIOGRAPHY Barbara Brown

I grew up on the prairies, live in Toronto, and yearn for the mountains. I write for pleasure and self expression. I spend a lot of time listening and trying to pay attention.

WHY I AM AN EX-CATHOLIC
Daniel Curzon

I left the Catholic Church when I was twenty-one and have never regretted leaving the least bit. If anything, I regret all the years I spent in the clutches of the Sisters of the Immaculate Heart of Mary at St. Rose of Lima, the four years under the sway of the Jesuits at the University of Detroit, another three years teaching at the same university. Okay, I'll give Catholic education this: it encourages discipline and postponement of pleasure, not totally bad things actually, especially in today's impatient, instantaneous McWorld. Nevertheless, mostly my Catholic education has made me roaringly anti-Catholic. I simply don't see how anybody would want to belong to this organization. I'm probably still listed on its rolls somewhere, god help me.

I was born into the church. I didn't ask to be a Catholic. It seems incredible to me that parents have the unquestioned right to impose their religions on their children, no matter how ludicrous or irrational the faith may be—a right that I suspect will be challenged in the next century. If I'd been able to speak up at the Holy Sacrament of Baptism, I would have said, "You're pouring this water on my head so that I can be admitted to Heaven? Required Water? On my head? What is this, somebody's idea of a joke?" All the mumbo-jumbo like this that I had to memorize and abide by during all those years might not matter so much if God or Heaven existed. Surely then all the hair-splitting and guilt-mongering might not have left such a bad taste in my mouth. But of course there is no God, never was, and never will be, and, if there is, He certainly couldn't possibly run Immortality like a fraternity initiation! I give Him more credit than that.

I've noticed that some people with a limited exposure to Catholicism sometimes are taken in by its trappings: the liturgy, the music, the incense. These people keep trying to drag me to Midnight Mass every Christmas Eve. They even think nuns are cute. Believe me, nuns aren't cute. They teach children awful things. They may have changed their habits, but old habits of dogma don't change even if the skirts are shorter. The instruction in my day was very thorough, guaranteed to ensure internalized guilt so that we would never be able to have sexual pleasure outside marriage without feeling sick about it. Get this—you're supposed to marry one person of the opposite sex and then want nothing more than to have sex with that person for the next sixty years, no ifs, ands or buts, and if this doesn't make you happy then there's something wrong with *you*. Nooo, there's something wrong with that mold. (It's moldy!) We even had to confess any enjoyable unmarried thoughts about sex to some man wearing a black dress as he sat in a little black box!

Even today the Pope continues to spout off about the evils of masturbation and homosexuality. (If I see that man on that balcony one more time on the national news I'm going to scream.) The church hates the flesh and tells virgins of both sexes that they'll go to Heaven for putting up with needless sexual frustration. They're even told that they'll earn eternal reward if they don't reproduce the human race because of being celibate. Of course those queers will go to Hell if they don't reproduce, but have some fun doing so. But men have far more sperm than they know what to do with, and all that unspent jism just turns men cranky, crazed, and pop-eyed. (Just look at leaders of the Traditional Nonsense Coalition or the Christian Colitis Association or whatever the hell it is.)

I was raised in a closed world, where one was punished for not believing the silliness being handed down. Do you know what some of the Catholic Church's other doctrines are? Just look at the following objectively: God decided to have his son born of a virgin in an obscure village and then crucified like a common criminal in order to save a bunch of human beings who were born damned—and why? Because they had inherited an Original Sin from two people who had eaten some forbidden fruit after God told them not to. Pardon me, but I wasn't in the Garden of Eden and I'm not guilty as charged. (The church didn't even read me my rights!)

Wait! There's more. The shedding of somebody else's blood is supposed to save people from this big sin which they didn't commit, and this event is now celebrated across the world in Holy Mass when God appears in a little piece of bread that looks, feels, and tastes like plain, old bread but of course is God Himself—not a symbol of God, but the God, the creator of the universe, the High-Price Bread.

If anyone said a cult in Guyana was teaching innocent children doctrines like this, the government would arrest the whole lot of them, and should. But as a matter of fact the Catholic Church (like all established churches) receives a tax-exempt status for spreading this sort of 'truth' to the world. So in effect, taxpayers subsidize political acts of discrimination against gays through such religious organizations. It's time this was ended once and for all. (And the money paid out in reparations to ex-Catholics like me.)

It wouldn't be so bad if the Catholics practiced something close to Christ's message about loving and forgiving and being humane, but the more common pattern (for Protestants and Muslims too) is to browbeat, crush, and kill, all in the name of some spurious goodness.

I can't honestly understand why any gay people would want to have anything to do with the Catholic Church, except to picket it. (Or maybe get a job in it.) And yet, amazingly, there are some who still trying to change its anti-gay pronouncements. They go into convulsions of joy whenever some pontificating Pontiff or other gives them a crumb, such as saying that homosexuality as an orientation isn't a sin, only having gay sex is. (Thanks, but no thanks, Your Holiness.)

Suppose the church does eventually change its mind (what mind?) about gay Catholics (as it has changed its mind about married priests, the Jews' guilt for killing Christ, Galileo, and the authenticity of any number of saints who never existed). Who can believe in a religion that changes its basic beliefs? Are people so desperate to believe that they'll believe in anything as long as they have spiritual direction in their lives? Apparently so. I believe it takes more courage to face the void that's there. God did not make us to know Him, to love Him, to serve Him, and to be happy with Him forever. Sorry, kids, but He just didn't.

As I've gotten older I feel as strongly about all this as I did when I was a youth full of argumentative vinegar. I once wrote, "All these gay Catholics begging Mother Church to accept them, while she keeps spitting in their faces and calling them sinners—it must be a little-understood form of S&M." Now I just sort of shrug that most people can't seem to accept that they simply are not important in some big-picture way. I shrug; therefore, I am. Just don't bring your Holy Inquisition into my back yard.

Yes, I remember those blessed days of yester-year in church when I felt the Holy Ghost hovering near my heart, when I lusted after the salvation that was going to be mine forever if I was just hardcore Catholic enough. But thankfully I was exposed to some ideas in the outside—the real—world and I saw the light at last. And may I rot in Hell if I ever forgive the goddamn Catholic Church!

BIOGRAPHY Daniel Curzon

Daniel Curzon is one of the principal gay writers to walk the minefields of literary and social criticism to make it easier for those who have followed. His works include the landmark angry novel **Something You Do in the Dark** (1971), **The World Can Break Your Heart** (1984), **Superfag** (1996), **Only the Good Parts** (1998) and **Not Necessarily Nice: stories** (1998) as well as the plays **My Unknown Son** (Circle Rep Lab, New York, 1987, Los Angeles, 1997) and **1001 Nights at the House of Pancakes** (San Francisco, 1998). Daniel Curzon has also written and published non-gay fiction and plays. His plays, both gay and non-gay (some of which have won awards) have been produced in several cities.

Daniel Curzon's latest novel **Only the Good Parts** is available through: http://www.xlibris.com/OnlyTheGoodParts.html.

AL FATIHA—THE OPENING
Mohammed Khan

I am gay. I am a Pakistani-Canadian. I am a Muslim. For as long as I can recall, these three elements of my identity have either been on a mission to break away and assert themselves as distinct entities or in a constant struggle for dominance. Thus far, being gay and a Pakistani-Canadian have taken on more significance in my life than being a Muslim. Maybe tomorrow things will change. In fact, I know that tomorrow things will change. I've come to rely on change. It is change that beckoned me to attend the First International Retreat for Lesbian, Gay, Bisexual, Transgender (LGBT) Muslims, and Their Friends in Boston on the weekend of October 9th – 12th, 1998.

I must admit that I went to Boston not knowing what to expect—although, I was hoping I would meet the perfect desi (South Asian) Muslim boy and that the nikah (marriage agreement) would be completed by the end of the weekend (just kidding). Like I was saying, I didn't know what to expect. However, it was brought to my attention by one of my close friends, that perhaps the whole event was being staged by some right-wing, Islamic puritan group, that was planning to gather all the queer Muslims in one location and exterminate us all at once. She actually went so far as to give me the name and number of a friend in Boston just in case anything happened.

Upon arriving at the location of the retreat, which was only disclosed to the attendees for security purposes, I soon realized that of the 200 or so people who had inquired about the event, only 30 were going to be in attendance, the primary reason for this being security as well as visibility concerns. So my dear friend was not off base at all in her assessment. By the grace of Allah, no such fiasco occurred. In my heart, I knew that nothing like that was going to happen, unfortunately, not everyone was so sure. But can anyone blame them for their fears?

Although I was born Muslim, I don't presently practice the religion. Neither does anyone in my immediate family. I was born in Lahore, Pakistan and lived in Rawalpindi with my phuppie (aunt) until the age of ten, at which point I immigrated to Canada to come live with my parents. While living in Pakistan, I had learned how to perform namaz (prayer), and to recite the Holy Quran, and all of the kalmas (blessings); however, I gradually forgot it all in Canada.

It wasn't until the age of seventeen, while I was struggling with my sexuality, that I decided to revisit the Quran, in order to find out what Allah had to say about homosexuals. I vividly recall reading the Quranic verses and feeling my chest close in on me. How could Allah be so cruel, so heartless as to punish people like myself? All I ever wanted to do was to love someone, and to receive that love in return. But it was hopeless; nothing I read allowed me to be who I am.

At that point, I put the book away and decided to abandon Islam. In fact, I started learning about other faiths, including Hinduism and Christianity. I figured that if these faiths had their own floats on Pride Day, that maybe they were more accommodating of queers. Furthermore, the people around me sparked my initial interest in these two faiths. Two of my close friends are Hindu and Christian. I have since attended my first queer Christmas mass, and have come to adore the Mahabharata and the Sermon on the Mount. Despite my increased understanding of Hinduism and Christianity, I was always aware that there was something missing. It was as though my mind was the only thing being engaged, leaving my soul unspoken for.

Spirituality is supposed to be an alchemy of the heart, something that is with you in every endeavor, in every aspect of life. Growing up Muslim, I was always taught that one should aspire to complete submission to the will of Allah. In fact, submission is the literal translation of the word Islam. For me, that feeling of submission is what was missing.

So there I was in Boston, Massachusetts on a rainy weekend in a room full of the most diverse people you could imagine. There were folks coming in from the Netherlands, South Africa, and Belgium. Others were from Arizona, Boston, Chicago, Washington D.C., and N.Y. City. Unfortunately, I was the only Canadian there. There were approximately five lesbian-identified women, one woman who refused to be classified, one female-to-male transgender and about twenty-three gay-identified men. They represented various class, age and cultural backgrounds. We had African-Americans, South Asians, Europeans, and Middle-Eastern folks, just to name a few. We also had a significant non-Muslim presence.

We participated in intense debates and discussions focused on various topics including: Islam and LGBT identity, what Islam really says about homosexuality, as well as the obstacles and challenges faced by LGBT Muslims around the world. In addition, we undertook cross-cultural comparisons of gender and sexuality in Islamic societies (both present and historic), and lastly, we addressed the issue of how to celebrate our lives as LGBT Muslims. The conversations were at times extremely frustrating, as everyone wanted a chance to share their personal experiences and struggles. The irony of it was that this was perhaps the first time they had been given a 'safe space' to do so.

For me, the most significant part of this retreat was witnessing that there were LGBT Muslims out there who had managed to develop and maintain a positive LGBT identity, while still following Islam. I also learned to separate the widely accepted interpretations of the Imams, which are riddled with heterosexist bias, from the truest form of Islam, which stresses the fundamental principles of equality and justice. I have to admit that at some level I was hoping to find some theological accommodation for homosexuality in the Holy Quran. I never found that. Time simply did not permit an exhaustive theological examination. However, what I did find was affirmation, affirmation for myself as an individual. I am gay, by nature, and I refuse to believe that Allah created people who are sinful by their very nature.

I have come away from this retreat feeling empowered, not only on a personal level, but also on a community level. I say this because never in my life have I felt such a strong sense of community, certainly not in the mainstream Islamic community.

We have all heard the term 'familiarity breeds contempt', but in this instance the opposite was true. I realized soon after the retreat that the 'feeling of submission' that was missing for me was a consequence of the strong sense of affinity that I feel not only for Islam the religion, but also for the rich Islamic culture. Islam is indeed more than a religion, it is a way of life.

As a community, we have taken it upon ourselves to partake in the development of an actual International Organization for LGBT Muslims. Preliminarily, the name will be 'Al-Fatiha' (The Opening), titled after the first chapter of the Quran. Due to the diversity of our group and our ideas, it was decided that our goals and objectives would be multi-faceted. We will address issues ranging from human rights abuses in Islamic countries towards LGBT Muslims, to setting up support groups and other community resources in North America and abroad. The work that lies ahead is tremendous, but this retreat proved to all of us that it is long overdue.

I liken my journey to Boston with the words of Rabindranath Tagore, who once wrote that, "The traveler has to knock at every alien door to come to his own, one has to wander through all the outer worlds to reach the innermost shrine at the end."

P.S. Look for me next year on Pride Day on the LGBT Muslims' float.

BIOGRAPHY Mohammed Khan

Mohammed Khan is an HIV/AIDS Educator living in Toronto. He helped start and is currently on the Board of Directors of Al-Fatiha Toronto. He is busy un-learning the homophobic values of Islam and trying to integrate a more progressive Islam into his day-to-day life. Similar versions of this article have appeared in **Xtra!** magazine and **Trikone** magazine.

KISSED BY GOD
Brian P. Frank

Once upon a time I was scared, and didn't know who I was. Queerboy, faggot, less than a man. Endlessly, hopelessly trying to father myself. Both longing for and hating the objects of my deepest manly desire. And lost.

But then God kissed me. Not the Christian god, god of love-thy-neighbor-turn-the-other cheek; but the God of the Forest, the Antlered One, Lord of the Dance. He came to me late one night, and he wore the face and body of the hunky male physique model whose pictures I've plastered across my bedroom wall.

The sun shone bright and warm on the wide grassy field and the old mountain cabin. Alone on the front porch, he sat in a worn rocking chair; buck naked, not even a pair of boots. He beckoned to me, and I went to him.

Smiling gently, he opened his strong arms and, with infinite care, wrapped my body in his. I could feel the warmth of him suffusing through me, could feel the rough hairs of his chest against my cheek. I could hear the deep beating of his heart, measured and reassuring. And at last, at long, lonely last, I was wanted. Wanted and desired by the God that lies within every man. Then he turned my face up to his, and kissed me gently on the lips while his strong fingers caressed my brow. And he told me that everything would be all right; that there was nothing wrong with me, that I was special. That I was blessed. Then he kissed me on the lips again. Firmly. With much tongue. And I fell asleep, safe in his arms.

Don't even say it. I know what you're thinking. I'm trying to turn a wet dream into a revelation. I've fallen so far under the spell of the commercialization of gay male sexuality, endless streams of go-go boys and skin mags and porno flicks, that now even my spirituality is being exploited. God doesn't have his own full-color, twelve month Man of the Year calendar. I realize all that, but it doesn't really matter. Because I know what I know.

God kissed me.

BIOGRAPHY Brian P. Frank

Brian P. Frank is a practicing Taoist and a Neo-Pagan. He lives in upstate New York with his partner Stephen.

POSITIVE FAITH: Christians WITH HIV
Matthew Link

> Call unto me and I will show you great and unsearchable things you do not know.
> JEREMIAH, 33:3

The funeral was refreshingly uncommon. There was not one, but three separate hula dances throughout the service, lovingly performed by brightly dressed men and women with smiles planted on their faces. The altar of the Victorian Church was adorned with tropical flowers. The pastors donned white robes with multicolored rainbow collars. Even though the gray fog rolled along its familiar course across the hills of San Francisco outside, a cheerful good-bye was being administered in true Hawaiian style.

This pleasant service was for Crayne, a Chinese-American man born in Hawaii. He had been HIV positive for at least fifteen years, but the disease finally caught up with him. I had the opportunity to get to know Crayne while researching my video documentary on HIV-positive Christians. His lover was Paul, one of the men donning the robes of the Metropolitan Community Church clergy. In happier times, Paul and Crayne had run a drop-in support center for HIV-positive people.

I watched Paul, sitting quietly in the pews during the service. His face showed the signs of his great loss. But at the same time, there was present a soft calm and understanding, as he watched the hula dancers tell their story.

I remember Paul's words just a few days earlier: "Sometimes I want to run and hide—I don't want to stick around. Death is ugly."

Even at that, he added, "Faith is the only thing that keeps me going."

Like many other Christians with HIV, they were also gay. Crayne's mother, a Charismatic fundamentalist, had been arguing with Crayne all the way up to his death about his need to repent of his homosexual sins—pleas often heard by many gay Christians. Of course Crayne loved his mother, but he also loved his life-mate Paul.

After years of similar problems with his own family, Paul summed it up this way: "So many people have tried to invalidate my beliefs, castrate me spiritually so to speak. But I am a follower of Jesus of Nazareth, and nobody can take that away from me."

In this age of convenient sub-groups and labels, HIV-positive people and people with AIDS have many of their own distinct categories. Not only are there the obvious ones like 'woman with AIDS' or 'HIV-positive African-American', but also groups on how you may have contracted the virus—such as hemophiliacs, IV drug users, bisexual men. But labels like these merely indicate what the person's actions or physicality might be. They don't give much indication of the more complicated arenas of what a person with HIV might think, or feel, or believe.

The label HIV-positive Christians indicates a spiritual category of people facing their own imminent death. To be sure, HIV-positive people are living longer—with more sophisticated medicine and tools which may offset the illness indefinitely, but many HIV-positive people must still pass through that core of time in which they visualize their own death in vivid terms, and face the possibilities of an afterlife. What could be more quintessentially spiritual than the age-old question of, "Is this the only life there is?" Yet HIV-positive people deal with these impossible questions everyday, often without much spiritual help or guidance.

As the media and politics and society draw the line between gays and fundamentalists as sharp and clear, many are left in the in-between category of Gay Christians, sub-categorized further as those with HIV.

Christians, of course, come in many shapes and sizes. Although it's easy to think of most as fundamentalist, there are actually more middle-of-the-road to liberal denominations than one might imagine. In fact, many Episcopal, Unitarian, Methodist, and Quaker Churches accept openly gay members. Some churches, such as Presbyterians, even ordain gay and lesbian clergy. There are also many Catholic organizations and charities set up specifically to help people with AIDS. (That's not to say that all "progressive" churches are pro-gay.)

Dan, a young man in his twenties who I interviewed for my documentary, ran a support group for HIV-positive members, straight and gay, at his Charismatic Church. He told me his belief was that "Christians are called to embrace hurting people, no matter how they are hurting."

Dan found out he had HIV during his enlistment in the Navy, as part of a ship-wide blood screening. After being discharged, he broke up with his lover, and with the help of his parents, renounced his homosexuality. He is now celibate, but hopes to one day marry.

"I realized that my sin of homosexuality was separating me from God," he explained. "I don't at all believe my HIV is a judgment from God, though. It was through my own actions."

Many gays that are drawn to Christianity may find similar pressures to "repent and change" their sexual behavior before their church accepts them. As many find this impossible, they turn away from religion in general, sometimes at a great loss to their own identity and spiritual life. With a diagnosis of HIV, the need for spiritual support is even more intense and vital.

A case in point occurred one Sunday some years back, when a pastor stood up in front of his Catholic congregation, and simply disclosed that he was HIV positive. Instead of gasps of shock from the primarily straight and elderly members, they rose to their feet and told the priest that they loved him and supported him no matter what.

That priest, Father John McGrann, now runs *Kairos*, an organization that helps support caregivers of people with AIDS cope with their stress and fears, and offers practical as well as spiritual support. Although he is gay, his fellow Christians do not bat an eye as they work beside him. Following Jesus' example, they help their fellow human without stopping to ask questions first. When asked where Jesus would be if he alive today, many of these Christians reply, "the AIDS wards."

Of course, not all Christians with HIV are gay, either. I talked to one young woman, Tara, who contracted HIV through her first sexual encounter at age thirteen. She's now twenty-three, and has already been through many disabling illnesses, in addition to coping with the suicide of her alcoholic father.

I asked her how she dealt with it all. With a beaming face, she replied, "I realized the forgiving and loving nature of God. No matter what we've done, or what we've been through, God still loves us and wants us to rely on Him."

During her last bout of illness in the hospital, Tara was unable to speak or walk, and the doctors thought she was in the final stages of dying. "I just kept repeating to myself in my head, 'The blood of Jesus runs through my veins and heals me.'" A few weeks later, she was up and living back at home.

She adds, "I saw that loving God didn't have so much to do with going to a church or belonging to a specific denomination, as it had to do with having a personal, day to day relationship with Him...You can't follow other people's interpretations blindly—you have to find out for yourself."

As a young woman close to death, Tara seemed amazingly optimistic. "Sure I'd like to go back and change things that happened. Sometimes I do feel cheated—I won't be able to have children, I live day to day. But I really do leave it all in God's hands...HIV has taught me so much about life. That life is learning about life."

In a way, death brings out all that is important in living. Dying is the last great phase through which we must all someday pass. What I found in the Christians with HIV that I met and grew to know was a profound vigor in the face of death. Not a proud nor overt strength, but a quiet and humble feeling, a kind of peace, like they were ready to continue their journey onward to other places. In spirit, it was similar to Christ at Calvary—accepting his own death, his own suffering, and proving it was not all in vain.

If Christians could give some kind of gift to terminal people, it would be this sense of continuity, a hearty anticipation towards death instead of the common ideas of death as a failure, or as shameful—or as the ultimate end. It would be a feeling that the universe is a bigger and more beautiful place than previously imagined.

I remember Crayne telling me one sunny afternoon, in his lilting Hawaiian voice, "When I'm afraid, when I'm so afraid, I feel Jesus' spirit embracing me...and telling me it is all going to be okay. Telling me this life is just a pit-stop. That this is not finality."

DECIPHERING THE "EX-GAY" MOVEMENT
Matthew Link

Ex-gay. The word itself sounds like a punchline to a bad joke. Ex-wife? Ex-boyfriend? No, *ex-gay*. According to a religious minority, a lot of gays would choose to come out of the 'lifestyle' if they were so moved. As preposterous and implausible as it may sound, the ex-gay movement is a reality for many homosexuals. And the awful irony is that the movement, for some gay men, may actually do some good.

You may have tripped across ads in the back of newspapers that asked if you were "Tired of the gay lifestyle?" or if you were "Ready for an alternative to the gay life?" Imagine if you were a married man, a closeted daughter, or a homophobic high school student—the ad could prove very attractive. An end to all the "torturous" feelings spinning in your gut. And for many members of an ex-gay group, joining may be their first step in publicly admitting their same-sex tendencies.

Ex-gay gatherings usually include intense worship, prayer, and fellowship with others going through similar 'cycles'. Members meet on a frequent basis to discuss their issues and attempt to change behavior patterns. A twelve-step program for Homosexuality Addiction, if you will. In some states, the main American organizations, Exodus, Living Waters and Love in Action, have even set up houses where male members reside and commune.

You would expect this new anti-gay movement to arise from an old, reactionary church out of the dark ages, yet, ironically, it comes from a modern, vibrant, and, it must be said, liberal vein of Pentecostalism : the Charismatic Movement.

If a gay person stepped into a typical charismatic church on any given Sunday, they would probably have a good time. The dress code is normally jeans and a T-shirt. Drums, electric guitar, and back-up singers accompany the hymns, which sound like soft-rock ballads about God. Sometimes there's outright dancing. The pastor's sermon is personable and moving, and women are especially encouraged to come up and share speaking time. There's lots of healing, and the emphasis is on the positive power of the Holy Spirit in people's lives. It's a church that hits people's hearts.

These 90's Pentecostal denominations often include support groups for recovering alcoholics, incest survivors, and men's retreats. In many ways they are what older, stilted churches should strive to be. And part of their daring tone is dealing head-on with one issue many churches have avoided even saying out loud : Homosexuality. And thus, the noble movement to help gays come out of the 'lifestyle'.

The bottom line to all this is, of course, does it really work? Do members actually turn from gay to straight? Roberto, who was born in Mexico and lived in an ex-gay house for over a year, says, "I didn't ever really see any hard proof...there was only one guy out of the whole house that actually went on to marry and have kids. Personally, I thought he was bi to begin with."

Roberto also adds, "It was known that certain leaders had slept with each other. It was weird too, because with all this talk about not being gay, there were never any straight women around. We always did activities with each other...Regardless of the fact that I voluntarily left without turning straight, I had an incredibly spiritual year...It was one of the most fulfilling times of my life."

Dwayne, who calls himself "an ex-ex-gay" (!), puts it this way, " It was like a whole bunch of gay guys being very close and intimate with each other, but trying not to actually be sexual with each other. There were guys in the group who were known to have fallen a lot, since confession was normal...there was a lot of sex shame that way. It was wonderful to feel that close to the spirit of God at the same time...and in the end, I didn't feel like my love for other men really interfered with that."

In fact, Dwayne says, "Those guys in my group were some of the best male friends I have ever had...I have rarely been in a situation of such honesty and spiritual fellowship with gay guys before, with no jealousy or sexual competition or bitchiness...it changed my heart a lot."

So why the push to turn good Christians to heterosexuality in the first place? Don't gay people have the same spiritual needs as the rest of humanity, perhaps even more so? Is it really necessary to change who you love before you can love God?

Moreover, aren't there many who tire of the 'glam' gay world of shallow bars and impersonal sex and long to relate with each other in a more spiritual and loving way? Gays have traditionally fled away from Christianity in general for its ostensible stance against their very existence. Many gays have been emotionally and spiritually abused by Christian churches. But is fleeing from Christianity perhaps a loss to our spiritual life as well? Maybe it's time to reclaim our right to be Christians as it was to reclaim being 'queer' in the first place.

Should we look at things through the eyes of humans or through the eyes of God? Even though some Christians' doors are cautiously opening to begin to accept gays and lesbians back into the fold, many churches have a long way to go in getting past their cultural preconceptions and seeing things clearly through the heart of Christ. Regardless of the few anti-gay Biblical verses (which many scholars say are misinterpreted and extremely over-emphasized), let's face it—Christ himself seemed to be quite the social revolutionary of his time. Who did he choose to hang out with during his short lifetime? Only the literal outcasts of the Earth—the feared lepers, the despised prostitutes, the dirtiest of the poor, the hated race of Samaritans.

As always, Christ was forcing humans to look at each other in a completely different way. "Why do you look at the speck of sawdust in your brother's eye, and pay no attention to the plank in your own eye?" He said in Matthew 7:3.

And what did Jesus have to say about the monumental sin of homosexuality? The Gospels record he said absolutely nothing.

BIOGRAPHY Matthew Link

I am a writer and videomaker living in Hawaii. I have written freelance for a number of gay publications over the years on topics ranging from queer spirituality to drug abuse in the gay world to gay cyber-life and more. I have also published travel articles on Nepal, Hong Kong and Hawaii for gay travel guides.

My award-winning interview documentaries on titles ranging from **Positive Faith: Christians with HIV** to **The Male Escorts of San Francisco** have aired on public broadcasting stations and in numerous international gay film festivals. I have resided in Hong Kong, the Philippines, New Zealand, Papua, New Guinea, Palau and Britain, as well as having travelled extensively. I have studied comparative religions in college and continue to explore the many facets of global gay religion and spirituality.

(RE)CLAIMING SODOM
Connell O'Donovan

I have been deeply envious of lesbians because of an important factor in their cultural existence: they have the Island of Lesbos—physical space which they can dream of and re-create and hope toward. I used to think that we Queer Boys had no such physical space to claim as our own. But then I realized that the biblical Sodom could become important space to (re)claim for our own designs.

There are three main mythologies concerning the twin cities of Sodom and Gomorrah: the original, etiological myth found in the Hebrew Scriptures (Genesis 19), other biblical/Judeo-Christian interpretations of that myth, and this newer, queer mythology.

The myth in the Book of Genesis describes how two holy men (commonly regarded as angels) came from the Hebrew god to see how the cities on the plain were faring, for the earth was crying out from the burden of the sins of the Sodomites. During their investigation of the small hamlet of Sodom, they were surrounded by a group of women and men who apparently wanted to gang rape these two beings. (Here, I must ask, what does male and female gang rape of two angels—even though called men, the Hebrew leaves their gender unspecified—have to do with modern acts of con/sensual Sapphistry and Faggotry?) For those of the right wing extremes of Judaism and Christianity, Sodom was a throbbing, thriving city (not a tiny hamlet) full of depraved, decadent, homosexual perverts. In their view, this god of theirs destroyed all those queers. (In my view, their god is a petty god because he guarantees free will and then punishes those who exercise it.) This god flattened the city in a devastating attack of fire from heaven, and leaving nothing but a salt-riddled, sulphurous wasteland next to the Dead Sea. And if he did it back then, he'll do it again! And that's where we get AIDS from (Anal Intercourse Destroys Sodomites is a graffito I read in the late 80s).

But I want to (re)claim Sodom for our very own, so I speak this new myth. I want that tiny hamlet of Sodom to be Queer Safe Space. And really, it's ours whether we want it or not. Enough of our blood has been spilled in its name to warrant ownership of that land several million times over. And all because that petty god hates us Bulldykes and Faeries—would rather kill us than look at us. So what's new? After all, he was made in the image of the white, bourgeois, heterosexual, able-bodied male, wasn't he?

Is it a coincidence that Sodom and holocaust both mean burnt in Hebrew and Greek respectively? Burnt, burns, will burn: us little Faggots, faggots for the fire of that god—our burning flesh is but sweet incense to his nostrils. He thrives on burning us queer boys up and that burns me up! Incenses me! All because we don't fit into his god/awful plan; because maybe we would rather dress and keep the garden (as artists, interior decorators, drag queens, poets, dancers, pagan Faeries with our faggot/wands and hard cocks burning bright, lighting up the darkness of the hetero-world, casting shadows and spells, illuminating the mirrors of heteros for them to see their own horrors) rather than "multiply and replenish the earth," as if we're all just a gaggle of ambulatory inseminators.

I love being in Sodom now. I feel very comfortable here. Of course that god destroyed it. That's what power-mongering, insecure, and fragile hetero-males like him do. They always give us wastelands and we always turn them into music and gardens. Out of the ashes of our dead brothers and sisters, let us sow a beautiful garden, till it with our passion, water it with our tears, and fertilize it with our cum and our desire. In that space, where a desert blossoms as the rose, we can stand our ground. From that space we can speak our bodies without fear.

Connell O'Donovan's biography appears on page 71.

DECONSTRUCTING LEVITICUS
Finding a Queer Spiritual Path Back from the Exile of Sacred Text
Avi Rose

And if a man lie with mankind as with womankind, both of them have committed an abomination: they shall surely be put to death; their blood shall be upon them.
LEVITICUS XX, 13

I was born into a rabbinical family for whom Judaism meant everything. For as long as I can remember, I was a Jew first and everything else second. The rhythm of Jewish life permeated my consciousness and directed most of my activities. Food, clothing, study, music and art, were all infused with Jewish content, story and meaning. No matter what I did, I saw the world essentially through Jewish eyes.

When I began to find myself attracted to men, at around age ten, I was confused. I understood our tradition well enough to know that these feelings were antithetical to my existence as a Jew and as such, were unacceptable. I ran from them, hiding my burgeoning sexuality deep within my soul, working as hard as I could at almost anything else in my life in order to avoid it.

For a long time it worked. I became an actor and a puppeteer, trying out fantasies and living out lives on the safe and sacred ground of the stage. I painted large colourful compositions, rife with adolescent pain and rage, hiding my passion beneath the brush strokes. Later, I took on the role of leader within our Jewish community, teaching and guiding, rather than living and feeling the things I could not allow myself to confront.

Almost twenty years went by before I began to come to terms with my sexuality. Twenty years of longing looks, private thoughts and personal pain. While I dated women, wanting more than anything else to have the kind of Jewish family and community that my parents and my younger siblings later had, love and passion never developed. No matter how much I tried to be the person I wanted to be, the person who I was burst forth and interfered.

At the age of thirty, the walls within me crumbled. While trying once more to make a relationship with a woman work, I was struck, one day, by a powerful, almost overwhelming daydream, an image in my mind. There I was with the family of my dreams, only this time the partner was a man. This flash of vision infiltrated my being to the very core, leaving me with less and less room for denial and distance. Finally, as I agonized over how to reveal the truth, a friend bluntly asked me if I was gay. The word "yes" came pouring out of my mouth, unleashing a torrent of emotion and insight from the deepest depths of my soul. That moment of coming out, stands as one of the most liberating, frightening, thrilling and meaningful events of my life thus far.

Since then, I have been on a journey of reclamation and reconciliation. Coming out to myself, to my friends and finally to my family, took a great deal of energy, along with repeated acts of courage. Thankfully, I was blessed with a community of supportive, understanding and loving individuals, who helped me work through some of the more complex facets of coming to terms with the loss and joy of being out. I am one of the lucky ones. I did not lose a friend or member of my family to the hatred and fear that clouds so many of the relationships in the lives of queer folk.

This is not to say that there hasn't been pain or anguish present in many of these relationships as a result of being out. At the heart of these conflicts was, often, the perception that to be queer was to be incompatible with the goals and values of the Jewish people. When I went public with my queerness and was photographed in the local Jewish newspaper marching in Pride Day, for example, members of my former work community (in a somewhat traditional and conservative branch of Judaism), seemed to feel that I had given up the Jewish piece of myself in favour of my queer identity. "I hear you're part of something else now", said one parent, whose child I had led in our youth group.

Truth was, that though I had no intention of making the choice, I kept hearing over and over that there was one to make. For, despite all of the incredible work that has been done by both queer and straight Jews to reconcile the inherent conflicts, there are still real barriers for gay and lesbian Jews to overcome. Queer Jews are still not accepted in a whole and complete manner by any of the major Jewish movements (with the exception of the tiny Reconstructionist branch [1]), even by those that are supposedly liberal and progressive. The Reform movement, for example—the first and so far only one of the large branches to accept gay and lesbian clergy and congregations—still cannot reach consensus among its rabbis to perform commitment rituals for same-gender couples.

The more out I was and the more closeness I felt with members of my family and community as they accepted my whole self, the less I felt comfortable with the dogma of Judaism and its stubborn refusal to allow me in. All of a sudden, I went from being the consummate insider, to the ultimate outsider, the 'other' of the Jewish world, condemned and isolated for the sin of being myself.

Over and over again, as I explored the roots of this homo-hatred, I kept coming back to the biblical text in the book of Leviticus. In these few sentences, there seemed to be great power and authority, which, to my horror, appeared to overshadow the rightness and reality of my own feelings. Surprisingly, this left me with a deep sense of hostility and resentment rather than shame or sadness. Whereas once, I questioned the validity of my sexuality because it seemed at odds with this text, I now became angry with the text for denying me the right to be the human being and Jew that I was.

As the years of my being out have progressed, I have found myself at various times more and more enraged with the text of Leviticus and by extension, with the entirety of the bible itself. My anger spread like an infection, colouring my whole understanding of my once beloved Torah. The patient I believed, could not be saved, the putrid limb prevented it from recovering.

The conflict reached a crescendo for me on the eve of Shavuot, sitting with friends and participating in a ritual that is thousands of years old. Together, we celebrated the festival of receiving the Torah with an all-night study vigil. Many speakers contributed their wisdom and insight and much discussion was held. Words flew around the room, empowered with intellect, emotion and spirit. Through it all though—even as the discussion turned to the problems inherent in the Torah—I felt distanced and removed. I could not, as some had suggested, love the Torah and accept it as my central document of humanity, while it stubbornly refused me the same courtesy.

Frightened by the place that I had so suddenly come to in my life of faith, I began to try and find a path back into the Torah. I knew it to be a document of real power and humanity—it changed forever the way in which people worshiped, looked upon the creator and saw themselves as members of the human race. I understood that though thousands of years old, its central messages still bring hope and meaning to millions, offering light and insight into the human condition. I also knew that without it, I could not continue to enjoy my sense of belonging and spiritual connection with my tradition. Though I was angry with the Jewish community for its rejection of its lesbian and gay family members, I was still a Jew and wanted very much to retain my deep connection. I knew no other way to be and had no intention of seeking alternate forms of spiritual practice and expression.

Thus, I began to tackle the heart of the textual conflict by asking questions and seeking out its roots and nucleus. While this is a process that will presumably take a lifetime, I have already begun to find a way around the roadblocks created by the Leviticus text and back to a place of comfort and growth. In order to achieve this, I have had to deconstruct the text, examining its origins, context and meaning. So far, I am pleased with what I have found.

What I have learned is that this text—so often used by both Jews and Christians—is most often misused by people who are unfamiliar with its foundation, subtlety or structure. Being that it is a biblical text, it comes with much baggage and meaning which must be slowly teased out and theoretically dissected, in order to grasp its true intentions. It must be understood as a document which emerged out of very particular political and sociological conditions, which was intended for a society in a specific context and time frame, and which had as its goal a very limited social order. What follows is a brief summary of how I have come to see the text in this new light—highlights from a journey of understanding on the path back into my biblical roots.

The Text
There are only two explicit references to male (and none to female) homosexuality in the bible, both of them in the book of Leviticus. In the first, chapter 18 (verse 22), the prohibition against a man "lying" (biblical lexicon for sexual activity) with mankind as he would with womankind, is regarded as a "Toevah", an abomination. The second reference—two chapters later (verse 13)—repeats the interdiction, adding to it that those who engage in this kind of behavior should "surely be put to death".

The book of Leviticus offers a lengthy listing of laws and practices which the People of Israel assumed as partners in a new covenant with God. Distinguishing themselves from the pagan cultures which surrounded them, Jews took upon themselves the worship of one God who was neither seen, nor represented in image or form. The tribe ended practices of hunting, ritual sacrifice of humans and temple sexuality, common to other religions of the time.

Instead, the Israelite community accepted upon itself a strict code which separated their world into sharp contrasts. Animal meat was either "kosher", or unacceptable for consumption. The Sabbath was a day of complete cessation from acts of work and creation. Humans were either pure if they worshiped one God or impudent if they worshiped many. Sexual acts were either heterosexual, monogamous[2] (at least within the confines of marriage) and not at all related to ritual worship ceremonies, or deemed offensive. Life was, in short, either defined as sacred or profane—few shades of grey were offered in this black and white reality.

Those who followed this tradition, apparently saw it as a starting point, choosing, almost immediately, to soften the harshness of Torah law. In the absence of great detail, scholars and leaders began a lengthy process of teasing out the subtleties which were understood to implicitly lie within the text. This led to the development of rabbinical discussion and interpretation, codified in the volumes of the Mishnah and Talmud. To this day, there is debate and growth within the Jewish legal community—the process of adding shade and hue continues. Christianity, which sees itself as the next step in monotheistic culture, abandoned these strict laws altogether, seeking instead a new spiritual understanding of God and the acts of human kindness, which seem to emerge from biblical tradition.

It is interesting, therefore, that long after they have both evolved away from the strictness of biblical precept, some Christians and Jews run back to the narrowness of the text when it seems convenient. Christians, who ignore biblical precepts related to dietary and Sabbath observance, still consider the Leviticus text as legitimate and real. Jews, who allowed their legal thinking to soften on many issues raised in the bible, adhere to its anti-gay sentiment with great ferocity. Even Jews who would themselves be liable for death penalties under biblical law for violations of the Sabbath, insubordination against parents and even adultery, freely use the Leviticus text to cut out queer Jews from their midst.

So, how am I, as a queer, committed Jew, able to live with this text? I cannot simply dismiss it as a piece of homophobic rhetoric, it does, after all, sit within the very heart of my spiritual and religious tradition. Neither am I content to live in its shadow, accepting its rightness and my wrongness, perpetuating the rift between my Jewish and queer selves.

What I choose to do, is to follow the example set by previous generations of Jews and deconstruct the text and its context. Rather than a work in stone, I see the bible as a mirror, a reflection of human thought and belief which emerged under very specific sociological, historical and political circumstances. This does not mean that I deny the divine inspiration of the text, for I do believe that on some level the bible contains in it the seeds of both Godliness and ultimate humanity. What I do hold to be true, though, is that humans (mostly male patriarchs) interpreted and compiled the teachings of Torah into a document which served both universal and specific (political) purposes. Thus, I believe that the fire of the Torah is both black and white, fore and background, seen and unseen. What is required is intensive spiritual detective work in order to clearly understand where the framers of the Torah text were coming from, and where they hoped that humanity was moving towards under their leadership.

The Biological Argument
Looking back at the needs of the newly liberated tribe of Israel, it is easy to see why exclusive man to man sexual contact might have been threatening. After all, the greatest weapon at the disposal of the patriarchal tribes was their sheer force of number. In fact, the whole story of Exodus starts with Pharaoh's assumption that the Jews had become too numerous and therefore threatened the safety of the Egyptian nation.

As such, the most common understanding of the Leviticus text is purely biological—for men to ignore their responsibility as progenitors would be disastrous. The fact that men spent a great deal of time segregated from women, along with a tradition of homosexuality in the surrounding cultures, is cited as proof of this view of the text. By extension, this argument is used even in modern times. In a post-Holocaust reality, it is argued, when the depleted ranks of the Jewish community face biological obliteration, could there be any other understanding of the law?

The answer is both a strong yes and no. While such a rationale has merit, it does not go far enough to fully explain the prohibition. This is because it is simply impossible that a man would have even considered an exclusively homosexual life, even if that was his primary orientation. Given the societal imperative for procreation, a man's reproductive role was likely never questioned. Multiple sexual partnering for men was, therefore, not only acceptable, but regarded as a symbol of wealth and prestige.

Homosexuality, if it were to occur, could only have existed as an accompaniment to marriage. If they were inclined to engage sexually with another man, it could occur only in such a way that would not threaten the biological survival of the tribe. As such, it must be concluded that though a partial rationale, the purely biological explanation falls short of clearing up the core nature of the Leviticus text. Obviously, there are other factors at work.

Keeping the Civil Order
If biology was not the main reason for the prohibition, it seems logical to look at the socio-cultural factors which might be useful in understanding the Leviticus text. Something about certain aspects of homosexuality seemed threatening to the social order of the community.

Two explanations for this can be found by examining the linguistic structure of the text. Torah text is usually very economical and specific, such that scholars look for clues in the words chosen, the context in which they are placed and the patterns which are common with other occurrences in the text.

Rabbi Dr. Michael Sammuel, an orthodox scholar, offers an understanding of the Leviticus text in his internet discussion of the subject[3]. He claims that the use of the Hebrew word for male, "Zachar", is used elsewhere in the text with great precision. In fact, he argues that it specifically refers to male children and not mankind in general. As such, it is possible that what the Torah is really stating is that an adult cannot have sexual contact with the younger male members of his clan. This would make sense, given the placement of the statement. The law pertaining to male/male sex is part of a string of prohibitions outlawing incest and sexual activity with members of extended family and community.

A related understanding of the text's civil order intentions is offered by Reb Zalman Schachter-Shalomi[4]. Reb Zalman is of the opinion that the text warns men not to substitute other men as sexual partners, when in fact, it is a woman that is desired. His proof for this is the fact that the text goes to the trouble of stating that what is prohibited is sexual contact like that with a woman. If the Torah had wanted to ban all sexual contact between men, it might have sufficed with a statement such as 'do not lie with a man'. Since it does, however, take the time to be specific and since it is well known that men spent a great deal of time together in isolation, it is possible to conclude that the Torah warned men not to forcefully use each other as substitutes for what they really needed. Issues of bisexuality aside, this argument makes a great deal of sense. Telling men that they could not have sexual contact with other males under certain circumstances—rather than not at all—would fit in well with the vision of civil order implied in the text.

Separating Judaism from Other Religious Practices
Judaism was a revolution in its time. The prevailing custom dictated belief in multiple gods, the sacrifice of humans and the use of sexuality as a form of worship. All of this was rejected by the Torah, which called for a radical shift in religious paradigms.

Several commentators, including Rebbaca Alpert in the classic work on queerness and Judaism entitled **Twice Blessed**[5], note that it was common for men in cultures surrounding the Israelites to engage in ritual sex with temple prostitutes of both genders. In fact, vestiges of these pansexual human rituals still exist in parts of the world.

These authors point once again to the language of the Torah in order to buttress their contention that what is prohibited in the Leviticus text is not a personal relationship between men, but rather a religious one. Noting that the word used to connote the negative image of homosexuality is "Toevah", the commentators state that this word is otherwise reserved for acts of ritual practice deemed outside the acceptable norms of Jewish convention.

Strength for this argument comes from re-examining the placement of the prohibitive law in the general text. The anti-homosex statute comes right after other forms of inter-family and community sex, and right before a statement which forbids sex acts with members of the Molechite tribe. The Molechite tribe was known to use sexual rituals as part of its idolatrous worship ceremonies. As such, it can easily be stated that what the text intended was for Jews to refrain from sexual activity known to be primarily for ritual purposes. Loving sex between two men did not likely enter the equation—either because it was not considered enough of a phenomenon to warrant mention, or because it was accepted as part of human nature. The fact that sex between women (which was not a common ritual practice) is not mentioned in a document which otherwise severely limits the sexual practices of females, adds validity to this view. If the Torah really wanted to ban homosex rather than ritual sex, it would have clearly told both genders to refrain from doing so.

The Feminist Understanding
For me, the strongest and most visceral reading of the Leviticus text comes from a feminist interpretation of the law. Rabbi Elyse Goldstein, in her upcoming book of Torah commentary[6], claims that male/male sexuality was threatening to the patriarchal framers of the bible, since it was, in many ways, a direct rejection of the patriarchy and the sharp distinctions between male and female necessary for its survival.

Rabbi Goldstien's argument is that, once a man allows himself to play the passive role in a sexual contact, he violates the very essence of patriarchal thinking. To be receptive as a sexual partner is to be female—to be lesser than and subordinate to the dominance of others. The fact that a man might choose such a role, part or all of the time, threatens the order of a society which believes that divisions of power necessarily fall along gender lines.

As such, the Torah might well have seen homosex as an act of subversion, something which it could not accept. It challenged the idea that at a basic genetic level, all men were aggressive and all women passive. It opened the door to women demanding more rights and primacy within the community. This, it feared, might loosen the bonds of tribal power which otherwise flowed in an orderly fashion from one generation of males to another, using women as conduits rather than participants in the process.

In the eyes of the patriarchs who framed the Torah, homosexuality's dirty little secret was that variation in roles fell along a continuum of humanity and not gender. Sexuality, as the great symbol of power, created the illusion that men would always be on top and women forever on the bottom. Men having sex with other men, sharing their power rather than lording it over women, threatened to pull down the whole house of cards which was the patriarchal system. In order to prevent this from happening, it was deemed necessary to place homosex in the cesspool of human sexual urges—with ritual blasphemy and incest—lest it be let out of its cage and reveal its deep, dark truth.

I can see the validity of this argument in the ways and means in which we are still grappling with the residue of patriarchy in modern society. Women are still being forced into passive, second class status—raped, beaten, threatened, starved and impoverished into submission. Men who dare to desire each other, or to act in effeminate ways, face ridicule, censure, isolation and similar consequences to those of women.

Even within the community of gay men, there are attempts to modify the patriarchy and unwittingly preserve its hold on society. The devaluing of effeminacy, the glorification of the macho, the myth of men's natural promiscuity and inability to maintain 'feminine' style monogamy and the strict separation of men into ranks of 'top' or 'bottom' are but a few examples.

So What Now?
The Leviticus verses, seen in the light of these explanations, lose much of their authoritarian power and absolutism. Behind the smoke and mirrors of their magic, they seem suddenly less monstrous, even puny. Yet, for all that we see it as mere bark, we have allowed it to have great bite. We are still, as both Jews and Christians, controlled and dominated by the text. For many, even the most rational and reasonable explanation of the verses is mere apologetics, a means by which to cloud the truth that God hates homos.

So, it seems to me that all the scholarship in the world is useless, unless and until we are willing to both give and receive of its wisdom. Without a chorus of voices from within the queer community and from our straight brothers and sisters, the message is lost in the apparent negative clarity of Leviticus. We cannot expect the rational mind to take in information which the emotional and experiential self deems as inauthentic. We need to believe and act upon the truth of these more enlightened views of the Torah, if we are to make it possible for a wider audience of religious followers to listen and treat queer members of society with respect and acceptance.

As such, I remain committed to my tradition and to my people, even when they try to criticize and isolate me. Simple or not, I choose to sew together my queer and Jewish identities, even if the pieces do not seem to fit, or even match in fundamental ways. I will do my best to create an environment of healing and reconciliation between the Jewish community and the community of queer Jews. Painful as it often is, I see myself and others like me committed to restoring our Torah to its true nature and Godly intention. It is my prayer that we can clean the lens of our collective eye and allow the Torah's light to bring humans closer together. As a Jew, I see it as my responsibility to repair the world and engage in an attempt to make of humanity the clearest reflection of the Divine that we can possibly be.

Endnotes
1. The Reconstructionist movement ordains openly gay and lesbian Jews and performs commitment ceremonies. Though gaining in popularity, the movement is still relatively small with fewer than 100 congregations worldwide.
2. Monogamy in Torah law is a relative term. Women are forbidden to have sexual relations with more than one man. Men were permitted to take multiple partners, so long as they either married or kept them as concubines. European Jews outlawed polygamy in the tenth century, though Jews in other regions continued to practice well into the twentieth century.
3. This comment is part of a wider discussion on re-thinking Orthodoxy's view on homosexuality offered by Rabbi Dr. Samuel. It was first posted on AOL in January of 1999 and re-posted in "Gay Jews", a queer/Jewish discussion group.
4. Reb Zalman shared this teaching with me in the summer of 1996.
5. **Twice Blessed: on Being Lesbian, Gay and Jewish**, edited by Christie Balka and Andy Rose is published by Beacon Press of Boston, 1989. Rebecca Alpert authored a further work in 1996 on Lesbian/Jewish issues called **Like Bread on a Seder Plate**, published by Columbia University Press of New York.
6. Rabbi Goldstein's book of Torah Commentary is due to be published in 2000. Her 1998 book **ReVisions: Seeing Torah Through a Feminist Lens**, is published by Key Porter Books of Toronto.

BIOGRAPHY Avi Rose

I am a recent graduate of the OISE/University of Toronto doctoral program in clinical psychology. I am a Jewish educator, teaching most recently at Kolel, a centre for Liberal Jewish Learning. I was, for seven years, the Director of Youth Activities for the United Synagogue of Conservative Judaism, Canadian Region. I am on the Board of Congregation Keshet Shalom, Toronto's lesbigay synagogue. I frequently lecture on issues related to Jewish Queerness.

In response to this anthology and after much thought, I wrote this essay which is both personal and theological in scope. Since much of the pain and conflict I experienced in coming out, seemed to me to stem from biblical law, I decided to journey into some of my encounters with the Leviticus text, a venerable and potent nemesis. The final result is a reflection of the deep and personal balance that I am attempting to create between my queer and Jewish selves.

SANCTUARY

DYKE/WARRIOR-PRAYERS is about being a
Black/urban/dyke/mother/Ancestral hearing/gurl
it's about walking through shattered images of self and learning to Love
this is a Work for Shango (Yoruba Orisha,warrior-fire)
Mother-Jesus/God/Black Madonna
this Work is about choosing to become a Spiritual warrior/to walk with Love

DYKE/WARRIOR-PRAYERS
(an excerpt)
Sharon Bridgforth
i
am
the child
of the daughter of a
just-waxed Moon gurrl who
birthed the African
that jumped ship
and flew back home
to seek him Ancestors
guard his seed destined
to walk through
the door of no return
into
the arms of slavery/i am
the gran-granny's/daughter
of the wo'mn
guided
to the Indigenous Chief that
took her people in to safety/i have
blood memories of
the Red Road
and
the African Way
   i can hear the drum
but
can't
recall
the chant/i
no longer know
the cry of names
that proceeded me/i
am
trying to remember
   Harriet Tubman
   Frederick Douglass
i am trying
   Old Gran Nanny
   Black Elk
to remember

    Tituba
    Marie LaVeau
i am trying
    Martin Luther King
    Malcolm X
to remember
    Huey Newton
    Ceasar Chavez
i am listening
    Langston Hughes
    Audre Lorde
and
praying
    Yemonja
    Tequantla
    Mother of God
    Keeper of the Waters of Life
OH MIGHTY AND DIVINE GUARDIAN SPIRITS
    WHO'VE GONE BEFORE
    WHO PAVED THE WAY
    WHO BLESS US NOW
have mercy
HOLY AND SACRED ONES
protect us and lead the way
i am

WE
sitting in the Sun
waiting
for the Moon
to come back
and carry
Us
Home.

i am
standing
firm-footed
in the blood
of my people.

BIOGRAPHY Sharon Bridgforth

Sharon Bridgforth is the author of the Lambda Literary Award-winning **bull-jean stories** published by RedBone Press and founder/writer/artistic director for the ROOT WY'MN THEATRE COMPANY. Bridgforth's work can be found in various anthologies including: **does your mama know?**, RedBone Press; **KenteCloth**, 1997 ed. North Texas University Press; **MA-KA: Diasporic Juks**, Sister Vision Press; and **Sinister Wisdom 58**. Bridgforth has been nominated for the Osborn Award (sponsored by the American Theatre Critic Association) for her **no mo blues** script.

Statement
I am a little bit Catholic, a little Baptist, a lot Indigenous/Ancestral and Geecheee. I pray that my work and actions be an offering for the will of the Creatress...Ache!

Sharon Bridgforth's poem *Blood Pudding* also appears in this anthology.

CONFESSIONS OF A TANTRIC ANDROGYNE
Ganapati Shivananda Durgadas

> If they see
> breasts and long hair coming
> they call it a woman
>
> If beard and whiskers
> they call it a man:
>
> But look, the Self that hovers
> in between
> is neither man
> nor woman
>
> DEVARA DASIMAYYA, 10th century CE[1].

My father often eyed me with distrust. During one of his frequent rages at my mother, he pointedly told me he doubted I was his biological offspring. I wonder whether his machismo allowed him the empathy to realize the irony in his breaking the news to me in a tone of concern for me. I think my father's concern was genuine, but I was beyond caring by the time of this supposed revelation. As a teenager, I had so successfully learned to numb myself against his almost uninterrupted stream of emotional, verbal and physical abuse that I felt only the dullest and haziest irritation in response.

I suspect what rankled my father was my not being the man he was. Fact was, I had only a vague notion I was a boy, some generic social group or category I was supposed to merge into, but which I was only doing a half-hearted job of accomplishing. From the start I was possessed by the sense that maleness was more like something imposed from outside rather than generated from within. I was aware of having a self, of being someone in a body, but not necessarily a boychild's body governed by an intrinsic male character. There was definitely an interior feeling of girlishness I knew I could not afford anyone else discovering.

Externally there was femme fleshiness because of my fatness, which I tried hiding because of a shame indoctrinated into me by others. I can't say I felt completely female because I didn't know what that was anymore than I knew what being completely male felt like. Yet I was terrified to realize I was past the boundaries, somewhere in between. I was frightened into secrecy.

> Look here, dear fellow.
> I wear these men's clothes
> only for you.
> Sometimes I am man.
> Sometimes I am woman.
> O lord of the Meeting Rivers
> I'll make war for you but
> I'll be your devotees bride.
>
> BASAVANNA, 10th century CE

For my Puertorriqueno father, maleness was definitely a predetermined hereditary repertoire of traits expected to be automatically passed on with his genes. He became repeatedly enraged that I did not meet his expectations, as if I purposely refused to do so. For me it was all a game: a series of roles played to keep my skin intact. I had secrets, like my love of dolls and my desire to trade my ugly green or gray chinos for the flow of skirts. By the early 60s I was able to make a poor compromise with baggy shirts over jeans. This improved with the hippie counterculture's inception: I wore gender-noncommittal clothes and third-world ethnic wear. This signified the physical and emotional space I was putting between my aging father and myself while I escaped his household via the release of drugs and sexual exploration.

With the glitter/glam of the early 70s, the pop-culture aftermath to Stonewall and my father's not-incoincidental death—I finally permitted myself to live fully within the borderland between male and female. From unisexual hippie through would-be Bowie boy. I moved on to semi, and then full drag. I relished all the stops along the way, but still felt not quite fulfilled. Reflecting this was my bisexuality. With innumerable male and female partners, I felt like a shifting presence within each of their embraces. I was a screen onto which they projected specific definitions of maleness and femaleness. What surprised me was their apparent certainty of being a man or a woman. I resented the accompanying demand, either implied or explicit, that I conform completely to their definitions of who I was or should be. Men either wanted me to be their femme, to service and nurture them, or else rejected my obvious androgyny because it suggested a feminine side to gayness which they escaped via hyper-butchness. Ironically, they sometimes carried that extreme into blatant drag in itself. Women, even those I thought ardent feminists, expected me to automatically top them; that is, to be an utterly phallic male in bed, if nowhere else. Almost every one of my lovers, with few notable exceptions, had shockingly rigid inner gender schemas, which they sprang upon me within moments of initiating intimacy.

By now I have become pretty blase about the regularity of this. It's become routine. Yet the expectation that I conform, be a man, still triggers a hesitation in me, while simultaneously dulling any incipient desire. It's back to playing the accustomed charade of childhood and adolescence: passing as the gender others want me to be, distilling whatever enjoyment remains while going through the motions.

Parallel to my sexual exploration has been my spiritual search. Gender outlawry creates an imperative to try to figure yourself out. A hopeless bibliophile, I sought solace in books during periods of often socially imposed isolation: Jungian psychology, gay liberation manifestos on genderfuck, bios of androgynous pop stars and coffee-table photobooks full of shemales. I searched for reflections of the inner that I was defiantly revealing to the outside world. I ransacked stacks of mythology featuring twin-sexed gods like Dionysos and Yemaya-olukun, or discovered anthropological ancestors like the hijra and the berdache.

The Divine Itself was a shemale. God appeared to be most at home in that borderland between male and female. Most human beings had fallen into spiritual exile because of their gender dualism, which they mistook for reality. For this reason, occultism and mysticism developed a seductive hold on me. I began practicing meditation and yoga, and studied Eastern philosophy after a long fling with Neo-Paganism.

Then I discovered Tantrism, a branch of Hindu and Buddhist spiritual practice. Tantra guiltlessly uses sexual symbolism and openly accepts androgyny as much as the West shuns and suppresses it. And it was with Tantric Hinduism that I finally felt that I had come home.

In Hinduism, the feminine is the dynamic creative principle while the masculine is the cognitive or conscious one. Shakti is the Divine Feminine side of God personified as the Maha-Devi, or Great Goddess of Many Names: Ambika, Parvati, Uma; Annapurna in Her pacific aspects; Kali, Durga, Tara in Her militant and even necessarily destructive aspects. She is the Universal Mother and the active power of the universe. Shaktism constitutes a separate yet affiliated sect of Hinduism that overlaps with Shaivism, the sect of Her consort, Lord Shiva. Both descend from the original matriarchal religion of the Indus Valley civilization that dominated the Indian subcontinent prior to the patriarchal Aryans who imposed the orthodox Brahminism when they gained power[2].

A Hindu counterculture that runs in parallel opposition to Brahminism, Tantrism disregards orthodoxy's caste and gender proscriptions. It's a resurgence of India's primal faith in Shiva and Shakti, and a religion of the masses. It is also a movement of social protest and school of esoterica. Its life-affirming, non-dualistic philosophy has provided a strong counterbalance to the mind/body splitting asceticism and social elitism that periodically overcome all Indian-based religions, Hinduism, Buddhism and Jainism included. Tantra returns one to the borderland between male and female, not as patriarchally[3] defined mistake of nature, but as an emanation of Sacred Reality.

Tantra is not just an assortment of esoteric schools, nor is it the ancient collection of sex manuals that some Western populizers might have it seem. It's a mindset, a way of life in which one gradually withdraws from dualistic and compartmentalized perceptions of ourselves and the universe—a universe were intimately a part of, but which we've been brainwashed into thinking is opposed to us.

Hinduism thrives heartily upon contradictions. The most ascetic sects live alongside the most sensual, with nothing more than a mild philosophical debate or vigorous rejoinder between them. More a way of life than a religion per se, conservatism co-exists with the broadest sorts of tolerance. You can find the most sharply defined sex-roles assigned to biologically defined men and women, as well as the changes exerted by feminism, modernism and international youth culture, along with sanctified castes of transgendered people[4], all existing and accepted within the same spiritual and social spectrum[5]. It doesn't hurt that Hinduism's main deities, such as Shiva, Durga and Vishnu, are omnierotic and pangendered.

Within this religious context, I can acceptably wear multiple earrings and nose rings, cosmetics and extensive jewelry not to mention my torso and arms full of God/dess tattoos along with a waist gown (called a dhoti, and usually made of cotton or silk).

> Locks of shining red hair
> and a crown of diamonds
> small beautiful teeth
> and eyes in a laughing face
> that light up the fourteen worlds.
>
> I saw His glory
> and seeing I quell today
> the famine in my eyes.
> I saw the haughty master

for Whom men, all men
are but women, wives.

I saw the Great One
Who Plays at love
with Shakti.
Original to the world
I saw His stance
and began to live.

MAHADEVIYAKKA, 10th century CE

By helping us withdraw from the false, imposed dualism that attach constricting and alienating identities upon us, Tantra offers a healing philosophy and set of practices. These enable us to tap into, even merge with the underlying Divine Wholeness that sustains the incessant flow of phenomena we mistake for a static, sharply categorized and divided world. Through Tantric Hinduism, I achieve a fulfillment never felt before. There were occasions where I came close, but those other times were hemmed by a fear created by the clear and present fact that such fulfillment was only acceptable among fellow outlaws, along with a realistic danger accompanying it. The difference here is that I am given tacit spiritual approval.

Sometimes I am even given explicit approval as well. Six years ago, during a temple festival commemorating the completion and consecration of several shrine areas and the installation of the deities within them, a visiting Vaishnava brahmana (or priest of Vishnu) repeatedly expressed curiosity about me. At first, I thought it was about my appearance, one of the few times I've felt self-conscious about it among my Hindu peers. However I learned it was instead my distinctly non South-Asian ethnicity that piqued his interest. Explaining my obvious androgyny, my adopted brother, Balu, the assistant temple priest, explained that I was a convert and an Ardhanarishvara, a bhakta or devotee of God, in His/Her half-male/half-female form of Ardhanarishvara. From that moment on, the visiting priest treated me with the the most affectionate courtesy.

It's difficult to correlate our dichotomous Western culture with India's polycentric one, and Western categories of sexual orientation and gender generally do not translate very well into those in India. For example, those the West classifies separately as strictly gay, lesbian or categorically transsexual all constitute the third nature (Tritiya Prakrit), or intersexually intercaste (intercaste because the logic goes, none is consciously prone to actively seek to procreate and thus, unlike strict heterosexuals and rigid biological-sex adherents, are unbound by hereditary caste guidelines)[6].

Moreover, I fall into the spectrum between categories because, although androgynous in gender variation, I am bisexual. This raises the ante in Hinduism's categories of sexuality and gender to four, compared to the West's standard two.

If only my father could really see me now.

Endnotes

1. This poem and the succeeding poems are free-verse lyrics written by South Indian Shaiva bhaktas (mystics devoted to the God, Shiva), specifically from the Lingayat sect, collected and translated in A.K Ramanujan's **Speaking of Siva** (Penguin Books:1973, Baltimore MD).

2. See **History of Shakta Religion** (Narendra Nath Battacharyya, Manoharlal Publishers: 1974, New Delhi, India); **The Indian Mother Goddess**, 2nd Ed (same author, Manohar Book Service: 1977 Delhi, India); **While the Gods Play** (Alain Danielou, Inner Traditions International: 1987, Rochester, VT); and **Gods of Love and Ecstasy** (ibid).

3. See **The Tantric Way: Art, Science, Ritual** (Ajit Mookerjee and Madhu Khanna, New York Graphic Society: 1977, Boston, MA); **Shakti and Shakta** (Arthur Avalon, Dover Publications: 1978, New York, NY); **Kashmir Shaivism: The Central Philosophy of Tantrism** (Kamalakar Mishra, Rudra Press: 1993, Cambridge, MA); and **The Tantri Tradition** (Agehananda Bharati, Samuel Meisser: 1975, New York, NY).

4. Most noted in the West is the Hijra, a Persian-influenced North Indian term. Joggapa is the South Indian languages equivalent. They constitute a legitimate third sex, yet it is difficult to accurately characterize them in Western terms because gradations of transgenderism are classified in this category, including sacred transvestites, cross-dressing sex workers and transsexuals in various pre-,post-,and non-operative stages. South India's Joggap are a caste of transgendered person predominantly at the transvestite side and sacerdotal in vocation. The Hijra lean towards the transsexual side, and labor in various vocations. Individual variations are nearly legion, and the various subcastes transgenderly identified are often divided and at odds or in competition with each other. See **Neither Man Nor Woman: The Third Sex of India** (Serena Nanda, Wadsworth: 1990, Belmont, CA) and *The Hijras of India: Cultural, Social and Individual Dimensions of an Institutional Third Gender Role*, in **Third Sex, Third Gender**, Gilbert Herdt, Ed., (Zone Books: 1994, Cambridge, MA). Also Nicholas J. Bradfords *Transgenderism and the Cult of Yellamma: Heat, Sex and Sickness in South Indian Ritual* in **Que(e)rying Religion: A Critical Anthology**, Gary David Comstock and Susan E. Henking Eds. (The Continuum Publishing Co.:1997, New York, NY); and **The Invisibles: A Tale of the Eunuchs of India** by Zia Jaffrey (Pantheon Books: 1996, New York, NY).

5. In light of ancient India's well-documented omnieroticism, it's a sad commentary on colonial trauma that we've seen the right wing Shiv Sena political party try to prevent the mass-showing of the award-winning domestically made lesbian-feminist themed film, **Fire**, (written and directed by Deepa Mehta, 1997). Homophobia in modern-day India is a product of the still dominant nineteenth century education system propagated by the British occupier Lord Macaulay in an effort to re-educate the populace, in particular, a client ruling class away from their indigenous culture. It was the British who created the anti-queer Sodomy Act of the 1830s, and their Anglo-educated Indian Proteges who maintained it after Independence in 1947. Hence, the noticeable puritanism of such politicians, which flies in the face of their society's own erotic realities.

6. See **While the Gods Play** and **Virtue, Success, Pleasure and Liberation: The Four Aims of Life in the Tradition of Ancient India** (both Alain Danielou, Inner Traditions: 1992, Rochester, VT). The contemporary fading of caste is likely to effect added modifications to this schema, but this all only confirms much of the social construction behind gender.

BIOGRAPHY Ganapati Shivananda Durgadas

Ganapati Shivananda Durgadas is a fifty-one year-old Hindu with a Masters in Psychology. After more than fifteen years in Human Services and Social Activism, he is more than ever convinced that lasting solutions to suffering can only be found spiritually. A former welfare rights activist, ActUp and Queer Nation member, under his birthname of Leonard Tirado, he's travelled extensively through India, Malaysia and Singapore and spoken publically at both les, bi, gay and transgender events, and in Hindu temples in the U.S., Asia and Canada.

COVENENT

Ari (Arlene) Istar Lev
For Geniebud, with all my love.

Loving Jewish womyn is always a challenge—a play of light and shadow. They are Jewish through and through—the inflections of their voice when angry, the tilt of their head when thinking, the massive curls jiggling when laughing. They eat kasha mit vanishkas, know the subtle distinctions between mishugana and fedrayt, and collect information as insurance, just in case.

Yet they hate being Jewish—hate being from Long Island-Brooklyn-Queens. Hate patriarchal synagogues and hate explaining them to non-Jewish dykes. They profane the Sabbath with the glee of the newly released, or even worse, hadn't noticed that it was the Sabbath, or even worse yet, don't even know what it means. They find Jewish gatherings boring.

That's why finding her was so sweet.

She was not the first Jewish womon I have loved. I have loved many other Jewish womyn. Mostly I have loved Jewish womyn. I used to be embarrassed about this. A sign that I was provincial and stuck in the shtetl. Now I search for them.

She says we met at a Jewish gathering. I find it hard to remember not knowing her.

She was one of those womyn who just appear on the periphery. Slowly, over many years, moving into a central place—suddenly, in your heart and bed, watching **Star Trek** at 2a.m. We spent a year loving full-circle.

First we were friends, not even close friends, but what an ex would've called community buddies. Womyn who know we are connected by deep cords and ancient karma, but who rarely have time for coffee or a walk in the park on a new spring morning, but who always enjoy it when we do. Sincerely, we say, "Let's do it again," but, sigh, "again" could be another year or so away.

I remember the first time I saw her incredibly hairy legs. The chutzpa of this womon to prance through the streets of Middle America with thick furry legs. "Wow," I said, "Can I touch them?" hardly knowing her. "Yes," she said with glee, and I knew we were destined for wonderful things.

Once we drove home from a lesbian festival together. It was a warm night with a gentle breeze and I longed to take her hand.

One spring I planted some seedlings for her, while she and her male lover biked through the Northwest. When she came home, she picked up the baby plants and returned a lesbian mystery novel. I was struck by her wiry beauty, her self-contained joy.

My lover and I invited her and her lover to dinner one night. He and I talked into the night, long after our lovers fell asleep. I found him intelligent and easy to get along with.

Another friend interviewed us for an article on bisexuality. Interviewed me to find out why I stopped sleeping with men fifteen years ago, interviewed her to find out why she stopped being a lesbian after meeting him seven years ago. It was an interesting juxtaposition, and after we had become lovers, our friend quipped that she wanted to write a postscript. Our stories flowed one into the other in her article, as did our life stories.

I understood that she loved him and I understood all too well how hard living bisexually could be. I understood what it meant to love a man and find ease there. A lifetime of womon loving—intense, passionate, transforming has yet to birth that kind of ease. Although I understood her life choices, she understood also why they could never be mine. I made a decision to be a supportive dyke friend.

When I left my lover and moved into town, she was my first visitor in my new apartment. With my front door still unhinged and boxes everywhere, I found her amid the mess, watching a fuzzy tv picture, eating take-out Chinese food, my dog cuddled on her lap. I took a picture of her, thinking how wonderful it would be to have friends like her to come home to. In the picture, still hanging on my fridge, she was reading **Dykes to Watch Out For**; perhaps it was a warning I didn't heed.

Once I thought we went out on a date, but I wasn't sure and nothing happened.

Then she called and asked if I was planning on going down to the March On Washington and of course I was. Before you knew it, we were driving through a snow storm in Pennsylvania and discussing SM sex. I found myself getting excited and I said, "Am I allowed to want you?" "Yes," she said, quite emphatically, and I knew then that we were going to be lovers.

There we were in Washington at the freedom march for Lesbian, Gay, Bisexual and Transgendered Civil rights. We had become lovers the previous day. For twenty-four hours, I'd been swimming in her juices, basking in the sun and living the queer fantasy of falling in love with one million queers to cheer us on. We decided to attend the vigil at the newly completed Holocaust Museum. The crowd was large and I didn't know anyone. Somehow this scared me. Didn't I know all of the queer Jews; didn't I know any of them?

The speeches were powerful. Starhawk—Jewish, bisexual, witch sister—conducted a moving ritual. It could not have been easy to lead a ritual this large; I was surprised when I opened my eyes and realize how many people were joining in. I too reached for the sky and touched the earth. I lit my candle, so fragile in the wind. I heard the voices of my queer ancestors, dead, murdered, tortured for loving. Could they have loved as simply as I was then loving? I could not keep my hands off her body. Could they have felt this too?

As I held her, suddenly I remembered the story she told at the last Jewish feminist brunch. She had said, "My mother escaped the Nazis as a young child. My grandmother persuaded a Nazi to let my father out of prison. She sat on his porch for days until he gave in." (Am I making this story up? It sounds unreal even as I tell it. Did I read it somewhere? Did she say this in the cool air, eating a bagel?) She showed me a picture of her great grandparents standing on their land. Later, they died in the camps. Her mother came to America as a little girl, to have a little girl who I was then holding. I shielded my candle, so fragile in the wind. Her candle would not stay lit and she gave up trying, which somehow broke my heart. I saw a tear stream down her face. Thousands of lit candles, thousands of dead Jews, thousands of nameless faces of Jewish queers and allies, and one womon whose presence was a simple twist of fate. A feisty grandmother, an agreeable Nazi, a fragile thread of luck, a womon in my arms.

We made love about two weeks later. She came from my mouth and afterwards I lowered my body, buried my face in her belly. While she was still writhing on the bed, unbeknownst to her, I said a prayer from deep within me, screaming silently. "Thank you, goddess. Thank you for this fragile thread of fate that has made this love possible."

I had never celebrated Shavuot before. Honestly, I didn't even know what it was. "Something to do with Moses and the Ten Commandments," a friend said. "I think you're supposed to stay up all night and study," said another. I asked my friends because I didn't want to appear stupid when I called her back to say, "Yes, I'll spend Shavuot with you."

She wanted to go to an alternative-type shul. I took the night off (something I wouldn't do for just any woman) and prepared dinner. I have to confess that my interest was not in Shavuot, but another night in bed with her. Frankly, I hoped we wouldn't go to shul, but was too shy to say so. We ate and talked and cuddled. She kept looking at her watch. We were already late and I bravely said, "What if we stayed here and studied." "Okay," she said. Just like that. She was so easy, it was an enigma.

Just so she knew I was serious about this Shavuot thing, loving ritual and loving her, I pulled my how-to-be-a-good-Jew holiday book off the shelf and we began to study what it was we were supposed to be studying. "Where should we study?" I asked, meaning which room. "In bed," she said. I smiled.

We lit candles first, waving our hands to bring in the light. It was a hot spring night. She was naked. I was wrapped in a father's tallis (My father's? My grandfather's? Both long dead and no one seemed to know). It was silk and felt cool next to my skin. She lay next to me, reading Torah. She read, "If you will now listen to me and keep my covenant, then out of all peoples you will become my special possession for the whole earth is mine." She threw the holy book on the bed. "I hate this God," she said. We had been studying for three minutes. "You wanted to study the torah," I reminded her gently. "This is the torah." She explained about hating patriarchal Gods and their possessions. "They don't own the earth," she reminded me. I picked up the holy book and read, "I carried you on eagle's wings"..."on eagle's wings," I repeated. Slowly, she nodded and resumed reading.

We discussed the commandments. She discussed which ones she followed and which ones she didn't. I was amused when she came to "Thou shalt not commit adultery," and said, "I wouldn't do that." I reminded her that I share her with another lover. She nodded. "But I would never commit adultery." I knew that somehow this made perfect sense to our god.

I read Ezekial to her. Despite it having been my first time celebrating Shavuot, I had studied and pondered mystical biblical experiences. I read, "The heavens were opened and I saw visions from God, and the Lord's hand was upon him." "Wow!" she kept repeating. "Wow!" We discussed visions of god and what that meant. We discussed our visions and how they compared. We studied Ruth and Naomi. She read the words, "Whither thou goest, I will go." This was, of course, not true, but oh, the words sounded so pretty. We were both annoyed that Ruth ended up with a man, even though she too would leave me and go home to one.

All this while, I was wrapped up in my grandfathers tallis (I was thinking that it was his then). I began petting her. "Pet me," she said. I rubbed my hands up and down her legs, her belly, over her breasts. I played with the hairs between her chest, below her belly button, under her arms. I took the strings on the tallis and teased her nipples. I played with her pubic hair, unconsciously, the way I play with my own while reading. I played with her labia, my fingers darting in and out of her wetness while she read the holy book. "Is this okay?" I asked. She smiled warmly. Her eyes lit up and she kept reading.

At some point, she put down the book. It was in the middle of the night. "I want to stay up til dawn," she said, her eyes closing. We made love wrapped in my grandfather's tallis (I was sure it was his then.) "Do you think my grandfather would mind?" I asked. "Is he dead?" she wondered. "Yes," I nodded. "Oh, then he'll understand. When you're dead, you go to a place where you understand all kinds of things. He'd like it," she said. I tried to imagine my grandfather's approval, and I made a mental note to find out more about her afterlife theory. Since my grandfather did not get buried in his tallis, what could have been better than having womyn make love in it?

As the morning sun rose in the sky, we rubbed tzitzits together. Seeing the lightning and hearing the thunder, we were joined with our ancestors once again at Sinai. We too had known a revelation of sorts, shared an oral torah.

I have lived my whole life for such worship.

Our Rosh Chodesh group met. I wore the new silk tallis she made for me, while she drummed the heartbeat of the mother. We prepared for the mikvah, just a hot tub, but as the womyn gathered under the darkened sky, we chanted the mournful melodies of protection.

We are done now, over. She said that he can no longer bear for her to sleep with me, and she can no longer bear his pain. What of my pain? I wondered. How can I live without her touch? She cannot commit adultery though to love another when it hurt her partner—for that would be a sin against god. The dog whimpered as she left. Tears fell from my eyes. Only one shabbat candle still glowed, the other had went out, leaving only a hint of the smell of burnt offerings, and I alone with the queerest of Jewish memories.

BIOGRAPHY Ari (Arlene) Istar Lev

Ari (Arlene) Istar Lev is a therapist, educator and activist who specializes in working with queer families. She is Sundance's wife and Shaiyah's momma. She is thrilled to be a Jewish dyke and grateful for the year she had loving a Jewish byke. Ari identifies spiritually as a Jewish pagan yogini and is passionately in pursuit of all mystical experiences, but is especially fond of those that are embodied.

MY JOURNEYS INTO FAERIE AND WHAT I FOUND THERE
Connell O'Donovan

While others have covered the history of the Radical Faerie movement, I wish to relate my own journeys into (and through) Faerie—that mystical site of Magick[1], shadows, extraordinary reality. The intense individualism and anarchy of the Radical Faeries prevent me from speaking for or representing the Faeries as a whole.

Long before I heard of the Radical Faeries (or much understood my own sexuality and spirituality), as a young teenager and a stranger in my own house, in order to escape the taunts of other children; the disgust of my parents (for having birthed this effeminate 'crime against nature'); and the opprobrium of leaders of my childhood religion (the Church of Jesus Christ of Latter-Day Saints—or Mormonism); and having read many books on archaeology, anthropology, and ancient history, I began to create an imaginary land that lay far away from my daily misery—a magickal island populated by wondrous folk: Fairies, Elves, Amazons and Giants, as well as humans who lived close to and loved the greenness and sanctity of the world far more than they feared each other. I drew maps of this island, wrote histories of its peoples, and even plotted out a rather complex cosmology and theology for these folk.

And of course, there were two human Heroes on this Island—ageless, handsome, strong, gentle, virtuous, mischievous, and magickal. I called them Berek and Khail[2], created elaborate epic prophetic poems and riddles foretelling their births and destinies; and recorded tales of their trials and their lives together. Through these Heroes, the guilt-ridden, fearful and powerless boy I was back then, lived a life in which I had power and control. I was strong and brave, and yet I was valued more for my gentleness and passion than for violent might.

Now I am 37 years old, surviving and thriving in the Plague Years. I'm tall and strong, gentle and brave. My hair is long, my red beard thick and full—looking like some barbarian warrior who has stepped out of the pages of my childhood tales. I live a blessed life, balanced and harmonious, full of joy and love, very engaged in a balance of the physical, mental, spiritual, intellectual, and psychological—healthy, healed, whole, holy—embracing both the Light and the Dark, fearful of neither. I have arrived here at this holy site via my sporadic, often tentative forays into Faerie.

I first heard about the Radical Faeries in 1989, when I read Mark Thompson's book, **Gay Spirit**[3], which turned my frightful, depressing, confused life around. The photo on the front of the book, of a large group of naked gay men covered in the mud of the Arizona desert, sent shivers down my spine—a reawakening of something deep, tribal, fulfilling. Opening the book and reading just the words "Radical Faerie" for the first time sent me into a mystical experience that left me physically and mentally drained but weeping tears of joy. I had found a Home at last. The intervening years of my explorations with the Faerie Folk have healed my despair, giving me hope, a sense of self-responsibility, empowerment, expansive love, and enough courage to joyfully explore the juxtaposition of sexuality and spirituality through loving Fae Ritual.

While I cannot speak for anyone else's Faeriness but my own, during the past decade I have experienced Faerie dynamics at work during large and lengthy Gatherings, smaller evening Heart Circles, solitary rituals on the beach or in the desert or in the forest, and intense moments in cyberspace via the Radical Faerie e-mail listserve. And this essay tells what I have found there—what 'speaketh to my condition' in Faerie.

It seems to me that as a Radical Faerie I readily assume (or at least desire) a site of fundamental liberation, which informs all of life's activities. We have a paradoxically anarchist and communal utopian eschatology. In the introduction to **Gay Spirit**, Mark Thompson writes that "Chaos, terror and uncertainty seem the only true human inheritance in this, our age." However, he feels that the Radical Faeries (and other queer folk influenced by us) are a teleological response to a post-modern (homo)sexuality: "These gay people finally stand at the edge of our time, resilient and resourceful, tending to the new life necessary for the future" (p. xiii). I see Radical Faeries joyfully and (rather) successfully integrating (even centering) this utopian ideal into their liberated lives. We know that we have not been expelled from the Arcadian Garden. We take this burned-over wasteland of Sodom and through our love, we make the desert "blossom as the rose" in so many ways and on so many levels that others do not understand.

As a Fae man, I seek to live an Idea(l) of constant "Heart Space"—where there is full and mutual respect for Self and Others (indeed All Existence). My mystical journeyings (through High Camp ritual, playful sex, exuberant nudity, song, dance, poetry, art, and many other magickal acts) have brought me visions of my connectedness to Nature, to the vast and complex web of All Existence, which in turn is the firm basis of my Fae Ethos.

And I speak of an Ethnos as well—feeling that in my sexuality lies the basis for important societal roles that I must play out. Two of the roles that seem to resonate with many Faerie Folk are those of the Shaman and the Berdache, which I define as Technicians of Sacred Ecstasy and of Sacred Mediation, respectively. Together, they emphasize our marginality and our liminality—our outness and our inness, if you will, for Ecstasy is literally a "standing outside of" (the Self, the community, the mundane, the ordinary, etc.) and liminality is a mediation that occurs from the threshold betwixt two distinct spaces, a building of bridges over whatever dichotomies alienate the individual from the whole (be it gender, class, race, sexual orientation, etc.). Or as Thompson calls it (p. xvi) "entertaining irreconcilable differences."

Summer Solstice, 1996 The Homo-Hex Ritual, 18th and Castro, San Francisco
In the midst of the crowded street party the night before the Queer Freedom Day Parade, some 75 Radical Faeries and friends gather together just before midnight. We link hands and form a circle in the intersection of the road, at the heart of this Queerest Mecca, to publically give our deepest thanks to the Goddess for one more year of fabulous Queer Sex. Casting the circle, clothes come off, drums come out, and the beat begins. The crowd of curious (and often scandalized) mainstream gays gather around us to see what the ruckus of these freaks is all about. Naked in these streets, we raise our voices in chanting, we move our bodies to the rhythm of the drums and whistles and bells, flowing into and through the music and the Magick and the Love that are fully present.

I have come to this place to lose and find myself, to heal from old wounds, to be vulnerable, to (re)claim the heroism of my childhood, to find power (the kind that is unrelated to the prevalent 'power over' paradigm), to be extraordinary (not merely queer), to remember Magick, to learn to spread my wings and fly free, to encounter ecstasy, to fuck and be fucked, to embrace my mortality (the authenticity of bodies), to make peace with decay, to love and be beloved, to remember what I wanted to become. Expelled long ago from the Mormon Temple, I have finally found my truest Temple, and find myself as a Sacred Whore there.

I lose all sense of ordinary reality—and in this Perfect Moment, I encounter and am enraptured by the Faggot-God, and we make Love in this Circle of Dance. And I am become His lover, His bride, His friend, His queen, His hero, His high priest/ess, His beloved, and of course His god.

For I am (in love with) the Cosmos.

Endnotes

1. I use the archaic spelling to distinguish this from "magic" tricks of professional, modern magicians. I recently defined Magick to my best friend (and fellow Faerie) as "the mechanics whereby we embrace paradox".

2. These are two reconstructed Proto-Indo-European words I took from the American Heritage Dictionary's appendix, which have the modern English descendants of "bright" and "whole", respectively—purposely echoing the Hebrew divinatory items found on the priestly breast plate, the Urim and Thummim, which literally means "lights and perfections."

3. Reference to the Radical Faerie movement, see:
Mark Thompson's essay *This Gay Tribe: A Brief History of Fairies* in **Gay Spirit: Myth and Meaning**, Mark Thompson (ed.), St. Martin's Press, New York, 1987.

4. **The Trouble with Harry Hay: Founder of the Modern Gay Movement**, Stuart Timmons, Alyson Press, Boston, 1990. **Radically, Gay: Gay Liberation in the Words of Its Founder**, Harry Hay, with Will Roscoe (ed.) Beacon Press, Boston, 1996.

Connell O'Donovan's biography appears on page 71.

BISEXUALITY AND THE SPIRITUAL CONTINUUM
Brian Utter

I questioned my God as I walked down the aisle of the church during my confirmation. I had always been a faithful and upstanding Catholic. I had always followed and believed the words and the doctrines I was taught by my parents and priests, but as an adolescent confronting his sexuality, the dichotomies of right and wrong and of good and evil seemed too simple. These divisions were stressful because homosexual thoughts were not supported by my church. Above everything else I feared that I was, at best, wrong and, at worst, evil.

I accepted these divisions of right and wrong as truth because they were the basic tenets of the moral education I received as a child. Being raised in a Catholic household does not necessarily mean there is no freedom or choice, but in my experience there were definitive boundaries established to distinguish right from wrong. The Bible delineated morality and adhering to the Ten Commandments was requisite for a devout life. Sins could be repented, but not ignored. As a child, I viewed my religion as authoritative and absolute, but as long as I followed the rules I felt supported and justified by my faith. The simplicity of the choices I had as a child was harmonious with the dictates of my church. Since deciding what game to play or what to eat for breakfast did not raise questions of morality, I tried not to lie and kill and felt vindicated in my ability to comply.

During adolescence, the world seemed less clear than I was taught to believe. I interpreted my sexual attraction to people of my sex as a significant personal failing because I thought the church regarded heterosexuality as morally correct. I suppressed thoughts about boys because at that time it seemed there were only two options—heterosexual and homosexual—and so I pursued girls as everyone expected of me. I really did enjoy pursuing girls, but it was at the expense of denying attraction to boys. There was a great deal of attention and emotion devoted to the interaction of boys and girls by peers and adults alike and any slipping from this heterosexual paradigm might mean I was gay.

It was socially debilitating to conflict with the established gender roles and this climate was intensified because there was no discussion of diversity in sexuality. Maybe my classmates thought that if they discussed anything other than a man and a woman in the missionary position, they would be labeled queer. Perhaps talk of gay concerns was not common because one shouldn't think twice about who to have sex with. My same-sex thoughts continued despite my attempts to ignore them and it soon became clear to me that if I was not entirely straight, I might be gay. The way that romantic feelings were regarded by people around me was too simplistic. Most people were heterosexual, and people who had same-sex thoughts were homosexual. There was nothing in between as far as I knew.

However, I could not completely reflect either homosexuality or heterosexuality, because I could identify with the attractions and desires felt by each group. It would have been as unlikely for me to accept the label of gay as it was to accept that of straight; either way it seemed that I would have to deny part of my desires. It certainly seemed that given the two choices that my religion and society left me, there was part of me that was gay. However, what that meant was unclear. Queerness is an entire identity, not just a hobby or activity, and being partly gay is as implausible as being partly human. Without understanding the complexity and fluidity of the world, there was little option left but to admit that I was somewhat gay and according to my spiritual guides, somewhat wrong and somewhat evil. But I couldn't understand how I could be evil for being who I was. It disturbed and depressed me that it was not enough to do good.

For many people in my home town, sexual thoughts of same-sex partners seemed to indicate some malady or condition termed homosexuality. Regardless of what my same-sex attractions meant to others, something seemed amiss. It didn't seem right to determine my entire sexual identity based on only some of my desires. Of course, it also didn't seem to make sense to admit to only my heterosexual desires and identify as straight, but it was easier to err on the side of social acceptance.

Raised in a town that vocally supported heterosexuality, I was tainted in some way by these feelings. I was tainted and I did not know how to repent. Stronger than fears of rejection from my friends, though, was rejection from my God. So in a desperate realization that I could not comply with the absoluteness of my church, I chose to take the initiative and reject my God. As unsure as I was about how to be partly gay, I was even more perplexed at the thought of being partly sinful. In disregarding those who might label my sexuality based on my same-sex thoughts, I felt forced to disregard those who might question my morality. Sexuality exemplified to me that my church was not a refuge for those that might break accepted classifications. In a bipolar world that segregated right and wrong, I saw no choice but to reject religion when I did not feel acceptance.

Questions about sexuality raised further questions about the church in areas that initially seemed unrelated. The realization that Catholicism was not infallible in discussing sexuality led me to question the truth of other issues. Is the story of Adam and Eve at odds with scientific theories of evolution? Is the Bible divinely inspired and beyond question? My confusion was based on the absoluteness of the church and its teachings. It seemed there was no room for error or disorder, in stark contrast to the way the world appeared. Perhaps religion was supposed to be a way to move beyond the world as it seemed, but I could not relate to a belief that did not understand my life or my sexuality. My life and sexuality included confusion and disorder.

As my adolescence came to a close, I had lost a great deal of faith in organized religion. This change arose completely from my experiences in church and permeated my views of Catholicism and religion in general. It wasn't until attending college that, for the first time, I encountered a wide variety of views and ideals that I had not confronted in my suburban hometown.

As quickly as possible I moved into the most liberal residence hall, which was composed of special interest groups from a range of artistic and academic areas. With varying degrees of conviction, it was labeled the 'gay dorm' since the community was accepting of its openly gay residents. Most people living there were identified as straight, as I was at the time, but it was a forum in which my confusion could be explored. The other residents possessed an outlook in social, political, and sexual realms that was similar to mine and consequently, this was the first time I truly felt a sense of community. I considered myself very liberal politically and accepting of individuality in personal expression, and my fellow residents vocally agreed with these views. This community was filled with people that, in my childhood, would be classified as perverse based on their sexual attractions, and I was comforted because I could relate to them. I met gays, lesbians, bisexuals, and many others fascinated with sexuality and gender play. After always being taught what should be, I saw what was—and more importantly, what is—possible.

Courses in the philosophy department allowed me to question who I was and why I felt alienated from the perceptions of my childhood. As trite as the proposition seemed in Philosophy 101, *who am I?* remained a poignant and unanswered question. The responses of both religious figures and nonsecular philosophers provided outlooks that were unfamiliar and new. More importantly, learning how to think philosophically allowed me a chance to critically sift through the teachings I had received. Rather than accepting the prevalent beliefs, I learned to question all assumptions, including what I was taught as strictly good and bad in religion and sexuality.

I saw that there were other people around me who were clearly caught in the same trap and told that what they felt was wrong. Rather than being just a confused adolescent who did not fit into the way things ought to be, I was one of many who did not fit. In examining the myriad of complexities and distinctions in people around me, especially in gender and in the expression of sexuality, I became aware of the continuum.

This continuum was bisexuality on one level, but also a completely different conception of the world and my place in it. The world seemed to open into one that did not necessarily fit the restricted confines of my childhood teachings. I acknowledged the continuum as truth not because it was taught to me by elders, but because it felt right on a very personal level. In seeing and feeling the many possibilities, I realized that the fluid space of perception and expression is more than just an anomaly between opposites. Exploring a personal philosophy outside the expectations of my home and the Catholic Church emphasized the importance of being true to myself. There was a drive stronger than rejecting or accepting Catholicism, which was understanding myself. This understanding did not seem to be a focus in my experiences at church, which emphasized general guidelines that never spoke to me personally. To myself and a few close friends, I began identifying as bisexual and reveled in the blurring of distinctions between the accepted norms of 'boys like girls' and 'girls like boys.'

Starting from an assumption of only two sexual orientations, bisexuality seemed diffuse and indefinable. The realization that polar opposites could not describe the fullness of life helped explain my earlier confusion and disenchantment with religion. I decided that my faith and outlook must be as intricate and entangled as the life I've experienced. It must allow for variety and change, and avoid the denial of different outlooks.

I had already established that Catholicism was too absolute for me, but atheism suddenly seemed just as extreme. I could not justify a denial of spirituality any more than denying a piece of myself. There seemed to be a realm of spirituality that was wholly beyond the rituals of organized religion, which emphasized living well rather then practicing correctly. I could not find an organized religion that admitted the inherent confusion of life and acknowledged that we don't know most of the answers. In addition to the Western religions that were more familiar to me, the mysticism of Eastern religions, emphasis on the Goddess and existentialism all seemed to have something to say, each with a distinct perspective. Each world view offered clues without yielding the final answer.

I have now resigned myself to seeking clues without expecting to find the final answer. Far from being a defeatist attitude, I expect to learn more and I am open to new experiences. The life that I feel and the intensity I experience are very personal, which is compatible with a nebulous spirituality that does not define good and bad in passages or hymns.

There is a spiritual continuum that feels as unassuming as the world that surrounds me. This spirituality, though, is not any less real or inspiring than that found in a church sermon. This continuum is more than a vague agnosticism or religious confusion in which I would claim to not be able to discern the *truth* from the many possibilities. If that were the case, the problem would still be limited to the simplistic task of finding the right choice. Rather, the spiritual continuum actively affirms that *truth* includes many possibilities, beyond diametric opposites. For me, this has led to the avoidance of the definitive and opposing claims of atheism and organized religions.

This is paralleled in sexuality, as bisexuality exists in a society where straight and gay are viewed as distinct opposites. Bisexuality is not a denial of the validity of the straight and gay labels, but the realization and acknowledgment that more than these categories is important. In this sense, bisexuality involves a rejection of extremes and the rigid classifications that exist today. Ideally, we will eventually move beyond the need for categories and sexuality will be an individual form of expression rather than a choice among competing lifestyles.

The congruence and interplay of spirituality and sexuality then support each other and motivate a general life philosophy. The intertwined implications have led me to view my bisexuality as a philosophy and my spirituality as based on fluidity and possibilities. This philosophy seeks to elude extremist definitions and bimodal thought and leads to the denial of sharp lines and distinctions in daily life. Individuality is then raised at the expense of rigid boundaries, a direction I support as a person disenchanted with the established lines. Categories become merely guide posts and the only definitions that are ultimately meaningful are self-definitions in which we affirm our own identity. Bisexuality is a sensuality rooted in a discomfort with the dichotomized gender roles as much as it is a positive regard for people of both sexes, because dichotomies tend to ignore or disregard the continuum. As an integral part of who I am, this lends itself to the observation of the complexity and blurring of the spiritual world and disenchantment with the dogma of organized religion.

BIOGRAPHY Brian Utter

Brian Utter is currently a graduate student in the Department of Physics at Cornell University. His current ambition is to understand the world a little better tomorrow than he did yesterday. After frequently pondering the issues of religion and sexuality, his spirituality has evolved into a form that reflects the fluidity of sexual expression.

WICCA: From the Perspective of a Religious Transsexual
Mikki Maulsby

I was brought up and trained as a hardshell Baptist in the late 1950's. What this means in a nutshell is that Pat Robertson, Jerry Falwell and I spoke the same language.

Then I discovered that I was queer. At first I tried mightily to reconcile what my training said with what I was, but no amount of self-delusion could hide the truth that the religion I tried so hard to stay in, truly had no place for me. This brought on what I call my closet years, as I could not yet cut my ties to the religion or stop being who I really was. I just stopped going to church, but continued to call myself a member of the church. Since my spiritual beliefs were strong, this caused even more pain for me, both spiritual and emotional. Suicide became an ever-present thought in the back of my mind.

To ease the pain, I tried other denominations, shopping around so to speak, for a Christian church I could be a part of. In time I found the Church of England, also called the Episcopal Church, which had a priest who seemed understanding, even if he did not agree with my life choices. As long as I went to confession before partaking of communion, he seemed to let me be part of the church family. After a year or so, I began to feel so comfortable in this church that I began to open up and let other members see me as I was: a good and decent person who also happened to be a transsexual. This turned out to be a grave mistake or an eye-opening revelation, depending on your point of view. The priest pulled me aside one day and made it very clear that I could stay only as long as I stayed in the closet. I never went back there.

What saved my spirituality and my sanity was Wicca. Its precepts were simple, no more ethically demanding that the religion that I was brought up with, but still allowed me to be me. The spirituality, the rightness of Wicca, at least for me, was something I felt almost instantly. Wicca made me welcome as a person with utterly no regard or concern about my gender or gender orientation. To Wicca, what was important was my spirit.

From the start, Wicca has taught me that my queerness is just one facet of who I am. Wicca embraces the total person. Even now, it is difficult to describe the great feeling of warmth that I felt at my initiation. All I can say is that it was total and without reservation. As a solitary practitioner, I had no other Wiccans to deal with, no societal prejudices to cope with. This welcome came from, I believe, the Lady and the Lord directly. Such a welcome is not easily forgotten.

Wicca also allows a person room to express spirituality in any of an endless number of forms. One needs only to study and learn just what works for them. For example, my altar is fairly normal with items easily recognizable to any Wiccan. The one thing that would most clearly express my queerness is on my altar cloth. The cloth is something I decorated myself, where prominently in its centre is a pink triangle: my small way of expressing connection and personal contact with my knowledge of persecution of both Wiccans and queers.

Christianity is a lot like a one-size-fits-all suit, even when it rarely does. Wicca is a custom-made suit, easy to wear, because it fits you perfectly. Using Wicca as my foundation, I have invented a set of spiritual traditions, which blend Wiccan sensibility and transsexual activism. This allows me the honest expressions of both spirituality, the bedrock of my existence, and the day-to-day realities of who and what I am.

So much energy is wasted in the effort to force other religions to accept us. So much pain is caused in these attempts to fit in, to be accepted, that little spiritual energy remains. It is a heart-breaking thing to see loving, spiritual souls made sick and useless, when our world so desperately needs these loving souls, whose energy could turn to tasks of improving the human condition.

Consider a religion that offers no other constraints other than this: *And ye harm none; do what ye will*. These words saved myself and my spirituality. Both have grown and blossomed into rich fruit following this simple precept. I share my story in the hopes that another soul, in pain and in search of peace, may find the great wisdom within them that I found, as well as the healing of both life and soul that I did.

Blessed be.

BIOGRAPHY Mikki Maulsby

Mikki Maulsby resides in Pennsylvania.

BIRD FLOCK AND BERRIES
Ann Marie Wierzbicki

"My wedding,"
shouts the little girl
observing the sky dance of birds.
Many in one
enclosed
by boundaries unseen
swirling in air
wheeling against a blue sky.

"I listen," prays the woman
standing solitary before the bush.
Wizened and dry
dark berries cluster
at each fork
of gnarled twigs
branching out
on the wind-swept
snow-white rise.

"I shall continue," cries the soul
translating the creak and scrape of limbs,
hearing the blessed promise
and whispered possibilities
in this minute dance of aged wisdom.
"I shall be crone."

BIOGRAPHY Ann Marie Wierzbicki

Ann Marie Wierzbicki is a middle-aged lesbian mother of one son. After a Catholic upbringing, she drifted out of touch with any soul-nurturing practice. She has, over the years, cobbled together her own spiritual practice from assorted feminist, pagan and First Nations sources. She's much happier now.

CLAIMING CHRISTIANITY
Gloria Kropf Nafziger

Remembering is easy as I sit staring out the window. I can see their eyes and hear their voices, eyes filled with disappointment and anger, voices filled with disagreement and judgment. "It is a part of the journey," some voices concede. "God will show you the way through as long as you don't act on your feelings." "If you act on them," I hear, "you will be separated from God and His will." I wondered then why this separation was not my experience because, you see, I had already "acted."

My coming out as lesbian within the Mennonite Church was a time filled with much loss. It was also a time of tremendous growth and expansion within my own being. It was a time of reading and rereading Biblical and secular texts on the question of sexual orientation. It was a time of conversation with friends. It was a time of misunderstanding and pain for my children who loved their mother but could not understand why she was breaking up this 'perfect' family. It was a time of much questioning and being questioned by myself, my family and my church. It was a time of coming to terms with the reality of rejection by some of my closest friends who said they could no longer be my friend because we disagreed on basic Christian principles. It was a time of arguing:

"...how can you say that...",

"...you have other friends who disagree with you...",

"how can you not allow your children to come to my home?! I was like a second mother to them...I love them like my own...I am NOT a different person...I am just more honest with who I am..."

Today the arguments have subsided, the losses, while still real, are no longer my daily companion and my faith which was being challenged has become stronger and surer, as sure as the foundation of Christianity on which it was built.

So what is my story? How has change taken place? How have the questions been replaced by faith unshakable? I ask myself the same questions and then I realize that throughout my life prior to my coming out, I had a faith unshakable, a faith that was soundly based on a God of love. This faith has not changed, it has become stronger and has been tested by flames of doubt and human judgment. In the midst of the doubt and of the judgment, the God of Jesus the Nazarene has been present with me showing me a way, introducing me to people, helping me to recognize the people of God in a variety of settings and leading me profoundly and directly. I have come to believe, with the prophet Isaiah, that nothing, absolutely nothing[1], can separate me from the love of God.

My story is a story of community. The community of people spread across the North American continent. A people searching for the Divine reality in their lives and willing to share their search with the larger world. As I have come to recognize and to know a variety of people with a variety of spiritual/theological/religious beliefs and understandings, I have come to feel a part of a larger spiritual family.

This Divine being who helped me to claim my sexuality also helped me to reclaim my family of faith, helped me to see that the acceptance of the earthly body is not the basis of the heavenly kingdom. The acceptance of all people is the work of the Divine and the challenge to all people who choose to follow the calling of the Spirit.

The Divine's presence in my life has helped me to see and to embrace community, at times of need. It has opened me to trust when I have not wanted to trust and in the trust I have found reassurance of my presence in the family of God. I have become aware of the work of God's people as they embrace and live the words of Jesus. Through the words of writers and poets, I have come to recognize and feel at home with my own writing and poetry and I have come to recognize this and come to see God or the Divine in the written word. Through the work of artists, potters and painters, I have received a creative challenge to claim my spirituality through physical media. As I have listened to speakers and songwriters, I have come to feel affirmed and to recognize the Divine presence in the spoken and sung word. As I have walked in nature and as I have heard and read environmentalist concerns, I have begun to experience the Divine in the natural environment. The willingness of a variety of people to express both doubts and conviction, to share both hopes and fears, to feel both rejection and acceptance has given me permission to express, share and feel the continuums of the universe as well.

I have experienced oppression and have been ministered to by a variety of gifts within the community of God/Goddess, and I have been able to minister to others. I have come to see and to celebrate the Divine in the lives of those around me, both those with whom I am in agreement and those with whom I struggle. I have come to see that the church of God cannot exclude me because God does not exclude me, therefore I am included. This experience of being in the margins has opened my eyes to the reality of many others who live in the margins due to race, class or disabilities. I will choose my battles and I will celebrate and live in harmony, the harmony of a loving God ever-present with me.

The North American Mennonite Church struggles as it attempts to understand the experiences of a sexual minorities. The Biblical texts are read and reread and fear, the fear of difference, continues to dictate. I too fear those who are not like me until I get to know them, and in the knowing, fear is removed. As I have come to know God/Goddess in increasingly personal ways (through an increasingly wide range of community members) I have come to claim my own knowing and have come to reclaim my historical understanding of the Divine in my life. I have come to recognize that the God of my father and mother; the God who invited in the 'outcasts' to dinner; the God of the oppressed is my God, is the God of justice, the God of peacemaking, the God of love. I have also come to see that the church, which in my childhood challenged me to walk with the outcast, the hungry and the frightened, is my church. No one can take it away from me. This church, this community, this God live in my soul and I celebrate all of who I am in this context.

I long to offer my daughters, and all the sons and daughters of humanity, the gift of a spiritual life so rich and so free that they are able to claim all of who they are, body, soul and spirit. I also hope for a church community that can embrace them and welcome them regardless of their sexual orientation. For now even though the church struggles to embrace me, I will embrace it and claim the promises of the Divine for all who seek to walk in Her ways.

Endnote
1. As reminded frequently by my dear friend, the theologian/prophet Melanie Morrison.

BIOGRAPHY Gloria Kropf Nafziger

Gloria Kropf Nafziger is the mother of three daughters (ages fourteen, eighteen and twenty). She lives with her partner (Liwana Bringelson) and her daughters (Kaitlyn, Lisa and Lora), who also live half-time with their father. Since leaving her heterosexual marriage, Gloria's daughters attend and participate in worship in both their father and mother's churches. Both churches are Mennonite, albeit at opposite ends of the theological continuum. Mennonite Churches belong to regional conferences, however many decisions are made through a discernment process at the congregational level. Gloria attends Olive Branch Mennonite Church, which is a publicly affirming member of the Supportive Congregation Network (a network of Mennonite and Brethren Churches that are inclusive of all persons, regardless of sexual orientation). The church Gloria's daughters attend with their father (and the one Gloria attended until leaving her marriage) is fundamentally opposed to non-heterosexual relationships. Some common tenets of both of these churches are emphasis on non-violent conflict resolution, importance and strength of community, adult baptism and a belief in following Jesus the Christ toward justice for all people. Gloria's faith has been a significant part of her life journey, from a rural community church through a traditional marriage and into her current spiritual jumping-off place: mother, therapist, lover, friend, writer, facilitator, partner, daughter…and the list goes on.

MY LIFE AS A JEWISH QUEER PRIESTESS
Alina Ever

As a young child, I loved going to synagogue, singing, feeling part of a loving community and sensing something bigger than myself. I remember praying to god as a child. I needed help living with my many fears. I am a child of Nazi holocaust survivors. I don't remember the word "Holocaust" ever mentioned in my family, but it was ever present in my consciousness. The silent, unspeakable horror. Images of hiding, of running, of blood, of small children with their hands raised, of gas, of bones upon bones upon bones. I have had many nightmares about the knock on the door in the middle of the night, of running from Gestapo, of taking my last breaths in gas chambers. I was confused by a god that would allow such horrors, and yet I wanted to believe there was something I could pray to that would allay my sense of the world as a scary place.

I grew up in a Reconstructionist synagogue where most of the time we had no Rabbi. The community consisted of highly intelligent, intellectual and Jewishly knowledgeable individuals who could rarely agree on anything, let alone whether to have a rabbi or how to choose one. We had one I didn't like when I was twelve years old, but he didn't last very long. I had a sense that rabbis were no more or less knowledgeable or closer to divinity than anyone else. And I witnessed wonderful services and drashes (interpretive talks) led by members, including my father. To me, Judaism never felt like a religion that needed intermediaries.

My parents, who were new immigrants to the United States, discovered that they were not automatically a part of the Jewish community as they had been in Europe and Israel. Only by joining a synagogue did they find other self-identified Jews. Community, whether propelled by oppression or from genuine human need, always felt primary. The synagogue we attended included many European Jews with accents like my parents. It helped to some extent in replacing the relatives and extended family that I yearned for.

When I came out as queer at twenty (first as bisexual, soon after as a lesbian, then years later as bisexual again), a lot of the draw for me was towards the community. Here was a group of people who shared values and visions to make a better world AND offered support to live a more integrated life. Here was the family I had been unknowingly searching for. At the same time, I had many misgivings. The lesbian community at my college looked so small and insular, back-biting and male-hating. I didn't want to feel any doors closing to me in choosing to declare an identity and becoming a member of this community. In the end, the pull to belong was too strong to resist. Although I never rejected my Jewishness, it slid down in importance. At the time, feminism and queer activism were more compelling.

I have always felt within me both an activist and a priestess. When I moved to Boston after college, I was led into a Jewish Renewal Community. Though there was still a male Rabbi in the lead, the holy days and Shabbats (sabbaths) were celebrated in a much more spiritual way than anything I'd been exposed to before. There was beautiful music, movement, dance and poetry. There was less emphasis on reading from a prayer book and more on opening the heart and feeling spirit. During that time, there were also some wonderful Jewish experiences: a Sukkot (harvest holiday) weekend when a group of us went to the country, built a sukkah (a hut), made many paper-strung decorations, danced and sang passionately for hours. I was discovering a vibrant, meaningful Judaism. Still, there was not a place where I could bring my political, queer and spiritual selves together.

When I moved to San Francisco eight years ago, I was invited to join a small lesbian/bisexual woman's havurah (Jewish ritual circle). It was here I started to take spirituality into my daily life and that I was encouraged to take leadership in creating and facilitating rituals. I began to learn about working with energy, about the power of chants, about the progression of services. I was also inspired to learn more about the Jewish holy days and their roots. We encouraged each other to adapt the liturgy, to make it more feminist, progressive, and meaningful in our lives.

As I entered more deeply into Jewish spiritual life, I became involved in a local Jewish Renewal synagogue, where I participated in holy days not celebrated by my havurah. And I was offered opportunities to learn from leaders in the larger community, as well as to lead High Holy Days services. I went to several conferences of the movement. At the first one, I helped form a queer affinity group and we decided to do an entertaining skit at the end of the week that educated the attendees about what it was like for us to be Jewish and queer in this community. The response was overwhelmingly positive. I was encouraged by the willingness of the community to welcome queer Jews.

Soon after, I and two others formed Queer Minyan, which still today meets the third Friday of every month to celebrate Shabbat. It is a wonderful group of women and men who have become mishpochah (family) for each other. We have created a blend of Jewish Renewal, Buddhism, Wicca and Radical Faerie paganism. Each service begins with singing "hinei matov umanyim, shevet haqueer gam yachad." It means "how good and sweet it is for us queers to be together." The original has "achim" (brothers). Something about replacing the Hebrew word for brothers with the contemporary English word "queer" evokes powerful feelings. Then we cast a circle and invoke five directions (there are several Jewish holy days where we call in directions).

In the last five years, there have been several other influences on my spiritual life. About three years ago when a friend of mine was dying of AIDS and I was suffering with emotional illness and repetitive strain injury in both arms, I was taken to a weekly meditation class taught by Sylvia Boorstein. Sylvia is one of those JewBu's (Jewish Buddhists) who is warm and grandmotherly and teaches a totally down-to-earth Buddhism. It was just what I needed. One thing I love about Buddhism is that it puts everything in a larger perspective. My suffering is important AND everyone is suffering. This is the nature of human existence. Meditating offered me a way to be with my pain moment by moment. More recently, I have discovered ancient meditative practices in the Jewish religion. These practices, as well as the Vipassana Buddhism I have studied, have informed my Jewish ritual leadership. In High Holy Day services that I have been leading for several years, I incorporate both kinds of meditation.

The other major influence on my spiritual leadership has been the movement to reclaim earth-based European traditions. About five years ago, I joined a multicultural ritual group that was formed after a ritual organized by Starhawk, the well-known Wiccan writer and ritualist, and the Reclaiming Collective, a local Wiccan group. The group needed a Jewish presence. This was a group of people from diverse ethnic, racial and religious backgrounds who all shared an interest in the indigenous roots of their people. The challenge of working together was at times frustrating, and at other times, rewarding. We struggled to create a multicultural ritual in which European traditions were not dominating or framing the result.

Some members of the group were suspicious of my Jewishness. Christianity was the enemy of indigenous peoples, and Judaism, though not a colonizing force, was seen as another patriarchal sky-worshipping religion, but I was inspired to dig into the roots of the Jewish people and religion.

What I discovered should have been no surprise. Before the Rabbis, the Torah (the five books of Moses), the patriarchal god-in-the-sky, and all the rules, Jews were tribal-based peoples who lived in harmony with natural and agricultural harvests. Many of the holy days have customs that harken back to pagan roots. For example, during the holy day of Sukkot, we build branch-roofed huts decorated with fruit. We mark the space by shaking special branches in six directions. This was the major harvest in the fall and the huts were originally the agricultural harvesting huts that were built in the fields thousands of years ago. I learned about Asherah, the Hebrew Goddess, who was worshiped by the people on hilltops and had a place in the great temple for most of its duration. I learned that a number of our traditions and holy days were borrowed from other people around us. Some of the names for god in the bible are actually Canaanite divinities. The Jewish people and the religion is a creative mix of borrowed and adapted traditions from surrounding tribal and earth-based peoples.

Inspired by these discoveries, I spearheaded a new group called Pardes Rimonim, Orchard of Pomegranates, a Jewish feminist earth-based and inclusive ritual community. We are in the process of creating and returning to an earth-based Judaism. It is an amazing journey. In our recent High Holy Day services, I created altars in each of the directions (altars played a central part in the ancient Hebrews' religious rites), which incorporated Hebrew goddess sculptures, elements like flour, oil and frankincense that were described in the Great Temple of 5000 years ago, harvest fruits and elements of tikkun olam (social justice). We invoked directions, elements, divinities and ancestors at the beginning of our services. In addition to the traditional Torah-reading, we added non-traditional stories from women's oral history and a Canaanite myth from the city of Ugarit that describes the seasonal changes of autumn (which the High Holy Days and Sukkot celebrate). We replaced concepts of the divine as king and lord with nature-based and communal images. Pardes Rimonim is a collaborative venture that continues to discover and enliven earth-based Jewish traditions while creatively adapting liturgy and customs.

In recent years, I have been thinking about what it means to be a Jewish ritual leader. I have a problem with the term "lay leader," although I am a proponent of lay leadership. Lay leadership implies a leader with lower status—lying down even—underneath the Rabbi, and with lesser knowledge and power. When I think of the term "Rabbi," I think of book knowledge and top-down leadership. As a feminist, I have strived to be a different type of spiritual leader. What has come to me is a new and ancient role—that of a Jewish priestess.

We don't know a lot about Jewish priestesses, but there is evidence that they existed. The matriarch, Sarah, seems to have been a high priestess in her Canaanite homeland, and bought the traditions and duties of her role into her new land and the emerging Jewish religion. Savina Teubal in **Sara, the Priestess** (1984) posits that Sarah originated from a nature-based, non-patriarchal system emphasizing community over individuality. Sarah, as Goddess incarnate, held a tradition of self direction, whereas Abram (the first Jewish patriarch) acted as an intermediary between his god and his community. Sarah's position was internationally recognized and she had an important role in ensuring the fertility of the land and well-being of the people. In the ensuing years, the patriarchal system of Abram prevailed and subordinated women along with their tradition. Even the word "priestess" was eradicated from the Hebrew Bible.

I envision Jewish priestesses today incorporating new thinking within the construct of an ancient role. I believe that a modern-day priestess would, like Sarah, care for the land and the community. Priestesses access spiritual knowledge from the inside out, from tuning into shefa, the flow of divine abundance, and encouraging others to do the same. Due to the historical necessity, Judaism became a heavily intellectual and text-driven/based religion which led to an imbalance between mind and body. Priestesses with body and psychic knowledge (more than book-learning) can take the lead in promoting a major healing of the religion and the Jewish people.

One aspect of ancient priestess' role was as sexual initiates and healers. As part of my priestess work, I lead sexual healing classes for women. The way we are bound sexually in this culture is linked to all the ways that we are un-free. Sexuality is at our core. It is our life-force energy, the same as our spiritual and creative energies. When we heal this core, we become more authentic to ourselves and more in balance with others and the planet. And I believe that women can and should be leaders of the movement towards sexual healing and empowerment.

My spiritual path continues to evolve, I am an integrator. I take from many sources and I find a way to piece together what I hope is a meaningful whole useful to a number of people. I feel that this is my calling. There are no schools or academic institutions to train priestesses, but I have studied with many wonderful teachers. In addition, I try to maintain a willingness to learn from every experience, mistake and opportunity. I know this work is not easy, but I also know that I am not alone. As priestesses, we are in the process of midwifing in a new era, one that values the interconnection of all life on the planet.

BIOGRAPHY Alina Ever

>Alina Ever is a ritualist and community educator with a passion for fusing multicultural art/ritual and politics to heal and transform the world. She has developed and facilitated workshops and classes on sexual healing for women, as well as Jewish and women's spirituality, earth-based traditions and life-cycle rituals. She has led large and small groups ceremonies, and participated for five years in the creation of an annual event celebrating the ancestors of many cultures. She spearheaded Pardes Rimonim (Orchard of Pomegranates), a Jewish feminist, earth-centred/based and inclusive ritual community, and she co-founded Queer Minyan, a monthly Shabbat group.

YULETIDE PRAYER (1982)
Candis Graham

I am sitting at the kitchen table, staring at the black and white photograph propped against a bowl of bananas and tangerines. Fighting not to cry. Behind me, the apartment-size washer spins and whirls and shoots soapy water. A minute later, as noisy as Niagara Falls, clean cold water rushes in.

Liquid wax slides down the candle and lands in the tarnished brass holder. I take a deep breath. Close my eyes. See the children as they looked at the cottage on White Lake, the summer before last.

TJ will be seven in a month. Strands of soft blonde hair fall in her eyes. She holds a stick in the air and two raw marshmallows balance on the tip. TJ, I love you. Listen to yourself. Trust yourself. Know you are safe. Share my strength, oldest child to oldest child. Your father means you no harm. He wishes only to hurt your mother and your nana and your grandad.

Jason has long blonde hair that frames his handsome face. He turned six last week. He holds his stick with both hands, stretching toward the fire to toast a marshmallow. Jason, Feel my love. Reach out and link hands with me. Hold tight. You'll be home soon.

Jennifer is three. She is cuddly and warm, always smiling. She points a stick at her beloved grandfather, offering him a toasted marshmallow. Her arm extends beyond the view of the photograph. Her upper lip holds the lower one, and her toes curve toward her centre of gravity. Jennifer, I am with you, in love, always. Talk to me, in your mind. Tell me everything.

I blow out the candle and turn on the radio. A male singer croons, "Chestnuts roasting on an open fire." I hang wet clothes over the wooden rack in the bathroom.

Sometimes I pace. The length of the hall. Staring at the red wooden floor.

Other times I stand at the living room window. In the afternoon I watch a woman scrape ice from her windshield. Later, a man comes out of a neighbouring house, a brightly wrapped package under his arm. He steps over a snow bank and walks carefully across the slippery road to a parked car.

I believe in the power of things unseen. I take a long breath and close my eyes and chant to the living room window. T.J. Jason. Jennifer. I love you. Love you. Love you.

I try not to stare at the phone.

It rings in the late afternoon. He walked into the Ottawa Police Station with the children, the voice says, then turned around and walked out. Alone.

FLYING AT A SLANT:
Candis Graham
For Judy, Gordon and Thelma

It is a long room, bare
with hardwood floors
and dull white walls.
Commencement of Tai Chi
Three tall plants
congregate
in the front alcove.
Carry Tiger to Mountain
A wooden altar, draped
in marigold and apricot,
stands in the back corner.
White Stork Spreads Wings
The altar is dedicated to Kuan Yin, Chinese
Goddess of Compassion.
Move Hands like Clouds
Eleven women
and two men
move thoughtfully
in unison.
Step Up to Seven Stars
Then pause to sip tea
from tiny cups.

VOICES
Candis Graham

I'm modern magic
believing in myself on sunny days
it takes time but it's happening
I'm learning about
wanting too much
   like who needs ten pairs of earrings
   and five pairs of cotton tights?
talking too much
   like who cares if I have only
   $70 in my bank account
I'm learning to listen
to the murmuring voice
You always know what to do
be quiet
wait for it
I recognize her
heart-and-soul wisdom
she has a voice that can cancel cancer
a voice that can turn fear into freedom
it's a voice (just beneath the surface) whispering
Listen to yourself
and love me
love her
then the world
Do it now
before the clouds appear

BIOGRAPHY Candis Graham

I am trying to be a consciously spiritual person, although I have to admit I'm still trying to figure out what that means. Some people attend a formal gathering once a week in a place called a church, synagogue or mosque. Others gather outside and stand in a circle when the moon is full. For me, being spiritual is more primitive than a church and more sophisticated than a moon circle. It has to do with thoughts and feelings, beliefs and actions, intuition and guidance, and energy in all her forms.

Imperfect Moments, my second book of short fiction, was nominated for the 1994 American Library Association Gay and Lesbian Book Award. My third book, a collection of creative nonfiction pieces about health and spirituality, will be published in 1999.

WHEN THE SAINTS GO SNEAKING IN
Irshad Manji

This year, the Toronto chapter of the Metropolitan Community Church, North America's most open house of worship for gay men, lesbians and our families, celebrates its 25th birthday. At a time of plunging affection for so much of the Christian world, MCCT's growing congregation seems like a minor miracle. Maybe more surprising is this: I find myself eminently comfortable in its pews and I'm Muslim. (Not a very good one, some would thunder. But given the daily struggle of coming out to my Creator, I long ago learned to laugh at any rush to judgement.)

What attracts me to MCCT goes well beyond its fight against homophobia, a noble cause, yet one that addresses only a facet of my being. Nor can my appreciation of the church be reduced to its non-alcoholic communion wine and its usually inclusive language. In fact when one of the choir members apologized for a closing hymn that proclaimed Jesus as a saviour, I confessed that I'd taken the loud liberty of changing that to Jesus, a prophet. Allah, I explained, would approve. The choir gal did too.

Which brings me to the real reason I attend MCCT. It embraces imperfection, offering the chance to graduate from religion to faith. Religion delivers us certitudes. Faith recognizes that life is messier. My life, your life even Christ's life.

Indeed, Jesus was born to a poor, unmarried Palestinian woman in an occupied territory. Today's arbiters of conservative morality would call him a bastard. A refugee criminal to be. Good with his hands, but hardly leadership material. (And typical, isn't it, that the son of a whore would hang around other hookers?)

Moralists from the opposite direction should be reminded that Christ didn't always live up to his compassionate billing. Take his rocky relationship with his mother. Observes Stephen Mitchell, author of **The Gospel According To Jesus:** Mary of Nazareth is almost completely absent from Jesus' life and words. The few times he mentions her, his words are cool, even hostile.

The exiled Jesus refuses to let his mother and brothers see him upon his controversial return to Nazareth. When a woman in a crowd yells, "Blessed is the womb that bore you and the breasts that gave you suck," Jesus reportedly cringes, then rejects her sentiment. He dismisses two others who wish to say good-bye to their families before following him. Decrees Christ in the Gospel of Thomas, "Whoever doesn't hate his father and his mother the way I do can't become my disciple. And whoever doesn't love his true Father (God) and his true Mother (the Holy Spirit) as I do can't become my disciple. For my mother gave me death, but my true Mother gave me life."

The painful point here is to lose myopic family attachments and merge with the universal—non-bastardizing—parent. Still, Mitchell points out: "However much I see all women as my mothers, I have a special bond with my flesh and blood mother, and if I don't honour it with my full attention, the flow of my love will be obstructed and a portion of my love will remain opaque." Translation: Christ had issues.

Such imperfections can give solace, even inspiration, to all whose hearts ache with resentment from being socially illegitimate students streamed into numbing fields, men on welfare, stay-at-home mothers, trannies, fags, dykes. That includes Muslim dykes who now go to a Christian church. Oy.

Given its connection to a community born into presumed hereticism, MCCT relates the lessons of Christ's struggles to the constant negotiating that gay men and lesbians must do with the wider world. Here's my favourite illustration. Reverend Troy Perry, founder of the worldwide MCC Fellowship, has rewritten his favourite hymn to read, "When the saints go sneaking in." No wonder. He once posed as a Catholic Priest so a hospital official would ensure that an AIDS patient received daily meals.

Lie? Love? Both? Because MCCT leaves us with questions as much as guidance, it provides incentive to keep faith. The church consequently elevates what could be a niche gospel into something that speaks to the confusions in most of us.

Which brings me to a confusion that I challenge the church to address, especially as it searches for a multicultural congregation. How can the humility that Christ ostensibly teaches be reconciled to the claim that Christianity is "The Path to Salvation?" Is this a humble claim? I ask these questions as a still-practicing Muslim. To truly fathom the value of Islam, I believe I must take the Christian and Jewish journeys. These monotheistic religions inspired the cornerstone principles of my own, so that much of what Moses introduced, Jesus subsequently embodied and Mohammed later codified. Islam thus provides for a multi-faith exploration, possibly even demanding it.

Does Christianity? Should it? If not, then what does the MCCT drive for diversity mean? Such challenges, affectionately issued, pay tribute to the church's mandate of spiritual growth.

In turn, I've learned that spiritual growth can happen anywhere. Hooligans once chased some MCC members through downtown Toronto. Their saviour that evening: a drag queen who appeared in an alley, raised her manicured hands with majestic authority and scared the bejeezus out of the thugs.

Let us pray that the saints sneak in for another 25 years.

Irshad Manji's biography appears on page 22.

ON BEING GAY (AND NOT STRAIGHT)
David Newhouse

Upon coming out I sought the advice of elders. They informed me that since gay people had been made by the Creator, they could not judge them. After all, they argued, since the Creator had made them, he (or she, I'm not sure which) must have had some purpose in mind. Who, then, was humankind to judge the work of the Creator? What mattered more, they told me, was how I lived my life and what I did with it. It was on that basis that I would be judged and not on the basis of my sexual partners. My life and my own attitude towards my homosexuality changed. While I am gay and likely will remain so, barring unforeseen circumstances, I no longer consider my homosexuality a disadvantage nor do I let it prevent me from doing what I want to do. It has become a part of me and my character. I expect that I will change with time, and that I will have to struggle with decisions regarding being visible in situations where there is real danger to others and to myself.

The questions I am asked most frequently are "Don't you wish that you were straight? Wouldn't your life be much simpler if you were not gay?" Surprisingly, I don't quite know how to answer these questions. First of all, I don't know if "not gay" is the same as straight. Observation tells me it is not so. There are many heterosexual people who are not straight. Secondly, my experience of living as an openly gay man for thirteen years hasn't provided answers to the questions but it has revealed much about the assumptions behind the question.

Most often my interlocutor is straight (or at least, I presume he or she is since I never ask) and, for the most part, has grown up with a presumption that heterosexuality is the way of the world and is to be valued over other sexualities. The questioner, in my interpretation, is asking me to conform to his or her view of the world and hoping against hope that I will do so. I do not do so, as you may have guessed. But the years have led me to think about that question: Do I wish that I were straight? At one time, I thought that I knew what that meant. Today, I'm no longer sure. The clear lines which I once thought existed between gay and straight have become blurred. But then, as one ages, the research indicates, one becomes more mellow and less prone to drawing lines in the sand.

Yes, I know what being straight means in the conventional sense: a progression from girlfriend to wife to family and children, white picket fence and suburbs. And yes, I know this is a stereotype. But do I really know what it is like to be straight and more importantly, at least to my questioner, do I want to be straight? The feelings and experiences are foreign to me, perhaps as foreign as the feelings and experiences of homosexuality are to straight people. I imagine that the pressure for straight people must be enormous: the pressure to conform, to marry, to produce children, to fit in, to settle down, to follow the well trodden path.

As a gay man, I feel none of these things except the pressure to conform exerted by the questioner and the urbancentric gay community and its overwhelming embrace of narcissistic consumerism. The truth of the matter is that I know of no other way of life. Despite my attempts at doing so, I cannot imagine being anything other than gay: whether I am gay through a happenstance of nature or through some combination of genetic programming and childhood/early adulthood experiences, I don't think matters. I did not control any of that.

What really matters to me at least is that I am comfortable with who I am. I do enjoy the advantages that being gay provides me (and I think that there are real advantages to being gay): the ability to look at situations from a different perspective, an instant sense of community in many different places, freedom to choose more readily between career and home, and above all, a sense of living at one and the same time within and outside of society.

I also understand that there are still many gay people who view their homosexuality as a handicap, as a disadvantage, or as something to be ashamed of. And in some cases, it still is. Recently, I listened, read, and watched a gay man struggle with the Anglican Church. He refused to become invisible. In that situation, others viewed his homosexuality as a handicap to administering to the spiritual needs of his parishioners. He didn't see it in the same manner. Thankfully, these situations are becoming less frequent. I don't know if, at any point in the ordeal, he wished that he was straight. It would certainly have prevented the situation from occurring, I agree, and have reinforced the assumption that heterosexuality is the preferred sexuality. The institutional forces are powerful and difficult to resist and to change. Without a strong sense of identity and self-worth, they can overwhelm.

Society in general still does not accept homosexuality. However, society has become more tolerant over the past twenty years as our understanding of the origin and nature of homosexuality increases and perhaps, the backlash from the HIV epidemic notwithstanding, will continue towards acceptance. Yet, I keep wondering to myself, will there be people who will still ask the question: Do you want to be straight?

BIOGRAPHY David Newhouse

David Newhouse is a professor of Native Studies at Trent University.

SWIMMING WITH APOLLO
Brian Day

Taking the arc of the air in my arms
And finding the press of the waiting water,
I'm chanting in the rhythm of my entering hands
As smoothness glides beneath my belly.
In this steady beat of heart and feet,
This rapid flutter of all my wings,
I'm ravished and entered in a single breath
By a sudden male and radiant motion—
Infused in my keen and streaming body
By a god who exults in the flesh he borrows,
Taking incarnation as the prize it is
And exerting himself in urgent play.
He's immersed in the blue, the cool of joy
And smiles in secret behind my face
At this meeting hidden in a sheath of skin,
This tryst of limbs and common lungs.
I've become the heavenly speed of his breathing,
The strain and soreness that forges his beauty.
He hums with the songs of waters inside me
And pumps to the reach of fingers and toes
The racing light that brims our body,
That gives to each smooth and fluid movement
The swell of the hymn we sing with one tongue—
Giving praise to this life in its blessing of flesh.

Brian Day's biography appears on page 73.

MOONRITE
Jane Inyallie

moon calls
a gathering
in the southern
midnight sky

clouds drift in
swollen with
phosphorescent bellies
dripping the sweat
of imminent labor

waves
shift
and
stretch
wet
luminescent
skin

moans
roll
to
thunder

a fluid burst
down to earth
in torrents of
warm
embryonic
rain

FIRE
Jane Inyallie

i drift
on a plane
of
sleep

your whisper
lures me
into
veils of silver

entwined
we
slide
the
spiral valley

we
spin
cry out
call
utsoo
keeper
of
eternal fire

she draws us
to her potency
we suckle
burning breasts
flesh and bone
melt away

flames
writhe
red
dancing
the sacred
womb
of
ecstasy

Jane Inyallie's biography appears on page 20.

BUDDHISM'S RAINBOW COLOURS:
Actualizing the humanistic Buddhist principles as they apply to human sexual diversity in the spiritual community of Nichiren Daishonin's Buddhism.

We wish to share our experience as gay, lesbian, bisexual and transgendered individuals in Soka Gakkai International of Canada, a lay Buddhist organization numbering some twelve million worldwide and based on the life philosophy of Nichiren Daishonin. This organization has shifted, from one dominated by the internal struggle between its humanistic principles and culturally supported homophobia, into an organization actively supporting acceptance and inclusion for people of all sexual orientations and gender identities. Adopting this new policy of acceptance clearly based on Buddhist doctrine,and the clarification of the principle that "all people attain enlightenment as they are" was accomplished harmoniously, without splintering the community. We have included the entire SGI Charter so that you the reader may understand its philosophical base and goals. Our purpose is to give an overview of our rainbow community's process of gradual integration over a period of 25 years. This process is ongoing. To enable you to have a reference within which to place our experience, we will include a brief history and description of the practice.

Fundamentals of Practice
The practice of Nichiren Daishonin's Buddhism consists of chanting the phrase Nam-myoho-renge-kyo, and the recitation of two key chapters of the Lotus Sutra, both to a mandala called the Gohonzon. The word Gohonzon translates as "the true object of worship for the observation of one's mind" and appears as a scroll with Sanskrit and Chinese characters, describing our many states of life and their potentials for enlightenment.

Studying to deepen understanding and compassionately sharing the practice with others are also fundamental precepts. The purpose of the practice is to understand the reality of one's own life and thereby develop an unshakable confidence, compassion and joy based on the fulfillment of our deepest life-enhancing desires.

A brief history
Buddhism, an eastern philosophy of humanism originating in India about 2600 years ago, arose from the teachings of Shakyamuni Buddha, also known as Siddhartha and Gautama Buddha. These profound teachings gradually spread throughout Asia in the ensuing centuries. In thirteenth century Japan, Nichiren Daishonin, a young Buddhist sage, came to an understanding of the true nature of his own life after years of study and prayer. He stated:
> Life at each moment encompasses both body and spirit and both self and environment of all sentient beings in every condition of life, as well as insentient beings—plants, sky and earth, on down to the most minute particles of dust. Life at each moment permeates the universe and is revealed in all phenomena. One awakened to this truth himself embodies this relationship...This truth is Myoho-Renge-Kyo. Chanting Myoho-Renge-Kyo will therefore enable you to grasp the mystic truth within you. While deluded, one is called a common mortal, but once enlightened, he is called a Buddha...**Once you realize that your own life is the Mystic law, you will realize that so are the lives of all others**. (Emphasis added)
> From **Attaining Buddhahood: The Major Writings of Nichiren Daishonin (Vol. I)**

His compassionate practice to enable all people to realize that "you, yourself are a true Buddha who possesses the three enlightened properties" and that "you should chant Nam-myoho-renge-kyo with this conviction," was passed down through the centuries primarily through the priesthood and small groups of lay believers. In the 1930's a Japanese educator, Tsunesaburo Makaguchi, took faith and started a lay organization, the predecessor to the current Soka Gakkai. This organization whose name translates to mean "Value Creating Society," devoted itself to helping people use the practice to alleviate their sufferings, and actualize their deepest potentials as human beings. During World War II the sect was outlawed and its lay leaders imprisoned.

Makaguchi died in prison, but not before transferring his passion for people's happiness to his eventual successor, Josei Toda. Toda emerged alive from the same prison and built a large organization before handing the leadership on to its current president, Daisaku Ikeda.

When at last, laws guaranteeing religious freedom were established in U.S.-occupied post-war Japan, the Soka Gakkai flourished. Its effectiveness in alleviating the sufferings of the people in those difficult times, including noticeably lowered rates of sickness and death among those chanting in the Hiroshima and Nagasaki areas, contributed to its rapid spread.

Eventually, emigrating Japanese brides of U.S. servicemen brought this faith to the western hemisphere. Provided with fertile soil for the spread of humanistic philosophies during the impressionable era of the sixties, it took firm root. It was on his first world tour to encourage international members that Daisaku Ikeda met Elizabeth Izumi in 1961. A young homemaker recently retired from a career in dance, she had emigrated to Canada. Out of courtesy and respect for her mother who was a practitioner in Japan, she agreed to meet Mr. Ikeda at the airport, because there were no members in Toronto at that time. Touched by his compassion and sincerity, she decided to chant, becoming the first person in Canada to do so. Eventually she accepted the responsibility for the leadership of the Canadian organization, a position she holds today, more than 30 years later. The Canadian SGI community has grown from a core group of compassionate and dedicated individuals of mostly Japanese descent, to one encompassing people from diverse ethnic backgrounds representing over 50 different countries and cultures.

The gay experience within the SGI Buddhist community.
In 1973, the first openly lesbian members began practicing with the organization in Canada. We were greeted warmly, and this reception enabled us to develop our faith despite the challenge that our sexual orientation represented to the majority of the leadership. We can only guess what their personal struggles might have been, coming as most of them did, from a repressive homophobic society, and living in Canada, where a similar, though somewhat less intense, homophobia existed. Nevertheless, we were all made to feel welcome and treasured on a person-to-person basis in those first years; no overt prejudice was exhibited. It was as a result of this attitude, and the indisputable fact that the practice profoundly improved one's daily life, that lesbians confidently joined in growing numbers during the late 1970's and early 1980's. This period also witnessed the appearance of the first openly gay males.

One of our leaders, a Canadian-born Japanese woman, Miyo Kozasa, sustained many of us, through her humanistic practice, as a mother sustains her cubs. While not a lesbian herself, her own experience during the 1930s, 40s and 50s, of being an outsider in whatever culture she found herself, translated into unwavering support and total acceptance. Unbeknownst to us at the time, she often protected and defended our perspective within the larger community, guided by compassion and her faith in Buddhist doctrine. The general Buddhist community grew, and by the mid 1980s, as we settled into the normal routines and demands of organizational life, we became increasingly aware that both subtle and overt signs of homophobia were beginning to appear. Restrictive decisions were being made, ostensibly for the benefit of the community at large. For example, an openly gay or lesbian person might not be appointed to certain positions of responsibility to avoid making other Buddhist members uncomfortable. The main structure for support within the organization consists of small districts of ten to twenty members. People usually practice with the person or persons who introduced them to the philosophy. In those days as now, each district had its own unique flavour and cultural composition, so that some districts were very open and not threatened by homosexuality, while others, coming from more sheltered backgrounds, had less tolerant views. This range of perspectives was common on all levels of the organization. What became disturbing was the lack of any guiding principles, which meant that decisions lacked consistency.

Even more alarming, however, were the instances where conflicted or closeted members were given guidance to live as heterosexuals. Though originally erratic, this position became official when a senior visiting leader from Japan described same-sex preference as a stumbling block to enlightenment. This event, occurring in the mid 1980s, marked the beginning of our active resistance to suppression and a quest for doctrinal support and clarification.

On various occasions during the following years, members from our Rainbow community approached individual leaders and priests with these doctrinal questions while on pilgrimage in Japan. In response, both the lay leadership and the priests consistently espoused the central principle of Nichiren Daishonin's teachings: "each person attains enlightenment exactly as they are." For example, a peach is a peach, a pear is a pear, and likewise all people, with their unique characteristics, are a reflection of the great law of life, Myoho Renge Kyo. In addition, any concept of sin in Buddhism is relegated to the intentional causing of harm to oneself or another. This concept does not apply to a preference for one's own sex; no doctrine exists supporting discrimination; it is clearly not necessary to change one's sexual preference in order to fulfill one's potential. Nevertheless, despite all doctrinal clarification, homophobic social conventions and privately held prejudices continued to guide the daily practices of the organization. We were painfully aware that though humanistic doctrines have existed for millennia, a compassionate "revolution of the heart" was our greatest challenge.

As we grew more vocal, leaders pressured us to remain silent about our orientation when speaking with the central leaders and the SGI press in Japan. On reflection, it is easy to see that they were attempting to shield both us and the organization from the scrutiny of a central leadership they felt might be judgmental, especially as our growing numbers made us more visible.

Our experience in our spiritual community was now mirroring our experience within the larger society. Despite our growing numbers, we became increasingly invisible. A heterosexual member's personal experience with the faith's impact on every aspect of his or her life might be published to encourage others. Our experiences, filled with the testimony of growth and increasing confidence, were heavily censored, lifting the experience out of its natural context; often they were not published at all in our community magazine. In our district meetings, sensitive to the prevailing homophobic undercurrents, we censored ourselves.

We rarely spoke our truths except to each other; we cast no shadows. Society's deep fear of individuals living with HIV in those days echoed in the halls of our faith. The few members who developed full-blown AIDS were forbidden from coming to the SGI Community Centre, the home base of our Buddhist community. This caused deep concern and pain for many practitioners, regardless of their sexual orientation. Their protests triggered the rescinding of this policy within a year.

By the early 1990's, our members had become discouraged. Many drifted away from participation in the larger community, resorting to practicing in isolation. However, Virginia Adamson, a lawyer/teacher/psychotherapist and Mala Teeluk, a pre-law student, both from Toronto, along with Cyndia Cole and Angie Joyce, health-care workers from Vancouver, and Carroll Holland, a community development worker and writer from Ottawa, began to talk.

These five were destined to change the course of the organization. In the fall of 1995, they wrote and presented a treatise to the leadership in support of same-sex marriage. Emerging religious, social and political trends, and their humanistic philosophical underpinnings, were presented for consideration. They engaged in numerous dialogues with the leaders to convince them of the importance of this proposal. Simultaneously, they circulated the brief among the members and rallied support in their respective cities. Despite sometimes painful and difficult sessions, the policy was adopted within a few months of presentation.

As a spin-off from this policy change, a group functioning as a home base for gay, lesbian, bisexual and transgendered members, called Pride Group, was established in Toronto and Vancouver. These two groups, the first of their kind in the entire international organization, were born in January of 1996. In June of 1996, the first same-sex marriage took place in Canada, signaling the beginning of a new era. Since then, Pride group meetings have been springing up in the U.S. and Canada.

Canadian meetings are currently being held in Montreal, Ottawa, Toronto, and Vancouver. The Toronto meetings are regularly attracting large numbers from the homosexual, transgendered and heterosexual populations within SGI, as well as interested individuals from the community at large. One of our Toronto members, originally from Japan, who maintains social and business ties there, has been instrumental in starting Pride meetings in Tokyo.

In 1997, with SGI's support, but without their official endorsement, we participated as Buddhists in our first Toronto Gay Pride march. The following year brought the struggle for rights to a hard-won climax: our parent organization in Japan gave its official name and full blessings to our participation as SGI Buddhists at Gay Pride 1998.

Conclusion

We applaud the courage of the central leadership for being open to the continuing changes necessary to make us feel truly welcome and at home. We thank the many heterosexual members for speaking up on our behalf, and continuing to support us with their actions. We especially thank all our rainbow warriors who, with faith and persistence, challenged insensitivity and injustice within our larger spiritual community. In a speech entitled *Peace and Human Security: A Buddhist Perspective for the Twenty-First Century*, President Ikeda describes three paradigm shifts essential

for securing humankind's peace and happiness in the next century. They are:
> from knowledge to wisdom
> from uniformity to diversity, and
> from national to human sovereignty.

SGI now honours the diversity of sexuality by proudly displaying its rainbow colours, serving notice that this profound life philosophy is for all people regardless of sexual orientation. The Pride members of SGI are indeed proud to be taking their rightful place among the champions of these humanistic principles.

Beverly Glenn and Evelyn Wolff
Members of Toronto Pride Group SGI Canada

SGI CHARTER

Preamble

We, the constituent organizations and members of the Soka Gakkai International (hereafter called SGI), embrace the fundamental aim and mission of contributing to peace, culture and education based on the philosophy and ideals of the Buddhism of Nichiren Daishonin.

We recognize that at no other time in history has humankind experienced such an intense juxtaposition of war and peace, discrimination and equality, poverty and abundance as in the twentieth century; that the development of increasingly sophisticated military technology, exemplified by nuclear weapons, has created a situation where the very survival of the human species hangs in the balance; that the reality of violent crime and religious discrimination presents an unending cycle of conflict; that humanity's egoism and intemperance have engendered global problems, including degradation of the natural environment and widening economic chasms between developed and developing nations, with serious repercussions for humankind's collective future.

We believe that Nichiren Daishonin's Buddhism, a humanistic philosophy of infinite respect for the sanctity of life and of all-encompassing compassion, enables individuals to cultivate and bring forth their inherent wisdom and, nurturing the creativity of the human spirit, to surmount the difficulties and crises facing humankind and realize a society of peaceful and prosperous coexistence.

We, the constituent organizations and members of SGI, therefore, being determined to raise high the banner of world citizenship, the spirit of tolerance, and respect for human rights based on the humanistic spirit of Buddhism, and to challenge the global issues that face humankind through dialogue and practical efforts based on a steadfast commitment to nonviolence, hereby adopt this charter affirming the following purposes and principles:

Purposes and Principles

1. SGI shall contribute to peace, culture and education for the happiness and welfare of all humanity based on Buddhist respect for the sanctity of life.
2. SGI, based on the ideal of world citizenship, shall safeguard fundamental human rights and not discriminate against any individual on any grounds.
3. SGI shall respect the freedom of religion and religious expression.
4. SGI shall promote an understanding of Nichiren Daishonin's Buddhism through

grassroots exchange, thereby contributing to individual happiness.

5. SGI shall, through it's constituent organizations, encourage its members to contribute toward the prosperity of their respective societies as good citizens.
6. SGI shall respect the independence and autonomy of its constituent organizations in accordance with the conditions prevailing in each country.
7. SGI shall, based on the Buddhist spirit of tolerance, respect other religions, engage in dialogue and work together with them toward the resolution of fundamental issues concerning humanity.
8. SGI shall respect cultural diversity and promote cultural exchange, thereby creating an international society of mutual understanding and harmony.
9. SGI shall promote, based on the Buddhist ideal of symbiosis, the protection of nature and the environment.
10. SGI shall contribute to the promotion of education, in pursuit of truth as well as the development of scholarship, to enable all people to cultivate their individual character and enjoy fulfilling and happy lives.

NAM-MYOHO-RENGE-KYO

BUDDHIST GRASSROOTS PEACE MOVEMENT IS A POWERFUL VEHICLE FOR SOCIETAL TRANSFORMATION
Carroll Holland

On March 24, 1999, fifteen years to the day after I joined Soka Gakkai, a police officer and myself, an 'out' lesbian community development worker, spoke to all the students at an Ottawa high school about the seriousness and unacceptability of hate-motivated crimes against lesbians, gay, bisexuals and members of the transgendered community. Two days later I sat in the auditorium of the same school, Woodroffe High, and, in the company of 800 students plus staff, watched a live play called **The Other Side of the Closet**. The graphic, fast-paced and unusually honest production depicted the living hell of a teenager named Carl whose life, at school and at home, suddenly became a nightmare of hostility, harassment and isolation as almost everyone turned against him when they found out he was gay.

For me, it was no coincidence that this was the convergence of the two highly significant events in my life: the anniversary of the ceremony when I accepted the mystic law of cause and effect as the foundation of my life; and the breakthrough stand against homophobia at an Ottawa school, in partnership with our community-based police project. Buddhism teaches that everyone has an inherent Buddha nature and a unique mission in the goal to achieve world peace. By making a focused effort in our chanting-based practice, we can rise above the delusions that characterize lower life conditions, bringing out a higher, more compassionate and wiser self to take strong appropriate action towards ending suffering. A writer and editor by trade and a social justice activist by instinct, the profound power of the practice has brought me to the right place at the right time for using my capacities to help create a fairer world. My contributions have come as one of the organizers of the country-wide queer lobbying initiative that evolved on July 3, 1986 into Equality for Lesbians and Gays Everywhere (EGALE); as a public relations worker with the Canadian Tribute to Human Rights in Ottawa; and in my work, since 1993 as an out lesbian involved in a queer community/police crime prevention—a project that focuses on hate-motivated crimes, unsafe schools and same-sex partner abuse issues.

So it was not surprising that in the constantly changing cosmos, in this universe of deep and intricate connections, these two threads of my life should converge in the temporal realm. The purpose of Buddhism is to enable all people to become happy and cultivate lives of supreme joy. "State of life" is its prime focus. Buddhism does not look at people in terms of ethnicity, race, sexual orientation or any other characteristic. The heart is what counts. The individual experience of growth is called "human revolution."

Buddhism is a struggle with all kinds of internal negative forces inherent in life. Without struggling against and overcoming such obstacles, there is no enlightenment. Unless we struggle with all our might against the downward pull of our own darkness and negativity, we cannot become Buddhas. The practice also fosters a deep appreciation of life itself and encourages us to create value every moment of our lives. Buddhahood isn't a far-off abstract goal, a distant place where we can, in a manner of speaking, sit down, put up our enlightened feet and bask in a high life condition for all eternity. Rather, it's a wise, compassionate and pro-active way of living that we can manifest in ever-expanding ways through faith-based efforts as we strive to change our dominant life condition from the suffering associated with states of anger, greed and ignorance to the joy of the highest Bodhisattva and Buddha states. Because everything is connected, positive change in oneself brings comparable change in the environment.

In 1998, an unprecedented anti-lesbian article and personal attack by an Ottawa newspaper columnist who's been a friend for thirty years gave me a chance to put my own personal growth to the test. I realized his irrational and grossly inaccurate statements came from a place of deep, distorting anger that is entirely his problem. It had nothing to do with me. I didn't respond and haven't lost a second of sleep. I chant, very genuinely, for his happiness, for an end to the anger that is eating away at his humanity. I know my spiritual practice enabled me to develop this perspective.

Our Buddhist practice encourages us to strive for self-control, not to control others. According to Daisaku Ikeda, our mentor and the current president of SGI,

> "...the 'invisible arrow' of evil to be overcome is not to be found in the existence of races external to ourselves, but is embedded in our own hearts. The conquest of our own prejudicial thinking, our own attachment to difference, is the necessary pre-condition for open dialogue. Such discussion, in turn, is essential for the establishment of peace and universal respect for human rights."[1]

Dialogue and reason are crucial to the process. As President Ikeda points out,
> "Genuine dialogue results in the transformation of opposing viewpoints, changing them from wedges that drive people apart into bridges that link them together."[2]

Nothing in my extensive experience as a journalist, travel writer and activist prepared me for the completely non-hierarchical reality of the SGI. The organization exists solely to support individual growth and empowerment. Everyone is equal. Everyone is treated with respect. Leaders in faith, who are volunteers, serve members and accept a lot of responsibility. There is no gap between the theory that everyone is equal and the practice.

In 1997, I had the privilege of going to Tokyo for a Buddhist training trip. SGI members came from distant parts of Japan to line the staircase leading into a study hall and, eyes glowing with joy, to welcome us. I walked slowly up the staircase shaking hands, returning the Japanese or English greetings with tears pouring down my face. It is this sincere, deeply-felt, one-on-one connecting that touches the core and literally takes one to a new experiential place—an awareness of our capacity to appreciate one another and to grow, individually and collectively. Respectfully inclusive, always acknowledging the Buddha within each person, young, old, lesbian, gay, transgendered, someone who speaks Swahili, drives a tractor, uses a wheelchair. Everyone. This profoundly anti-authoritarian, genuinely egalitarian and people-centred focus of the Soka Gakkai, is illustrated by the humanistic response of the leadership to the grassroots request for discussion on the need for lesbian, gay, bisexual and transgender visibility within the organization. It is a whole-hearted, not a token response. Information about our Pride Group activities is displayed prominently in our monthly, cross-Canada publication, and we organize meetings for all our members on topics such as celebrating our diversity. Our Ottawa Pride Group meetings were held initially at the home of a heterosexual member whose strong support extends to flying a Rainbow Flag, year-round, from her front porch.

Affirming the value of l/g/b/t members is completely consistent with Buddhist teachings. Moreover, President Ikeda urges us all to actively join forces with those who fight on the side of good for justice and truth. Martin Luther King Jr. would surely have considered us an ally. The clarity of analysis of the U.S. civil rights activist, expressed in a letter written in 1963 while in a Birmingham jail, has been a focal point of my activism for a long time:

> "I have almost reached the regrettable conclusion that the Negro's great stumbling block in the stride toward freedom is not the White Citizen's Councillor or the Ku Klux Klanner but the white moderate who is more devoted to order than to justice; **who prefers a negative peace which is the absence of tension to a positive peace which is the presence of justice.**"[3] (Emphasis added)

Likewise, in this decade the Soka Gakkai stood up to an authoritarian high priest who "excommunicated" all SGI members in a blatant exercise of old-fashioned power. The high priest claimed enlightenment was impossible without the intervention of priests. In a principled stand—the equivalent of Martin Luther's stand against the selling of indulgences by Roman Catholic priests that sparked the Protestant Reformation—the Soka Gakkai maintained that everyone has equal access through faith to enlightenment. The SGI, sans priests, continues to grow tremendously. According to Daniel Metraux, an American college teacher who contributed an article on the SGI to the book **Engaged Buddhism: Buddhist Liberation Movements in Asia**, "The priesthood...has extensive wealth and could well survive a prolonged cloistered existence, but it is doubtful that it will attract many lay supporters."[4]

For me there's an increasingly clear and visible contrast between "top-down" repressive power in general and the "bottom-up" popular movement that is the SGI, a movement of dialogue, empowerment and enlightenment. A movement based on honesty and heart-to-heart communication, one that is utterly devoid of hypocrisy. Furthermore, the SGI translates its principles into global community action as a non-governmental organization of the United Nations, in cultural exchanges and through educational projects on peace, human rights and the environment. In 1996, President Ikeda set up the Toda Institute for Global Peace and Policy Research, an independent, non-partisan, non-profit organization in Tokyo. Its Fall/Winter 1998 Journal contains an insightful article that identifies a transformation in the very concept of security. Increasingly, wrote Mahbub ul-Haq, security is interpreted as security of people, not just territory. This includes "security of all the people everywhere in their homes, in their jobs, in their streets, in their communities, and in their environment." "Human security," he wrote, "is a concept emerging not from the learned writings of scholars but from the daily concerns of people."[5]

Human security is the conceptual essence of my work as a lesbian activist. I know I will have an opportunity to infuse our grassroots experience in this global dialogue. I am also convinced, as a result of my personal experiences, that Buddhism is a more powerful vehicle for societal transformation than the queer liberation movement. Buddhism's foundation of respect for every individual, its emphasis on dialogue and its goal of world peace based on the empowerment and development of every individual, brings an unprecedented opportunity for genuine human revolution on a global scale.

Endnotes

1. Daisaku Ikeda. *Mahayana Buddhism*, in **A New Humanism: a Buddhist Perspective**: the University Addresses of Daisaku Ikeda; Weatherhill Inc., New York and Tokyo; 1996. Page 155.
2. Ibidem. Page 156.
3. Martin Luther King, Jr. *The Negro Is Your Brother*, in **Selections from 119 Years of the Atlantic**; edited by Louise Desaulniers; Atlantic Subscriber Edition, USA; 1977. Page 503.
4. Daniel Metraux. *The Soka Gakkai: Buddhism and the Creation of a Harmonious and Peaceful Society*, in **Engaged Buddhism: Buddhist Liberation Movements in Asia**; edited by C.S. Queen and S.B. King; State University of New York Press, Albany, N.Y. 1996. Page 391.
5. Mahbub ul-Haq, *Human Rights, Security, and Governance*, in **Peace & Policy: Journal of the Toda Institute for Global Peace and Policy Research**: Dialogue of Civilizations for World Citizenship; Tokyo. Fall/Winter 1998. pp. 3-10.

BIOGRAPHY Carroll Holland

Carroll Holland is a member of Soka Gakkai International (SGI), a Buddhist grassroots peace movement based on the mystic law of cause and effect. She lives in Ottawa where she works as an activist with the Ottawa-Carleton Regional Police Service.

BACK TO THE GAY GARDEN
Brother Christian Spiritus Zinzendorf and Brother Johannes Renatus Zinzendorf

Is there a place where you can grow? Is there a garden where your unique spiritual flower can take root in fertile soil and rise high into the sunlight of your potential?

For some queer folk, this place is not a fantasy or lost Eden. It exists today at the Hermitage of Mahantongo Spirit Garden.

The Hermitage is located on 63 acres of farm and woodland in a rural mountain valley in central Pennsylvania. It offers a place beyond dogma and belief, a place where each brother and sister has his or her own dwelling and can tend to his or her own spiritual development apart from the outside world.

The Garden is based on the Pantheistic concept that everything is both spirit and life. It is also based on the post-Christian idea that we are called as new Adams and Eves to return to the Garden and care for it, tend it, nurture it. For each of us here is both flower and gardener in the Garden, the three joined as one.

The Hermitage is not connected to an external power grid. It is self-contained in terms of water, heat and sanitation. We grow much of our own food. Each hermit provides for his or her own financial needs through a variety of means: an independent income, outside work, making and selling craft or food items, and offering workshops and retreats.

Communal buildings include a Gemeinehaus (community house), summer kitchen, barn, print shop, woodworking shop, and pottery shop. Only the barn existed at the site when it was purchased in 1988. Since then, more than two dozen structures, primarily log or timber-frame, have been moved to the site, either intact or in sections, and rebuilt.

A full range of summer workshops and retreats are offered, including open-hearth cooking, sourdough baking, flax to linen processing, and gay spirituality. Visits are encouraged, as are long-term residencies. Write for more information.

Brother Christian and I always had in mind a family of gay men. We had originally thought of it as perhaps a kind of Scottish clan, then as a faerie group. But it was a long defunct religious community that was literally little more than a footnote in Moravian history that gave us the blueprint and form we'd been seeking.

It took years to realize that gay men in general did not want what we had to offer, especially as we became more post-Christian and Pantheistic. If we wanted to form a monastery of gay Franciscans, there would probably be dozens of us. But even within the gay community, we have been far on the fringe, just too weird, for most to relate to. Our lifestyle is not trendy. It's hard. There is almost no support. We are voices calling from the wilderness.

Christansbrunn Brotherhood (now located at the Hermitage of Mahantongo Spirit Garden) was founded under the guidance of Christian Renatus Graf von Zinzendorf in 1749. The original site was a combination saw mill and grist mill in the Barony of Nazareth, in the Lehigh Valley of Pennsylvania. At that time, Christian was 22 years old and head of the Single Brothers Choir as established by his father,

Nicolaus Ludwig, Count von Zinzendorf. What little is known about Christian's life in English, and the somewhat more written about him in German, comes from second and third-hand sources. These are primarily Moravian apologists for the period in church history known as the Sifting Time, when church doctrines and practices considered inappropriate by its mainstream leaders were sifted out. Christian von Zinzendorf, in his own incarnation as the Second Christ, was sifted out. Our goal is to live in his spirit and his practices.

Christian was born in 1727 in Berthelsdorf, Moravia. That year was the Great Awakening in Moravian history, when the blessing and enlightenment of the Holy Spirit was said to fill the community established near Berthlsdorf under Count von Zinzendorf's protection. The Count and Countess were caught up in the fervent passion of the year and the Countess believed she was filled with the seed of the Holy Spirit. Her son was literally conceived as the Second Coming, the reincarnation of Christ. When he was born, she named this son Christian Renatus, Christ Come Again. The nuclear family was enthroned in the godhead, now with earthly representatives. There was God the Father, represented by the Count, the Holy Spirit as Mother—the Countess was significantly named Erdmutha, Earth Mother—and their son, Christian, the returned Christ. There was also his sister, Benigna, as Sophia, the Pietist representative of wisdom.

Christian was sickly as a child. He was slow in learning to talk and was said to be spoiled. One biographer, Edwin Sawyer, says, "He seldom played with other boys but was steadily urged into the role he should fill, namely, that of a religious wonder child."[1] Though considered gifted, Christian was not a good scholar. He was admitted to the Moravian theological seminary at Marienborn, but was rebuked for being proud of his position, for being too light-hearted, and for playing with a cat in class. By his middle teens, he was sent on a trip to Geneva, but by then he preferred the spirit to scenery. He returned to Marienborn and began taking an active role in congregation affairs. He began attending many religious and community meetings, gradually becoming a leader.

Christian's first Holy Communion was January 3rd, 1743. Writing to his mother, he said, "I never cried so much as there; I did not know where I was." When Christian turned eighteen, the Count pronounced him his "Joshua", his successor. Christian formed a choir of men and boys, to whom, as Sawyer writes, he became "the object of their unmitigated adulation."[2] He was intimately devoted to an officer in the Single Brothers Choir, who gave him the affectionate title of "Herzel", or Little Dear. Christian encouraged elaborate religious and birthday festivals, in which Marienborn was lit with so many candles that, according to a visitor, "at night the building seemed to be on fire".[3]

In this same year, 1743, Christian's father the Count gave a series of lectures in London. In one, he stressed that one can know Christ only by being filled with the Holy Spirit. The Count quoted from the Song of Solomon, "You have ravished my heart with a glance of your eyes," and "O that he would kiss me with the kisses of the mouth."

Christian took his father's advice literally, body and soul. With six of his most trusted brothers, he formed a "Society of Sweethearts". By 1748, Christian was made a presbyter. On May 21st of this year, he led thirty of his Single Brothers into an ecstatic experience in which several fell to the ground and could not stand up unassisted. At age 21, he insisted to his father that he was not interested in marriage. Many of the Single Brothers had begun to worship him.

Two months after his appointment as presbyter, Christian's father ordered him to London, rebuked him for his supposed excesses, and stripped him of all offices. The Count's political and religious enemies, as well as his own advisors, were stirring rumor about Christian and what was happening at Marienborn. His father's condemnation shattered Christian's spirit. He began writing penitential hymns. Christian's last service with his choir was held on August 10th, 1750. His fellowship disbanded and Christian stayed with his father, primarily in London. His health failed in the damp English climate. As Sawyer writes, "his inner frustrations slowly destroyed him."[4]

While Christian was in England, some of the remaining men from his choir came from Moravia to Pennsylvania and established a community, Christiansbrunn. The German name means "the spring of Christian", in honor of an ever-flowing spring at the site. The spring became even more important after Christian's early death. He became deified and it was believed the spring water was his blood and contained his spirit. Christian had planned to move to Christiansbrunn when he heard of its inception. Peach trees, his favorite fruit, were planted so that they would mature and bear fruit by the time he arrived.

Christian died in London on May 28th, 1752, at the age of twenty-five. His burial site is located on the grounds along the Thames River.

This is the mystery of Christiansbrunn: the divine marriage of each brother to the Holy Spirit. The symbolism that Christian used to support his motivations was drawn from the Song of Solomon, in which the Bridegroom expresses his desire and love for the Bride. Traditional Christian interpretation has desexualized this into a metaphor of Christ and his church. But Christian wasn't one for symbolism. He took things literally. We wait for the Bridegroom to come and He comes daily if we let the Holy spirit fill us. Christian did this, body and soul, becoming the Bridegroom and the Bride with his brothers.

The basic actions of sexuality are entering and being entered, of filling and being filled. For us, and, as we believe, for Christian's original brotherhood, being filled by another man is the physical equivalent of being entered by the spirit. Indeed, for us they are often, though not necessarily, the same. In the Judeo-Christian tradition, we are presented with this metaphor of the Bridegroom coming to the Bride. Gay men and women have the ability to be both the Bridegroom and Bride, both to enter and to be entered, to fill and be filled (literally full-filled). This is a special gift, not one that makes us better than straights but one that does make us distinctly different. For we can be both Bridegroom and Bride, both filler and filled. And how liberating that is! To be both the spirit that enters and the spirit that is entered. It gives gay people a remarkable and unique sensitivity and awareness—a blending, and a metamorphosis.

Christian was in the Holy Spirit, and the Holy Spirit was in him. There is no greater model for us to follow, not even Christ. Christian's spirit continues to live in the springs at Christiansbrunn and Mahantongo Spirit Garden. We merely continue the path he set before us and pass it on.

We were astounded by these findings, kept well hidden by the modern church as one can imagine. It took a great deal of reading between the lines but everything fits into this interpretation of what was happening then. What also fits was the adverse reaction to this by more mainstream, needless to say straight, Moravians, as well as the revulsion to this movement by non-Moravians in this country and

Germany during the mid-18th century. Why wasn't Christian's story well known? Why wasn't it a turning point in western religious evolution? Simply because the church was embarrassed by it. After 250 years, only the spring remains.

We went there, we drank the water containing Christian's spirit and realized that what had been thought destroyed so long ago was actually just sleeping, waiting for the chance to rise again. My partner and I looked at each other—we were the ones to do it.

In 1987 we incorporated Christiansbrunn as a non-profit, tax-exempt religious order recognized by state and federal governments. We started saving money for land. Most of the original 500 acres of Christiansbrunn was now part of a limestone quarry. We went farther and farther afield to find affordable land away from increasing development. We finally found it in an isolated mountain valley in the coal region of central Pennsylvania. We bought 63 acres, all we could afford, in 1988. Our goal was to reestablish Christiansbrunn and live as our early brothers had lived. That meant lighting with candles, heating with wood and rebuilding abandoned log and timber-frame buildings. Where only a barn stood in 1988, by 1999 there are over two dozen buildings of various sizes including a print shop, craft house, bake oven, bird houses, and a community house.

However, our devotion to eighteenth-century purity was gradually replaced by the reality of two men attempting the labor of the original 80 men and boys. eighteenth-century farming, for example, was labor intensive, though it required only a handful of different tools. We had the tools, but not the labor. We started hand scything a twelve acre field and quickly gave up. We found an old McCormick hay cutter and hitched it to our ox team. We went from storing loose hay to baling hay to having a farmer put it in large round bales for us. We learned that farmers are born, not made. Now our land is finally productive and we get half of the crop yield, far more than we could grow on our own.

The religion itself underwent its own changes. What excited us about our brothers' beliefs was not Christianity but their notion of the Holy Spirit as a mother (as Christian's mother, Erdmutha, signified). That seemed a truly evolutionary change and led us to describe our religion as post-Christian. We transferred the Holy Spirit to Mother Earth and saw ourselves as caretakers, as guardians of our 63 acre garden. We called ourselves Harmonists for living in harmony with the Holy Spirit and Mother Earth. Still later we recognized that we were actually Pantheists, for we had come to realize that everything has a spirit and must be respected.

All of these changes seemed very natural to us and the beauty and joy of the religion was self-evident. Or so we thought. But when describing it to others, no matter how clear and succinct we thought we were, most people stared at us blankly or just turned away. Or, as one early visitor said, "That's just your religion. If I live here, I'll have my own."

Well, that's not what we wanted. We wanted a brotherhood in the spirit, a shared spirit, not a bunch of gays all doing their own thing. So we developed an elaborate novitiate program to inculcate our beliefs into those who would join us. We went through it one time with a man who said he was born to be the third brother. He learned his lessons well and could repeat all our beliefs and theology. Only, as we later discovered, he really didn't believe them after all. He said he did, but we found out he was still Christian, still believed what he wanted to believe even after telling us otherwise.

This was traumatic. It looked as though all we'd attempted had failed, that no one really wanted to join us, that we would be used by people who wanted to get on the land but had no interest in the beliefs that led us to that land.

That was our deepest trough of failure. The two of us blamed each other, hated each other. We broke up and started living separately on the property. The brotherhood, as a cloistered community, died. Gradually what replaced it was a feeling that we had indeed gone astray in our emphasis on conformity and unanimity of belief. The more we thought about communal life, the more it seemed like an adult version of a college dormitory, which we'd hated anyway. By pressing for appearances, we'd stifled the spirit.

We learned that behaviour is more important than belief. It makes no difference what one believes; it's how one acts towards other life forms that's important. Kindness, caring, generosity, those create harmony, not spouting phrases. And it's action by which we are judged anyway.

We live in a society where we define our very lives through labels, like filling out a form for insurance. It was time to stop doing that here.

This realization led us to where we are now. Instead of a cloister, we are now a hermitage. Each hermit has his or her own hermit's house and then decides on one's own how to live in harmony with all these spirits. Now there is freedom here and more responsibility placed on the individual. We can share more, and grow like a myriad of different flowers in a garden, which is why we changed our name to the Spirit Garden.

We finally realized that we are for queers, not gay men. That can be a significant difference in that 'queer' means to take a different path and many gay men do not want to do that. They are quite satisfied with mainstream culture and there's nothing wrong with that. We connect with the mainstream on many levels.

We were also closed off from those lesbians, bisexuals, transgendered and, yes, even straights who are also seeking a different path. So for us, queer does not mean sexuality as much as the path we choose on which to reach our potential as human beings.

There are now two levels of membership. Some people need to be here to find their own path—perhaps to heal themselves—and may not now or ever be interested in the role of steward and gardener.

Those who do, and it's a matter of choice, follow the Six Fold Path, a process through which we connect to Mother Earth, and through which she uses us to know and to change herself, to become what she can be. She uses us to reach her greatest potential and, through letting her use us, we become one and whole through her.

And so we have come finally to this brave hill, less planned and knowing than stumbled, pushed, and blindly felt our way upon. And it is lonely here, sad and painful at times.

Mocked by other gays because we have so chosen to stay only with our kind. Shunned by many of the rural township folk, and through the secret veil of night, have heard the screaming hatred of the teenage boys in budding sexuality, and heard their rifles tear into our flock of sheep, and held one as his blood poured through his nose and bubbled from his mouth. And by the light of our old van watched pain and fear, then slowly lose their focus, his wide eyes. Eyes of endless curiosity when first we held him, just when he was born.

How had it come to this, for we had flowed like the water in a stream, we had gained fame and fortune then resigned, could we now take their curse and make it rhyme? Well, no, of course not. Armed with no outer support and no resources, what could we do but keep doing what it was that had drawn us here? What other choice did we have now but to continue? For once you have tasted life and growth, the rest is poverty. The boredom of living predetermined fag lives, ending up drunk in some wrinkle bar makes being shot at by some closet queers a welcome relief.

One won't feel warm fuzzies from incense, robes and altar settings here. We are the real thing, uncluttered by the fossil trappings of dead paper scrolls reinterpreted to induce shallow vanities to feel they have done service to the litanies of some castrated Christ.

Eighty-eight men flocked to the first hermitage in the eighteenth century with a need they could hardly describe. They only knew the lives they had come from did not offer the bonding and protection they needed. We sought to recreate this home for the brotherhood where gay men could grow in the spirit.

How naive that dream sounds now, years later, like seeing a rack of wedding dresses in a thrift store: meaningless relics of change, simply discarded. Ten years ago, the two of us were young, like those brides must have been, with stars in our eyes. We made a new life, like a marriage; building and creating a safe place for kinship and love to grow. Hadn't it been done before?

After a decade, our hermitage has grown to include log and timber-frame buildings that stun tourists driving along the road. They stop and gaze as if some ancient village, some Brigadoon, had suddenly appeared.

Yet there is a silence here. The gay spiritual retreats that we had planned were a bust. Not one person signed up except a college student who could not afford the fee, so we invited him just to come for a visit whenever he wanted to. We even paid for a classified ad in **The Advocate**, plus good publicity in regional gay newspapers. Either we are not advertising the right way, or we have a poor product to advertise. I've come to realize that most gay men, and probably most people in general, are not interested in spirituality—at least in a living, pervasive sense.

One man, Tim, has come here to live with us. He came in the middle of winter. He had been trapping for pelts in Canada, following trap lines for a week at a time, then returning to civilization with his catch. He wanted to become a hermit, leading a solitary life even more primitive than the pair of us live. Part Native American, he moved out of our log buildings and built a primitive lodge and a small enclosure at the edge of the property. At the very corner of our 63 acres, he chooses to remain isolated. The inclusion of Tim had a profound effect on our lifestyle here. It was nothing to experience the violence directed at us by our homophobic neighbours in the valley, compared to the internal division among just three people.

Tim's desire to create his own space in the Hermitage—both physical and spiritual—was the final step in our reevaluation of the very core of our existence here. It was like the biblical story of the wedding feast where those who were initially invited chose not to attend. The master of the house told his servants to go out into the streets and invite whomever they saw, so that the wedding hall could be filled. So, as the master said, "let anyone come who wishes to rejoice with us" (Matthew, 22:1-10). And so we have done here.

Tim longs to grow closer to Mother Earth, to lie in the lodge at night, hearing every natural sound. To make music on a sheepskin drum, a muted, heartbeat sound, and to draw the ancient spirits to this gentle place. The birds come already to the trees he has planted. He makes a garden plot and digs a pond. It is not just a finished home he seeks, but the act of creation.

Let anyone seeking growth in the spirit come here to express their inner self and to grow. The beliefs of our early brothers that brought us here have been ignored by those who have come after us, so let potential hermits express what a spiritual life means to them.

Reviving a 250-year-old gay religious order has not been without its perils: we've been shot at, our animals have been shot, we've been stepped on by oxen, crushed by logs and herniated from lifting bags of cement.
There have been other sacrifices too: lost friends, family, career.
Still, our founder's spirit is very much with us and in us. And we've needed all the help we can get. For despite our best efforts, despite making the desert bloom, despite creating a safe place where rare animals can live in peace, despite building two dozen buildings of various sizes, despite being self-sufficient and living without electricity or telephone, despite creating a garden where queer folk can live in harmony with the spirits as they see fit, despite all this and more, we are faced with the likely probability that we will ultimately fail. Not fail in creating our vision or in making it real, but fail in having it continue after us; fail in making this 63-acre site more than just a place where two fags live.
We've built a self-contained village in one of the most beautiful spots in North America, and no one seems to care. Apart from Tim, no one has come who has stayed. We give workshops, retreats, but no one wants to live here. And so we have finally had to think the unthinkable, what will happen to this place when we die? We built it so that up to one dozen brothers and sisters could live here—spinning, weaving, making furniture, printing, gardening, farming, taking care of the animals and growing in the spirit while sharing that spirit among ourselves. That's what we hoped for and now we realize it may never happen.
In that case, we hope to see it turned into a secular education center where students can learn about traditional crafts, sustainable agriculture, rare breeds of animals and other things. If the religious order must die, then education can keep the spirit of the garden alive. Of course, I'd prefer to see the garden grow, thrive and prosper in our original vision. And it may yet. You just never know.

Brother Johannes
On a still, cool summer's evening, after breaking flax, making hay or hewing logs, I take five minutes to look down the valley from my porch. The green, forested mountains are a backdrop to the fields of grain and corn. The cows, sheep and goats are lying together down in the pasture. The barn cats are playing in the wagon yard. The ducks are resting in one area, the chickens in another. Miracle, the lamb I raised after his mother died, is sitting beside me. Hawks are flying overhead. Nearer are the barn swallows. The creek rustles on its way to the river. The setting sun provides a benediction before it disappears and I am filled with the spirits. Our job is to live in harmony with these spirits, a difficult job at best and one at which I frequently fail but, on this evening, the failure is not a concern. It simply blends in with all the other things I feel on this mellow evening when I understand that it is possible to return to the garden and experience that primal oneness with creation on a daily basis.

As a gay man I am able to experience this evening in both masculine and feminine forms, for I contain both. Both fill my spirit and create it for me. In this garden where I live in central Pennsylvania, being gay is not always a blessing. But it is a distinction, and what we are creating here is distinctly powerful magic, the kind that dissolves appearances and the subject-object dichotomy into a wholeness, a holiness and a healing.

I realize that my religious vocation does not automatically make me a better or happier person. I'm still left with loneliness, despondency, despair, in addition to joyfulness. But I've also learned that those personal feelings in the long run don't really matter. Like an artist, it's the work that remains long after I've gone. I see religion as a metaphor to help us understand the world and our place in it. As such it needs to do more than merely make us feel good. It needs to challenge us, demand things of us. It should make us work. And in return? We should have a place in the world.

I've given my life to the spirits. Use me, I've said, fill me, make me an instrument of your wills. And they have. So I build this special holy garden for them. In return I get to live here, read my books, listen to my music, spend time with the animals and my brothers. Those are my rewards and I treasure and cherish them. A few moments of sitting in the tranquility of twilight, brings me peace and fulfillment. And that is my life.

Brother Christian

We believe that life is found in all that is. They call it Pantheist. That all things contain life. I walk along the yard and know the stout varieties of plant which stand among my feet. The small collections of our animals and mottled crew of half wild cats surround me. Buildings we have salvaged from decay of generations stand in testament of a time when the chisel, saw and axe were all that one required to make a home.

And I may sport a skirt or army green fatigues, depending on the male gay spirit which inhabits me, and which bright facet comes to light through some desire to express itself upon our mother earth.

I mark each new variety of plant upon the mountains which surround this farm, and learn their benefit and usage that we might enjoy a healthful drink, or tonic, or employ them for the dyestuff to color our wool, and to gain familiarity with such variety of life, for it is a pleasure to recognize old friends we have now come to know.

I watch the changing of the clouds and feel the force of wind from which direction, to predict the weather of our days; and follow in the night, the movements of Orion and his band of constellations through the season's sky. And never fail to find the one my ancestors had followed, old North Star, that most faithful guide, although forgotten by the modern voyager who hurls incomprehensibly to those below as some moving vapor trail or starlike dot at night.

I press into the earth our seeds of flax and corn, our kitchen garden laden down like some great salad squared off by heavy boards to keep my wooly herd from dining there.

I work the flax into strong linen thread by spinning on a wheel, which brings us to the heart of this small enterprise.

There are, like words unspoken, things the first men in this valley called out as spirits, and each in his own way, formed a union with this undefinable and invisible thing. They left chipped tools of stone as testament that they had been, and shared our mother earth in common with all living things.

Many are called, yet few are chosen for this craggy road, this pearl of great price, and yet many could do more who do not, and the edges of their conscience grow rounded and less painful through the tumbling of life, till they are ground as dust which blows across our fields, and cast like chaff upon the slightest zephyr, useless particles.

We are all this and more. And sometimes, we too blind ourselves to the beauties of each passing day even when we should express a flow of harmony as our early brothers did two hundred and fifty years ago, about whom was said, "They glowed like candles in their love."

We cling to this faint light of so long ago for it is all we know of value in this short space of life.

For I have heard the bridegroom is at hand and we must light the lamp, and be ready, that he may embrace us as his own, and make a peaceful garden of this wilderness.

Endnotes

1. Sawyer, Edwin. The Religious Experience of the Colonial Moravians. (Nazareth: Moravian Historical Society, 196_) p.98.
2. Ibid, 99.
3. Ibid, 97.
4. Ibid, 101.

BIOGRAPHY Brother Christian Spiritus Zinzendorf

Brother Christian was born in Maine in 1949. He graduated from the University of Maine, then moved west where he lived in a commune in Oakland during the '70s. He then earned his teaching certificate from Westminster College in Salt Lake City, Utah.

BIOGRAPHY Brother Johannes Renatus Zinzendorf

Brother Johannes was born in Oregon in 1951 but was raised in Mississippi, Alabama and Texas. He attended the University of Utah, obtaining degrees in film study, literature and educational psychology.

The Hermitage offers a variety of summer programs, workshops and retreats, including colonial flax to linen processing, open hearth cooking in a log house originally built in 1759 and sourdough baking in an outdoor brick bake oven. Visitors are always welcome as the Hermitage is just 15 minutes off Interstate 81. A free sample copy of The Spirit Garden, the Hermitage's newsletter, is available by writing: Brother Johannes, The Hermitage, Pitman, PA 17964 USA.

The Hermitage has a website constructed by the Oregon School for the Deaf and hosted by the Fellowship for Intentional Community. The address is: www.ic.org/thehermitage/   e-mail: brojoh@yahoo.com
The Hermitage is affiliated with the Fellowship through its network of queer and queer-friendly communities.

LETTER TO A LOVED ONE
Sulayman X

Dear Child,

I have waited a long time for the sound of your footsteps at my door. What joy it gives me to speak to you once again!

Before we were separated, I tried in so many different ways to tell you what happiness it had given me to create you, to watch you grow. But the voices of those around you raised in condemnation and the most foolish self-righteousness drowned me out. You could not hear me, but perhaps you can hear me now.

If nothing else, then know this: you are what you were intended to be. I do not make mistakes no matter how many foolish men might claim otherwise. You know this in your heart to be true so why not believe it?

And know this as well: our reunion is inevitable. One day you will return to me. If this causes you fear or apprehension, it should not, for you know I could never hurt you. And though I speak to you as a parent to a child, yet this is merely a device. I am not really your parent and you are not really my child. You are part of Me, you have always been part of Me, and you will always be part of Me.

There is a story about a little boy who, during the first day of school, shyly raised his hand and asked to be allowed to use the restroom. The teacher assented and the youth went off, only to return with much consternation having failed in his task. Again, he asked for permission to use the restroom, and again he received permission. He returned to the class yet again, not having achieved his goal. An older boy in the class volunteered to help the youth, and they set off and returned in short order. The older youth smiled at the teacher and said, "His pants were on backwards."

And that is what I would like to suggest to you: your pants are on backwards. You see judgement and hell-fire where there is only love and peace. You see confusion where there is only clarity. You are looking down and cannot find the sky and you don't know why but if you would look up, you would see.

During the years of our separation, I have watched you always, and, sometimes, with sorrow. You have sought with your body that which can only be satisfied with your soul. You have read much but learned little. You have believed that a profusion of words would lend clarity, and yet clarity is only found in silence.

But more distressing than all this is that you have too often believed what others have said about Me. They would have you believe that My nose is between the sheets of your bed, ever attentive as to what occurs there, when it is of no concern to Me. Why should it be? They would have you believe that you are an abomination. Imagine the arrogance of accusing Me of creating an abomination! They would have you believe that the sexual feelings that flow within you have some moral significance when they are nothing more than hormones and chemical reactions which I Myself created.

You must consider the possibility that they are wrong.

Humans so often cling to what they believe and whether those things are true or not doesn't seem to matter. It's a curious thing. Many times great men like the Buddha, or Jesus, or Muhammad, approach near Me and hear My words and then those words are twisted and used in such evil ways by the ignorant and the proud.

And yet My words are always available for the listener. If you would hear them, then listen. That is all. In silence, you will go a long way.

I am inevitable, and I am eternal so time has no meaning for Me. I will wait for you for as long as it takes for you to return.

You will not find Me in any church or mosque. They are brick and stone. They are not Me. You will not find Me in holy book or scripture. Those were words meant for other ears in other ages. You will not find Me in tarot cards or sacraments or monasteries or votive candles. If you would find Me, find yourself first, and you will see that we were never really separated at all.

Sulayman X's biography appears on page 55.

BLOOD PUDDING is a celebration of Life/based on the history of the New Orleans area and the culture's specific to this unique region. within the layering of language/the style of survival/the method of Prayer/the rhythms of song/and the history of Life of the people and culture of Louisiana, the story is told.
  This is an OYA Work (Yoruba Orisha of Wind/change).

BLOOD PUDDING
  (an excerpt)
  Sharon Bridgforth

>   my mother paints the leaves in autumn/fans
>   earthquakes and hurricanes beneath her skirts my
>   mother will clean for you/but
>   do not disturb her
>   if you are not ready for the visit/she cyclones destroys outward
>   structures when
>   she sweeps
>   maw'mn is ready
>   dancing by the tombstones
>   till changing time come/call

the old lady
walk cripple
   everyday shufe
      here
         and there
dont say nuthn/silence all round
her cause we no better
than speak she name.

when her sign is out we line
in crowds
waiting a turn/for
gris gris
   a charm
      a prayer
still no talk
she already know
how the future holds us.
they say she never died
jes stay   watch the livn.

one gurl hang round
young
supple sweet
and deliberate
   she know her power
we think silence is best for her too.

it is said they can cause the dust to stir
   Wind raise Her head
storm break loose/make lightning speak they

caldron, book and Spirits that keep
our stories live in the night round the house   those two
the old lady that shufes and the young wo'mn supple sweet
are never seen together/we know

they celebrate us
whispering our prayers to the Wind.
if you listen carefully/you will know
all there is
to know

                         Ancient breeze
                         softly send
                         my Soul fly home
                         with You/i pray
                         Heaven be here
                         on Earth
                         in my Heart and actions
                         please change me clean
                         for Thee/ THY WILL BE DONE
                         HOLY AND SACRED ONE
                         make me
                         a channel of
                         THE PEACE AND GOOD WILL OF THE CREATRESS
                         make me
                         a channel of
                         THE PEACE AND GOOD WILL OF THE CREATRESS
                         make me
                         a channel of
                         THE PEACE AND GOOD WILL OF THE CREATRESS/yeah!

Sharon Bridgforth's biography appears on page 128.

ABOUT QUEER PRESS

Our Goals

Queer Press is a Canadian-owned small press that publishes fiction, non-fiction, poetry and artwork. We are the first and only queer press in Canada. We define queer as lesbian, gay, bisexual, transgendered and transsexual. Our publishing objective is to promote and explore the literary expressions of these communities, with a mandate to include representation by women, people of colour and people with disabilities. Our current publishing priorities are directed at writers living in Canada with the exception of First Nations writers living in the United States.

Queer Press, P.O. Box 485, Station P
Toronto, Ontario M5S 2T1
Tel: (416) 469 . 5224

ALSO AVAILABLE FROM QUEER PRESS

ISBN 1-895564-05-0
$15.95

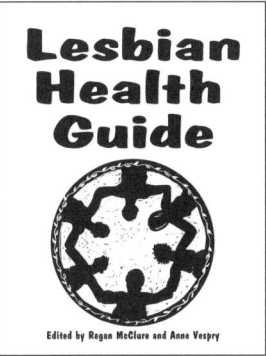

ISBN 1-895564-02-6
$18.95

ISBN 1-895564-04-2
$10.95

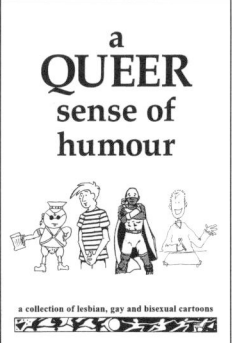

ISBN 1-895564-01-8
$9.95

ISBN 1-895564-03-4
$9.95

ISBN 1-895564-00-X
$9.95